CW01369075

AIRCRAFT OF THE ROYAL AIR FORCE
in service since 1918

Eurofighter Typhoon Two RAF Typhoon F1s demonstrate, in 2003, the ability to take-off and accelerate rapidly to provide a high launch speed for its weapons, in turn producing longer missile ranges and shorter fly-out times. No 17 Squadron will be the first front-line RAF squadron and a NATO declaration with FOC (Full Operating Capability) is expected by the middle of the decade.

Acknowledgement

BAE SYSTEMS

The Royal Air Force Benevolent Fund Enterprises is most grateful to BAE SYSTEMS for their generous support of the RAF Benevolent Fund through their contributory sponsorship.

AIRCRAFT OF THE ROYAL AIR FORCE

in service since 1918

Paintings by Michael Turner P GAvA

Main text by Chaz Bowyer
Consultant Editor Peter R March
Foreword by Raymond Baxter

AIR TATTOO
PUBLISHING

A division of
RAF BENEVOLENT FUND ENTERPRISES

To my late Parents, in appreciation of their unfailing support and encouragement.

Published by
The Royal Air Force Benevolent Fund Enterprises
Douglas Bader House, Horcott Hill, Fairford, Glos. GL7 4RB UK

© copyright Michael Turner 2003
Hardback ISBN 1 899808 965
Softback ISBN 1 899808 027

All rights reserved.
No part of this publication may be reproduced,
stored in a retrieval system or transmitted,
in any form or by any means,
electronic, mechanical, photocopying, recording or
otherwise, without the permission in writing of the publisher
and the copyright owner.

Produced in China by Jade Productions

Contents

Foreword by Michael Turner	7
Foreword by Raymond Baxter	8

Aircraft of World War One — 11

Bristol Fighter	12
RE8	14
Handley Page 0/400	16
Sopwith Camel	19
SE5a	20
Felixstowe Flying Boat	23
Sopwith Snipe	24

Aircraft Between the Wars — 27

de Havilland 9a	28
Supermarine Southampton	30
Fairey III	33
Blackburn Iris	34
Bristol Bulldog	36
Avro 504N	39
Hawker Fury	40
Handley Page Heyford	41
Westland Wapiti	42
Supermarine Scapa	44
Hawker Hart	45
Vickers Virginia	47
Handley Page Hinaidi	48
Avro Tutor	49
Hawker Demon	51
Vickers Vincent	52
Vickers Valentia	54

Handley Page Harrow and Fairey Hendon	55
Hawker Audax	56

Aircraft of World War Two — 59

Vickers Wellesley	60
Fairey Battle	61
Hawker Hurricane I	63
Bristol Blenheim I	65
Lockheed Hudson	68
de Havilland Tiger Moth	69
Supermarine Spitfire I	71
Avro Anson	72
Westland Lysander	75
Gloster Gladiator	77
Armstrong Whitworth Whitley	79
Vickers Wellington	81
North American Harvard	82
Bristol Blenheim IV	85
Handley Page Hampden	86
Boulton Paul Defiant	87
Miles Master	89
Supermarine Walrus	90
Short Sunderland	91
Supermarine Spitfire V	93
Westland Whirlwind	95
Bristol Beaufort	97
de Havilland Mosquito	98
Avro Lancaster	100
Bristol Beaufighter	104
Supermarine Spitfire IX	106

Hawker Hurricane II	106
Curtiss Kittyhawk	109
North American Mitchell	110
Consolidated Catalina	111
Handley Page Halifax	113
Short Stirling	115
Consolidated Liberator	117
Martin Baltimore	118
Republic Thunderbolt	121
Douglas Boston	122
Supermarine Spitfire VIII	123
Supermarine Spitfire Mk XVI	124
North American Mustang	125
Douglas Dakota	127
Hawker Typhoon	129
Hawker Tempest	131
Gloster Meteor	134

Post War — 135

Avro York	137
de Havilland Hornet	138
Avro Lincoln	139
Bristol Sycamore	140
Bristol Brigand	141
Supermarine Spitfire F22	143
de Havilland Vampire	143
Blackburn Beverley	145
Gloster Meteor F8	148
Supermarine Swift	148
Handley Page Hastings	149
de Havilland (Canada) Chipmunk	151
Vickers Valiant	152

Gloster Javelin	154
Westland Belvedere	156
Hawker Hunter	157
Westland Whirlwind	159
Hawker Siddeley Gnat	160
Avro Shackleton	162
de Havilland Comet	163
BAC Jet Provost	164
English Electric (BAC) Lightning	166
McDonnell Douglas F-4 Phantom	168
Handley Page Victor	170
English Electric Canberra	173
Hawker Siddeley Buccaneer	175
Lockheed Hercules	177
Hawker Siddeley Nimrod	179
Hawker Siddeley (BAe) Harrier GR1 and GR3	180
Avro Vulcan	183
Scottish Aviation (BAe) Bulldog	185
Hawker Siddeley (BAe) Hawk	187
SEPECAT Jaguar	190
Westland/Aerospatiale Puma	192
Panavia Tornado GR1 and GR4	193
Panavia Tornado F3	196
Boeing-Vertol Chinook	197
Shorts Tucano	198
Westland Wessex	200
Lockheed Tristar	201
BAe (Hawker Siddeley) 125/BAe 146	202
BAe Harrier GR7	205
EH 101 Merlin	206
Boeing C-17 Globemaster III	209
Eurofighter Typhoon	210

Foreword by Michael Turner

The major part of this book was published twenty two years ago and covered the period from 1918 to 1980. I am delighted that I have been given the opportunity by the RAF Benevolent Fund Enterprises, surely a most appropriate sponsor, to bring the subject up to date in this new version. The consequent opportunity to change to landscape format and the considerable advances in reproduction techniques has enabled better presentation of the paintings and a fresh new look to a subject which is close to my heart. Apart from re-scanning all the existing pictures, there are several new pictures and some substitutions, plus the addition of aircraft types which have come into service since 1980. The main text by Chaz Bowyer has also been updated, and Peter March has added text to cover the most recent types.

The sentiments I expressed in my 1981 Foreword are still relevant, and, apart from incorporating some revisions to accommodate the passage of time, they are repeated here. Similarly, I am indebted to Raymond Baxter for amending his generous comments to suit this new edition.

As a small boy living in the suburbs of London throughout World War two, I suppose it was not surprising that the exploits of the Royal Air Force in those heroic days captured my imagination, and filled me with an admiration which I have never lost. I still recall the seemingly endless nights under the dining room table, sheltering from Hitler's bombs, and persuading my indulgent Mother to take me on potentially hazardous journeys to airfields such as Northolt and Croydon, to peer expectantly through any available gaps in the perimeter at Spitfires and Hurricanes being prepared for battle. This, coupled with my fascination with aircraft and flying, which developed during this period, has no doubt led me to what is largely a labour of love.

In attempting to portray and record the aircraft of the RAF in their many forms and spheres of operation over a period of more than eighty years, space dictates that I have, regrettably, had to omit some interesting types and locations, and also to epitomise the many facets of some extensively used types with but one interpretation. However, whilst I have only scratched the surface of my self-imposed task, I hope this collection will provide a worthwhile visual record, enhanced by Chaz Bowyer's informative text, and the personal comments and anecdotes of those who flew the aircraft.

I have always believed that, to be able to convey the true feeling and atmosphere of any subject, there is no substitute for personal experience, and I have gone to considerable lengths over the years to acquire as many first-hand impressions as possible. In this respect, I have been fortunate enough to experience flight in a large variety of military aircraft - from Tiger Moth to Tornado, Lancaster to Nimrod: Fast and low with Harrier and Jaguar in Germany, to elementary flying in Bulldogs and formation aerobatics with the Red Arrows team. Of course, the majority of the aircraft types covered in this book are beyond the scope of my personal involvement, being as they are from times past, but, nevertheless, the feel of flying in an open cockpit, wire braced bi-plane, or the gut-wrenching G-forces encountered in modern high performance fast-jets, the wearing of often cumbersome and uncomfortable flying clothing and the nauseous smell of an oxygen mask, impart an essential understanding which can be applied to most situations I am trying to portray. In 1988 I finally learned to fly myself, and am privileged to own and operate an ex-RAF Chipmunk which has enabled me to continue to enjoy and better understand the wonder of flight and the natural habitat of the aeroplane.

In researching my subject aircraft, particularly those which were in service before my time, I have tried to ensure that the resultant paintings provide an appropriate interpretation and historically accurate record of the subjects, colour schemes and settings depicted. If some anomalies have crept in, I offer my apologies.

I would like to add my thanks to the Ministry of Defence, the Royal Air Force and the many Squadron personnel who have willingly assisted me in my quest for personal involvement over the years. In the process, I have acquired even more admiration and respect for those skilled enough to be capable of controlling an aircraft under the extreme conditions of flight demanded by military flying, and to those equally dedicated personnel on the ground who make such operations possible.

Foreword by Raymond Baxter

The philosophical distinction between artist and craftsman has long been debated by those far better qualified than me, but that Michael Turner is both seems to me self-evident. Having known him and his work for more years than perhaps either of us would care to calculate, my regard for both remains undiminished.

To reproduce with such consistency so broad a diversity of highly technical subjects to the standards of blueprint accuracy demands the skill and studious devotion of the engineering draughtsman. Observe, for example, the rigging wires in his Avro Tutor or Walrus, the aerials on his Demon, or the relationship between skeleton and skin in his Handley Page Heyford. This is the stuff to satisfy the most pedantic enthusiast for detail.

On the other hand, even without their primary subjects the background of so many of his paintings would constitute a work of art sufficient to satisfy more than one of his distinguished colleagues. The mountains below and above his Hawker Harts are awesome in their ice-clad majesty. Conversely the featureless monochrome behind his Vickers Vincent shimmer with mirages. Sky and desert merge in exactly the manner I recall as characteristics of certain days above Habbaniyah.

Sometimes perhaps, by purely aesthetic standards, his background is somewhat too cluttered. The famous Johnnie Johnson Spitfire painting is a case in point. Turner has attacked the chaos on the airfield with the boyish zest for action of a ten-year-old.

Yet his restraint in, for example, the Knapsack power station leaves us in no doubt where we are - if only for a few pulse-racing seconds.

It is unusual in my experience to meet an artist so skilled in the detail of technology who yet enjoys an equal facility with the human figure. The 'erks' in the foreground of his 501 Squadron Vampires are sprawled on the grass precisely as 'erks' and grass become inseparable for any length of time when nothing more demanding was to be done. On the other hand one can smell the sweat of the toiling airmen at Kenley during the Battle of Britain and the posture of the trio and pair about the RE8 freezes all five figures in a micro-second of their activity. The men in the tender approaching the Sunderland stand as only boatmen stand in boats, and the weight and restriction of flying gear hampers the aircrew at 4FTS Abu Sueir in 1938. Michael Turner was certainly never near Abu Sueir in 1938, but in this as in many other paintings of periods long before his time, he commands the authority of the eye-witness.

His choice and use of colour may be the key to his success in capturing the mood of the moment. The blurred golden light above the horizon and its echo superimposed on the dark grey-blue obscuring the ground add tension to the Tornado on operations over Iraq, and the white foam surrounding the Soviet submarine overflown by the Nimrod, focuses the immediacy of the encounter and reveals the artist's ability to capture sea as well as sky. The blue and white sky-scape pierced by his Lightnings is high-altitude, high-performance flying. I can almost hear the hiss of the spray as his Blackburn Iris turns into wind, and there is a dream-like quality appropriate to the Far East created by the greys and mauves of his formation of four Supermarine Southamptons.

A quality which will strike sympathetic chords with any pilot who has experienced low level operational flight is exemplified by the streaking of the sea below his Harrier GR7 off 'Illustrious". The same contrivance in 'Spitfire Special Delivery' almost startled me in my recall of the images stamped indelibly into my mind by those few minutes of timeless experience almost 60 years ago.

Michael Turner's ability to capture moments-in-contrast could not be more dramatically exemplified than by 'Boeing C-17 Kabul' and 'Typhoon Coningsby'. In the former we see the stark dazzling clear-light images of a hostile, dry, forward airfield. The contrast to 'Typhoon Coningsby 17 Squadron' comes, frankly, as a shock. The attitude of the aircraft, the display of their weapons, the burning thrust of the engines piercing the scatter of low 'cumulus fractus' cloud, is literally breath-taking.

There remains one outstanding characteristic common to all his work. All his airborne aeroplanes are flying. Just how this is achieved I cannot say. It is a quality instantly apparent by its absence from the work of lesser aviation artists, and instantly recognisable to anyone who has flown.

Michael Turner is above all a pilots' artist.

Without a deep and undying love for flying and aeroplanes, none of his demonstrable skills as artist and craftsman could combine to achieve the evocative impact of his pictures.

The jacket photograph of Michael Turner speaks volumes. The smile framed by his 'bone-dome' is that of a man happy in his work. I know the feeling well, and that is why to anyone who shares it, his work commands the particular affection reserved to that of a fellow spirit with whom communication is in no way hampered by time or distance. The sounds, the smells, the feel of the controls, the squeeze of the G and the weightlessness of inversion - above all the quickening of the pulse - all come flooding back from every encapsulated moment of experience.

Aeroplanes come closer to being 'alive' than any other machines. In this collection Michael Turner has ensured the immortality of the aeroplanes of the Royal Air Force, and that is no inconsiderable contribution to bequeath to posterity.

Raymond Baxter

Supermarine Spitfire XVI *In foreground is the machine flown by Flt Lt Raymond Baxter - picture depicts No 602 Squadron making a low-level precision attack on Baatsher-Mex building in The Hague, HQ of German V1/V2 research, on March 18th 1945.*

Felixstowe Flying Boat

Aircraft of World War One

The advent of the war in 1914 diverted all aeronautical development into military aircraft. Designers produced two major types of reconnaissance aeroplane: the two-seat biplane with reasonable range and endurance, and, in much fewer numbers, small, single-seater, 'high speed' (sic) 'scouts'. Nevertheless, ideas for different tasks for aircraft were already being mooted, in particular for pure bomber and fighter designs; major examples of these being respectively the giant Handley Page O/100 and the optimistically-titled Vickers 'Destroyer'. War Office and Admiralty orders were spread among a varied selection of private manufacturers throughout the war, resulting in a myriad of aircraft concepts ranging from excellent to frankly ridiculous. Even so, near-standardisation of aircraft types was relatively swift, and most were designed under one or other title - bombers, reconnaissance, scouts (to be later known as fighters), trainers, and various types of maritime floatplanes and flying-boats.

From 1915 to 1918, the urgent exigencies of wartime quickened the development of each major type of aeroplane design for its succinct war role, and by April 1918, when the RAF was 'born', its first-line squadrons were well equipped in respect of specialised roles. Fighter units were flying Sopwith Camels, SE5as, Sopwith Dolphins and the two-seater Bristol F2b; while day and night bomber squadrons were equipped with Airco DH 4 or 9 two-seaters, Handley Page O/100 or O/400 behemoths, and even the obsolescent FE2b or 2d two-seat 'pushers'. 'Artillery Observation' squadrons for direct tactical support of the army relied on the RE8 or Armstrong Whitworth FK8, and former RNAS units employed a variety of floatplanes or flying-boats for maritime purposes. Even the UK-based instructional organisation was by then receiving aircraft specifically designed for training roles, while Home Defences had been allotted a number of squadrons equipped with crudely-modified fighters for night interception of German raiders.

An SE5a in combat

Bristol F2b Fighter

A rugged 'fighter-reconnaissance' design introduced to squadron operations in France from April 1917, the Bristol Fighter - known to its wartime crews as the 'Biff' and its post-1918 owners as the 'Brisfit' - quickly earned a fighting reputation which also led to its universally recognised title of 'King of Two-Seaters'. Strongly constructed, with excellent controls' response, manoeuvrability and overall performance, the Bristol F2b allowed its pilot to handle his machine like any normal single-seat fighter, with the advantage of a gunner to protect the tail; the latter adopting the age-old classic 'back-to-back' fighting stance with his 'driver'.

Had the F2b rested on its many wartime laurels alone, it would have secured a niche in any list of classic aircraft designs; yet the aircraft was destined to continue in first-line service with RAF squadrons until early 1932. During those years, Brisfits gave sterling service on operations over Egypt, Palestine, Iraq and northern India (now Pakistan); they were virtually unaltered from their original concept, yet they successfully undertook almost every possible role.

Crew reactions to this aircraft were unanimous in their praises. The late Major W F J Harvey, MBE, DFC, TD, who fought in F2bs of No 22 Squadron in 1918, said of it: *"This was a classic aeroplane in looks, in performance for its period, and of a curiously perfect tactical design at a time when the future requirements of a fighting aircraft were not fully understood"*. Another 1918 pilot expressed his enthusiasm in equestrian terms, calling the F2b *"a thoroughbred hunter, with a delicate mouth and a stout heart."* Such was the appeal of the design that some 50 years later the test pilot Godfrey Auty, after piloting F2b D8096 of the Shuttleworth Collection, said of it: *"From the moment of placing one's left foot on the root of the lower port wing to hoist oneself into the cockpit, there is a feeling of unity between man and machine."*

Lieutenant Whipple was a young American who served in E N Griffith's Flight. In this account, written shortly after the event took place, he describes a dogfight between Bristol Fighters and the Richtofen Circus in August 1918: *"My first fight was with a Hun two-seater who was directing his artillery fire from his side of the lines. All five of us dived on him firing as we went and if it had not been for his armour plate he would have been a sorry wreck. As it was, I was on the tail end of the formation and got last shot at him and saw him go wobbling down to the ground. All of us had shared equally in his ruin so no-one could claim official credit, but it put new confidence into me. I was sure my bullets had been effective and now I felt ready for anything at even odds.*

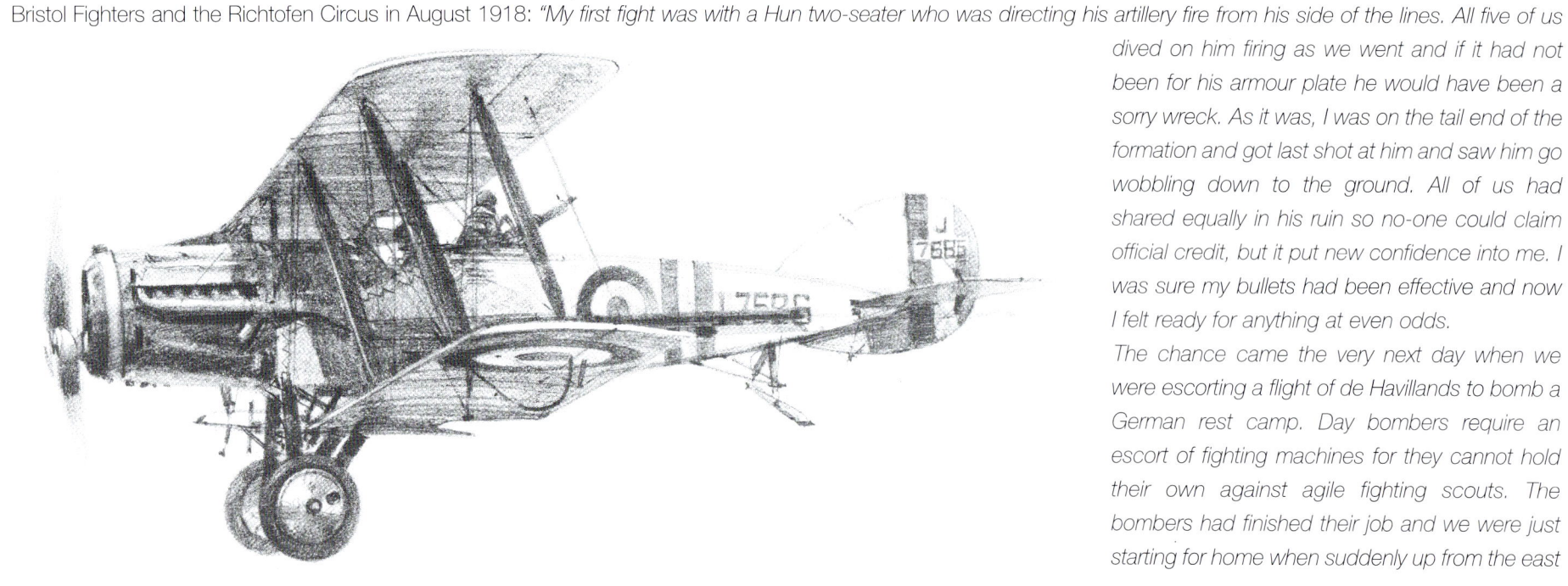

The chance came the very next day when we were escorting a flight of de Havillands to bomb a German rest camp. Day bombers require an escort of fighting machines for they cannot hold their own against agile fighting scouts. The bombers had finished their job and we were just starting for home when suddenly up from the east

Bristol Fighter *A Bristol F2b of No 11 Squadron in combat with a patrol of Albatros DVs in poor weather. This aeroplane was as fast and manoeuvrable as many contemporary single-seater fighters, and was one of the most effective fighters of World War One.*

came 14 Fokkers, all painted a brilliant scarlet except the leader who flew a silver tri-plane. The bombers raced for the lines leaving the five of us to fight it out and cover their retreat. We did nothing but stick even closer together and wait for our flight commander to give a signal. The Huns were right up to us by now and started firing. Their method of attack was very peculiar. One by one they circled up to us, firing as they came. We paid no attention to them but kept on steadily climbing so that while they were losing height by so much fussing around we were gaining height. At last our commander Captain Griffith judged we had the height on them then, without a single warning of our intentions, we wheeled and dived on the whole formation.

My own gun jammed and would not fire, and there was no time to fix it. The German I had picked out for myself slipped away unscratched. I was just pulling out of my dive when some instinct made me look over the side down to my right, just in time to see the big tri-plane getting into position to shoot me from underneath. My own gun was useless so I nudged frantically at my observer's elbow and pointed down at the Hun. He lost no time in turning his gun on him and the German changed his mind about attacking us and turned for home, but too late. Captain Griffith had seen my predicament and had come up to help me just in time to plunge after the fleeing leader of the German Circus. I turned to get a better view of the running flight. It did not last long. Inside of a few seconds the tri-plane was falling like a shooting star leaving a trail of smoke and flame a mile above it. We *lost no time in getting home after this and when we landed and tallied up the score we found that we had shot down three of them and not one of our machines was seriously damaged. The next day we read in our secret intelligence files that 'On 10 August Lieut. Loewenhardt commanding the Richtofen circus was shot down by a flight of Bristol Fighters on the Somme front. Lieut. Loewenhardt had just achieved his 52nd victory'. Thus perished the crack German air fighter of that time. I could not help thinking how very near I came to being his 53rd victim."*

RE8

Known universally as the 'Harry Tate' (one of the leading contemporary music-hall artists) the Farnborough-designed RE8 was one of the great workhorses of the RFC and RAF during the latter years of World War One. Its intended role was reconnaissance in aid of the infantry, a task which included photographing enemy-held territory behind the trenches, low-level contact patrols with forward units of the Allied armies, and constant assistance to the artillery on spotting patrols for the heavy guns. Plodding in performance and sluggish in manoeuvrability, the RE8 was no real match for the sleek Fokkers and Albatros Scouts of 1917-18, and its crews suffered high casualty rates. Yet one of the commonest sights of the aerial war in 1918 was of lone RE8s doggedly flying monotonous figures-of-eight paths through a flurry of anti-aircraft shell-bursts, as their courageous crews maintained faith with the earthbound infantry they were supporting.

Standardised for army co-operation duties by 1917, the RE8 was nevertheless by no means ideal for war operations. With its longitudinal and lateral in-built dihedral it became known as the 'Rigger's Nightmare', while its all-round mediocrity in performance meant that its many solid achievements in daily routine tasks were a tribute to the fortitude and sheer courage of its crews, rather than any credit to the aircraft or its designers. That it continued in front-line service until the end of hostilities was a mark of the irresponsibility and ignorance of RAF higher authorities of the day.

RE8 *The crew of an RE8 of No 16 Squadron prepare to set off on a dawn patrol over enemy lines in 1918. In many ways, the RE8 resembled the BE2 which it began to replace from early 1917; by the end of hostilities the RE8 was in service with 19 squadrons and over 4,000 were eventually manufactured.*

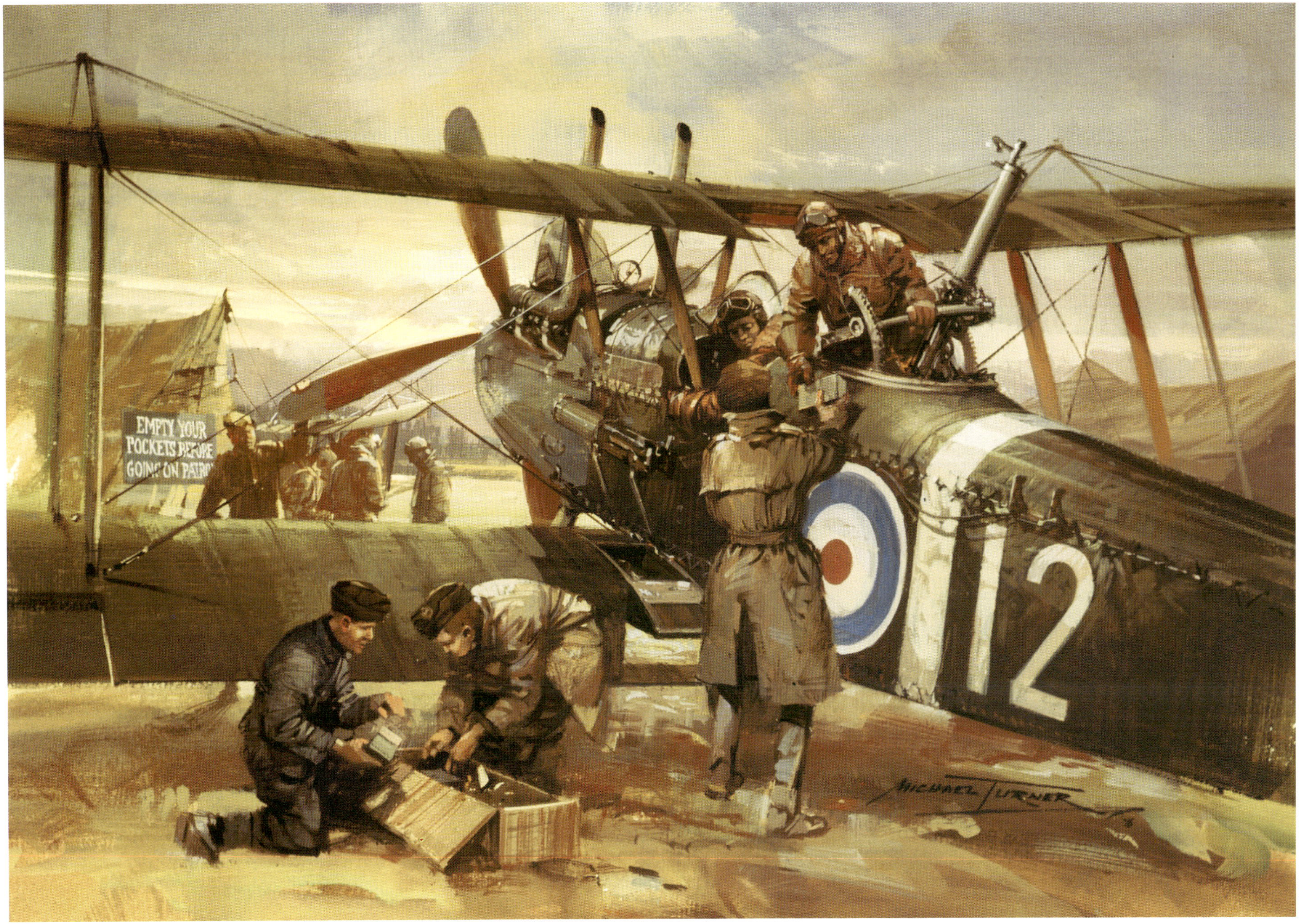
EMPTY YOUR
POCKETS BEFORE
12
MICHAEL TURNER

Handley Page O/400

The HP O/400 was a giant of an aeroplane in every way. With a wing span of 100ft, length of nearly 63ft, and height of 22ft, it overshadowed every other operational aircraft of the RAF in 1918. Derived from a 1914 design, the O/400 first entered service as the O/100 bomber with 3 Wing RNAS in 1916 and continued in service as a long-range night bomber until the end of the war; some 400 examples being delivered ultimately to the services. Its massive wings were designed for folding back to ease ground handling and field accommodation, and it carried a normal bomb load of 14 or 16 bombs of 112lb.

It was the only aircraft to drop the largest, heaviest Allied bomb of the war, the 1,600/1,650lb SN (some 40 of these giant missiles being dropped in the closing months of the struggle). Post-1918 use of the O/400 was mainly confined to the emerging passenger and freight carriage airlines; the last RAF examples were replaced in service by 1922.

In the current era of supersonic aerial transport it may seem quaint to recall the first impassions of flying in an HP O/400 by a national newspaper reporter in September 1918: "The roar of the two engines becomes a perfect inferno as we start to climb. The pressure of wind on my face makes me wonder if it will yet behead me. On each side of me a brown line of exhaust gases flows from the motors. The gale of wind thrust past my head by

Handley Page O/400 *Two Handley Page O/400s from No 215 Squadron bomb the Badische Anilin Chemical Works at Mannheim on the night of 25 August 1918. The two aircraft attacked at a very low level (250 and 500ft).*

the whirling screws is so tremendous that it seems as though I was being forced through something solid like butter... All this at a speed of little more than 60mph!"
First of the true heavy bombers for the RAF, vehicle for the genesis of strategic night bombing, and faithful pioneer of the first peacetime airlines in Britain; the HP O/400 holds a unique position in British aviation annals.

Leslie Blacking was 19 years old when as a Second Lieutenant he flew O/400s on No 27 Squadron at Ligescourt near Abbeville: *"I remember this big bomber chiefly for the heaviness of its control and the height of its cockpit above the ground. It had to be flown all the time and it was particularly heavy on lateral control. When you put on bank it didn't respond at once. When it did you had to reverse the joystick wheel immediately to take the bank off, and if you went over 45° you were in trouble. I've actually had to stand up to exert all my strength to get the 'bus' back on an even keel.*

The 'Handleys' were used for night bombing attacks on strategic targets, such as railway marshalling yards, and ammunition and fuel dumps, to help stem the German offensive of 1918. I had done only ten flying hours on O/400s before joining the squadron and had previously flown the tricycle-undercarriage FE 2bs; consequently I found it difficult to judge my height before touch-down. The observer helped my landing problem by leaning over the side and yelling, 'Back, back, more - OK!' As we always switched-off the engines and glided in I could hear him quite clearly, and knew when to pull back on the control column wheel to get the tail down.

Our grass airfield wasn't very big, but it had a wide valley on two sides, where the River Authie ran, and this helped us to get our heavily-laded planes into the air.

The instrument panel was quite simple: compass, airspeed indicator, bubble, altimeter and clock. There was a larger compass on the floor beside the pilot who sat on the right. The counters were outside the cockpit - on the engine nacelles.

We had no armour-plating or parachutes, just fabric and wood around us and thin duck-boarding under our feet. Our greatest fear was fire in the air, if we were to be hit by any of the green 'flaming onions' or white phosphorous balls which arched up through the darkness from the ground defences.

Normally we carried a number of 112lb bombs but sometimes just one 1,650lb bomb, and when we let it go the O/400 rose about 50 feet".

We could stay airborne for about four and a half hours - if you could stand the cold; for it was intense, despite our heavy flying gear (which could be electrically heated), in that big, open cockpit."

18

Sopwith Camel

Ask anyone to name just three aircraft of the 1914-18 aerial war and the answer is certain to include a pug-nosed, waspish little killer called the Camel. This 'popping firecracker' emerged from the war as the most successful individual fighter used by any nation, its many pilots claiming almost 3,000 combat victories. Its aerobatic qualities were legendary. It could be flick-rolled at grass-cutting height without loss of altitude and looped from a low speed with complete confidence. Yet its most significant characteristic was an ability to turn left or right and reverse flight path under perfect control with the speed of a greased pond-skater. Thoroughly unstable and wilfully independent, the Camel offered little sympathy to any ham-fisted tyro, but those who mastered it found themselves equipped with probably the greatest dogfighter of the war.

Veteran Camel pilots were unanimous in their praises of the Camel. Major W G Moore, OBE, DSC, said of it: *"A skilled pilot could not wish for a better mount. To him it was like having a pair of wings strapped onto his shoulder blades"*, while Henry Woollett, a 36-victory ace, gave his opinion that: *"The Camel could dictate a fight and turn inside any scout the enemy used, if it was operated at the right altitude, usually around 12,000 feet."* Major Oliver Stewart, MC, DFC, summed most pilots' regard for the type succinctly: *"Gifted with a more strongly developed personality than perhaps any other aeroplane, the Sopwith Camel inspired pilots who flew it with respect and with affection. It set a new standard in powers of manoeuvre and even today (1936) it probably remains the most highly manoeuvrable aeroplane that has ever been built'.* Such were the quicksilver qualities of the Camel that the fears of student pilots and the praise of combat veterans are best described by the blunt phrase of one veteran when he said of the fierce little beast: *"It left you with three choices: Red Cross, Victoria Cross or wooden cross."*

Cecil Lewis, MC describes one of the first night operations: *"After being wounded and returning from France in the summer of 1917, I was posted to Hainault Farm, a Home Defence aerodrome just beyond Ilford. It was there I met the Sopwith Camel, so called because of a slightly 'humped' top line to the fuselage. The pilot was hunched in behind the flat engine, the tanks were the full depth of the fuselage just behind the pilot - and all this meant the weight was highly concentrated and made for very lively handling characteristics. The Camel, in fact, was a beauty. It was sturdy enough to stand rough flying in a dogfight, handy enough to outmanoeuvre anything it came across. In addition it had two Vickers guns firing through the propeller and soon proved itself a very offensive weapon indeed. Beyond all this, it had all the Sopwith characteristics of viceless, well-balanced handling. It was light, responsive, comfortable and pilots loved it.*

The forward stagger of the main planes gave the pilot a good forward and downward view which served him well in a dogfight; but later, when the machine began to be used as a night fighter, to attack enemy bombers at home or overseas, the positions of pilot and tank were reversed. This brought the pilot out just aft of the main planes and gave him an excellent forward and upward view. Although we did not think the Camel handled quite as well with this arrangement, it was better suited to the job."

Sopwith Camel *Sopwith Camels from No 65 Squadron attack an enemy observation balloon near the Flanders front in September 1918. This single-seater fighter was named 'Camel' because the top line of the fuselage was slightly 'humped' to accommodate the breeches of its twin Vickers guns.*

SE5a

Of the many aeroplanes designed at the Royal Aircraft Factory at Farnborough before and, especially, throughout 1914-18, very few were received with enthusiasm by the crews who had to fly them in combat. One of the rare exceptions was the SE5a. The result of several years of progressive development, the first SE5s were taken to France by No 56 Squadron in April 1917. Combat experience quickly led to much modification and improvement in engine power, and the resulting SE5a came to be regarded as probably the finest wartime product from Farnborough. Though having a tendency to nose-heaviness in ground handling, in the air the SE5a had no vices. It was immensely strong in construction, permitting high speed dives with confidence, had positive control responses in almost any attitude, and withstood the inevitable rough handling associated with close dogfighting without undue stress on the airframe. Its relatively high speed, excellent ceiling performance, and all-round robustness made it a near-ideal vehicle for the 1917-18 mode of air fighting, and it became the mount of a high proportion of the many top-scoring fighter pilots of the Allied air services.

The SE5a's huge contribution to ultimate air supremacy over the Western Front particularly may be gauged by the opinions of two men who flew the type. Oliver Stewart said of the design: *"It is of all aeroplanes the richest in the associations of aerial fighting, of hard-contested and long drawn-out*

SE5a *A pair of SE5a's from No 56 Squadron on dawn patrol near Valheureux, France. Typically the aircraft was fitted with one Lewis gun firing through the propeller and one Lewis gun mounted on the upper plane to fire over the propeller arc.*

'dogfights', of battles against heavy odds, of extraordinary escapes."

Cecil Lewis, who led the first SE squadron to France, said of it: *"The SE5 was probably the first fighting aircraft to be produced which was reliable enough and steady enough to stand up to the rough and tumble of 30 or 40 aircraft milling around trying to shoot each other down ... Slammed into a dive, yanked into a climb, pulled hard round in a very tight turn, the aircraft structure had to stand up to enormous and sudden strains. The SE came through this ordeal triumphantly and justified the belief of the top brass that it would give the Allies the supremacy of the air that year. It did."*

J V Gascoyne, DFC described how the SE was used in the closing months of the war for groundstraffing: *"It was the practice to take off singly, carrying four Cooper bombs and fully loaded with ammunition. I found it most exciting to fly over the enemy trenches and batteries, some times at a height less than 200 feet. This was not as dangerous as it appears for we were moving very fast (for those days) and so were difficult to hit, particularly as we were firing our own guns most of the time. The danger came from crossfire and field guns using shrapnel. On the top centre-section of the SE, a Lewis gun was carried with a drum containing 97 rounds. To reload this gun one had to pull it down on a slide into the cockpit. The pilot was given a certain amount of protection by a small wind-screen, measuring 11 inches by three inches. To fit a new drum was therefore a work of art and very few pilots attempted it. It was not only very difficult but it took quite a time and left you open to attack by an enemy machine. We had no bomb sights but it was astonishing how near one could get to the target after a little practice and experience. My own plan was to decide on a target while flying at low-level and so gain experience as to how far the bomb carried. One had to be careful, however, with the bomb moving forward at the same speed as the aircraft as you both arrived at the target at the same time if the pilot flew in a straight line. It was therefore necessary to turn away from the target before the bomb arrived."*

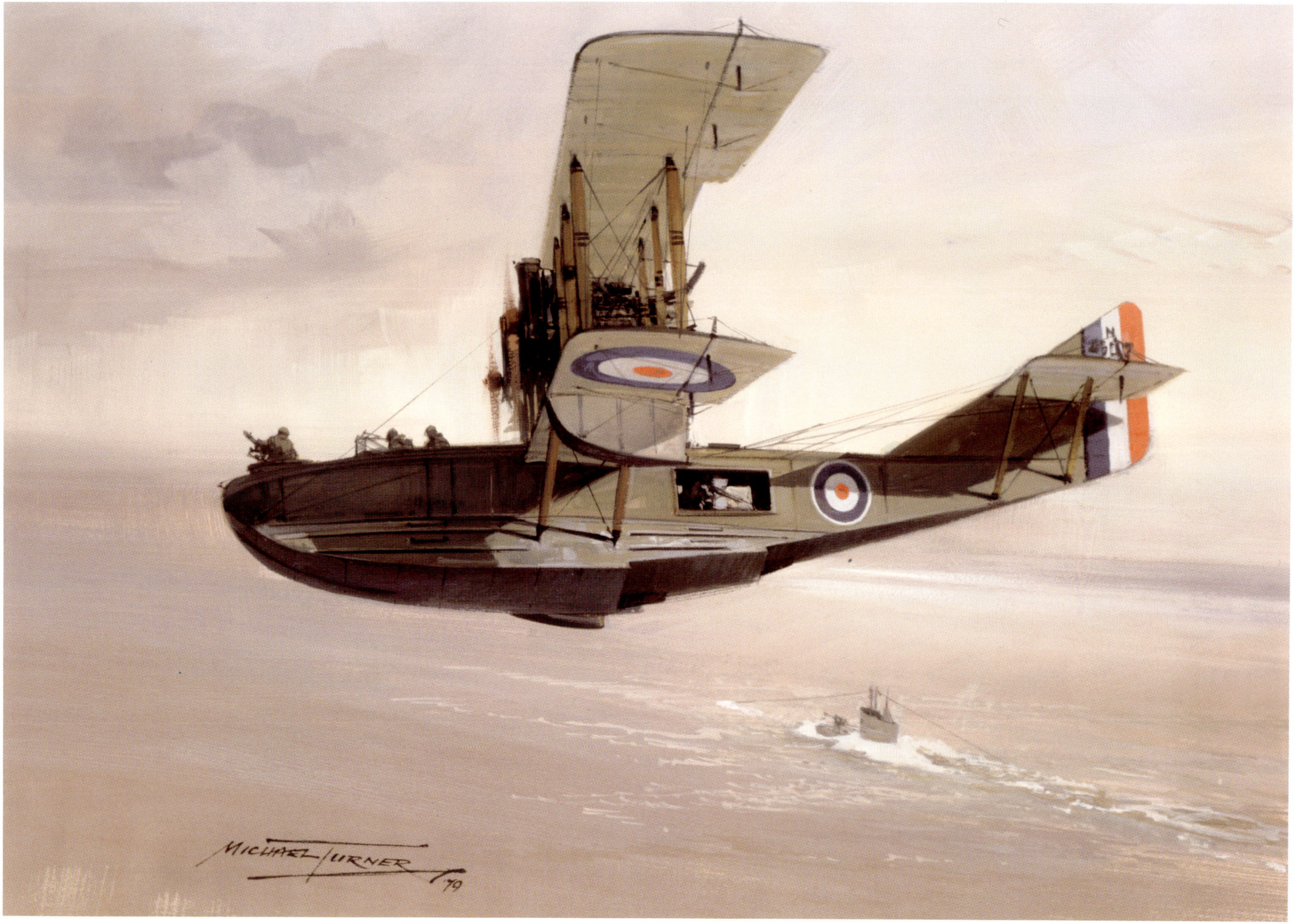
MICHAEL TURNER
'79

Felixstowe Flying Boat

Once man-controlled flight had been accomplished it was perhaps inevitable that Britain, with its age-old maritime traditions, should adapt the aeroplane for sea-going roles. The most outstanding examples of a true maritime design were the various large flying-boats produced during 1914-18, collectively known as the Felixstowe or 'F'-boats. Directly derived from the ideas of the noted American aviator Glenn H. Curtiss, the F-boats were designed by John C. Porte, a British naval officer serving in the RNAS. Porte's unceasing efforts to provide the RNAS with bigger and better flying boats continued until his death in 1919, and his legacy to Britain was the long line of practical designs which formed the foundation for several decades of RAF flying boat design.

Intended mainly for patrolling coastal waters, to protect Britain's mercantile lifelines of imported goods and materials, the F-boat crews were never content to play a mere watch-and-ward role, and took every opportunity to get to grips with any enemy which came within fighting range. At least two Zeppelins were destroyed in air combat by F-boats, while the many pure dogfights between British flying boats and German seaplanes during 1917-18 epitomised the offensive spirit of all F-boat crews.

F-boats were big by any standards, with wings spanning 100ft or more in several cases, weighing in excess of 10,000lb fully loaded, and capable of patrols of six hours or more.

Professor Sir Austin Robinson, CMG, OBE, FBA flew Felixstowe Flying boats in the RNAS and RAF before beginning a distinguished career as an economist: *"At the time they were built, the F2As were the largest operational aircraft apart from the Handley Page O/400. They were beautiful aeroplanes, although with hindsight their defects can be seen. For example, although the F2A had a rather short tail, rudder and fin, it had very long wings which meant that the ailerons were further from the centre of gravity than the rudder was; the obvious consequence was that if you tried to pick up a wing, you found yourself swinging off your compass course. However, one learnt by experience to give the rudder a hefty kick while using the ailerons, and on that basis a fairly accurate compass course could be maintained. The F2A also had difficulty in taking off in a heavy swell when fully loaded, although it could take off in less than 15 seconds when lightly loaded in calm conditions.*

The functions of the F2As differed at each station. Felixstowe and Yarmouth frequently encountered German seaplanes, because they were battling to keep control of the air in the lower North Sea. Throughout the war important trade took place with the Netherlands, which was neutral, and frequent convoys we knew as the 'beef trips' had to be defended by them from German attacks. At Killingholme, we seldom encountered German seaplanes; instead we had two main tasks. First, we undertook anti-submarine patrols, which were usually fairly close in-shore. Secondly, we undertook fleet reconnaissance and intercepted and frightened off Zeppelins.

Zeppelins had a higher ceiling than the F2A, and so we could only hope to catch one unawares or, more often, scare it away by making it drop its ballast and fuel in gaining altitude to avoid us and return home. The only Zeppelin that Killingholme has been given credit for was the L62, which was shot down by Pattinson, although others believe that this to be doubtful."

Felixstowe Flying Boat *An F2A May Harden May flying boat spots an enemy U-boat while on an anti-submarine patrol in 1918. In action the second pilot would operate the two guns in the nose, the engineer the gun next to the pilot and the radio operator fired through a porthole.*

Sopwith Snipe

The Sopwith 7F1 Snipe first appeared in prototype form in mid-1917 intended as a replacement for its stablemate, the Camel. In the event, it was almost a year later before production Snipes became available for issue to squadrons. First to replace its Camels was No 43 Squadron in September 1918, followed by No 208 Squadron and No 4 Squadron of the Australian Flying Corps. By November 1918 less than 100 Snipes had seen operational service. One Snipe, E8102, gained fame as the Snipe in which Major George Barker, DSO, MC won a Victoria Cross for a single-handed combat against great odds on 27 October 1918. Just 497 Snipes had been built by the Armistice, production continued post-war when the type became a standard RAF fighter and final production amounted to 2,103 Snipes.

The late Air Commodore Allen Wheeler, CBE, MA, FRAeS, Dutch DFC, as a junior officer at No 2 FTS, Digby in 1925 flew Snipes and described the type as: *" a delightful aeroplane to fly with light and effective controls. The trouble with the Snipe lay in its heavy and powerful rotary engine which gave a gyroscopic kick at right angles to any turning force applied to it. This meant that if the pilot pushed the stick forward to get the tail up on take-off the Snipe immediately tried to do a smart turn to the left which needed a significant rudder force to correct it. As one came off the ground and pulled up to a climbing angle the Snipe tried to turn smartly to the right."* The Snipe remained in RAF service until 1927.

Sopwith Snipe *flown by Major W. Barker, engaged in the dogfight in October 1918 in which he won his Victoria Cross.*

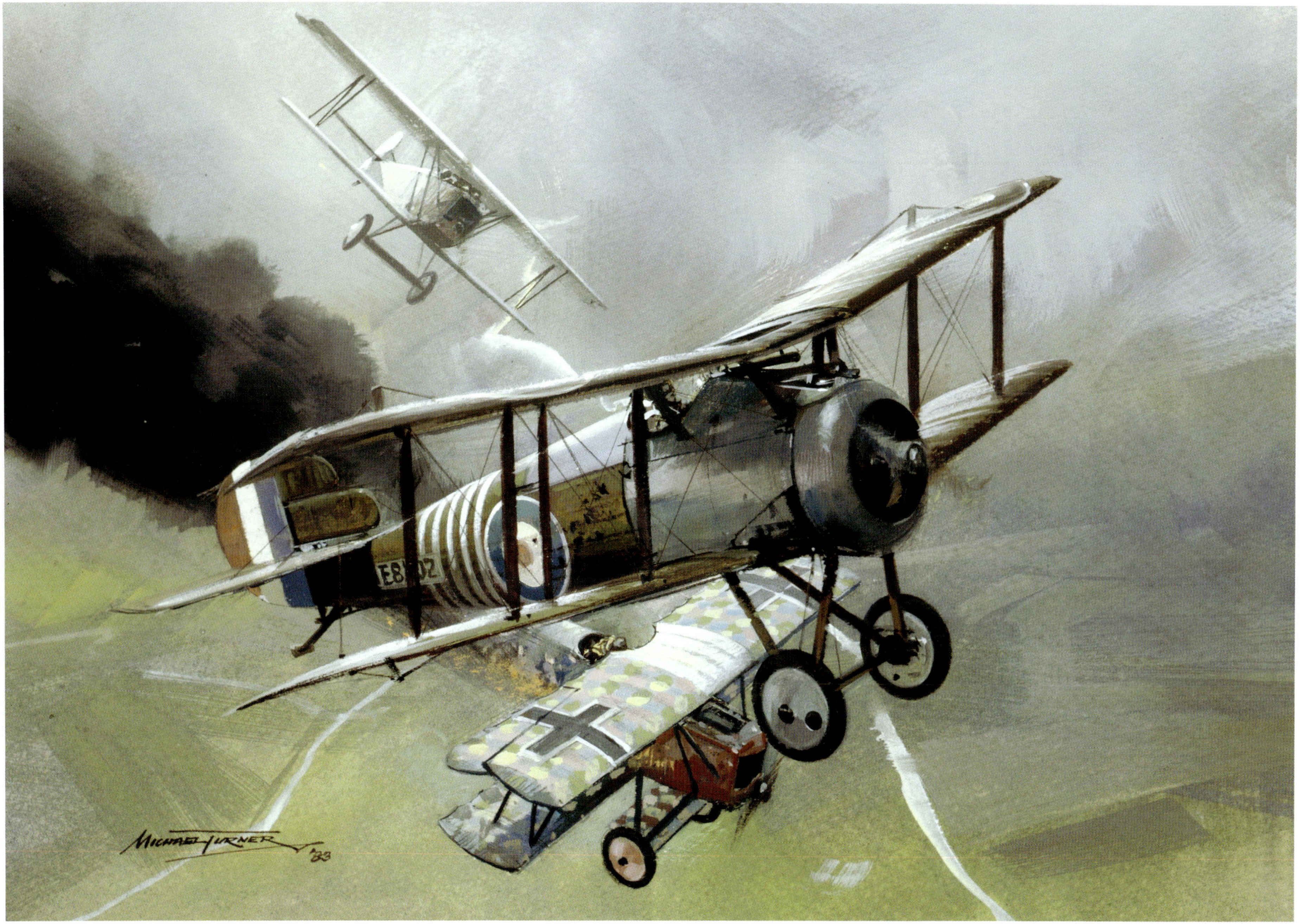
E8102
MICHAEL TURNER

A Supermarine Stranraer flying boat

Aircraft Between the Wars

By the Armistice of November 1918, a number of promising new aircraft were in embryo for the RAF, but as peacetime demobilisation and severely reduced financial backing decimated RAF strength, Britain's new air arm was forced to compromise in all matters of equipment. The few remaining squadrons in 1920 relied on wartime-designed machines such as the Bristol F2b, DH9A, Vickers Vimy and Sopwith Snipe. In the event, the F2b and DH9A were to soldier on in front-line operational use until the 1930s.

Continuing this policy of compromise through the 1920s, the RAF contracted aircraft manufacturers to produce a series of 'General Purpose' designs - a broad description indicative of the multi-varied roles each was expected to undertake - resulting in such aircraft as the Westland Wapiti, Vickers Vincent, and a line of Fairey III variants. On the bomber-cum-transport scene were lumbering biplanes like the Vickers Virginia, Vernon, Valentia and Handley Page Hyderabad - all little better in performance or conception than their 1918 predecessors.

In the fighter-interceptor role, for defence of Britain, the RAF continued to rely on twin-gunned biplanes until well into the 1930s, equipping first-line squadrons successively with Grebes, Gamecocks, Bulldogs, Furies, Gauntlets and Gladiators - neat, highly manoeuvrable little biplanes which were delightful to fly, but increasingly obsolescent in design concept for the more modern requirements of an aerial arm.

Bristol Bulldog

de Havilland 9a

The DH9a, or 'Ninak', as it was more familiarly known to its crews, shared with the Bristol F2b fighter the brunt of the RAF's first-line operational duties throughout the 1920s. Entering squadron service in the closing months of 1918, the 'Ninak' was then chosen as the main day bomber to equip many of the much-reduced RAF's overseas units attempting to maintain air control of Britain's empire and mandated territories; particularly in the Middle East zones and in India. A development of the much-criticised DH9 of 1917, the 'Ninak' showed a significant improvement in engine power and consequent high altitude performance over its predecessor. In the heated thin air of Iraq or India, however, the 'Ninak's' all-round performance suffered badly offering a fast landing speed but a laborious rate of climb.

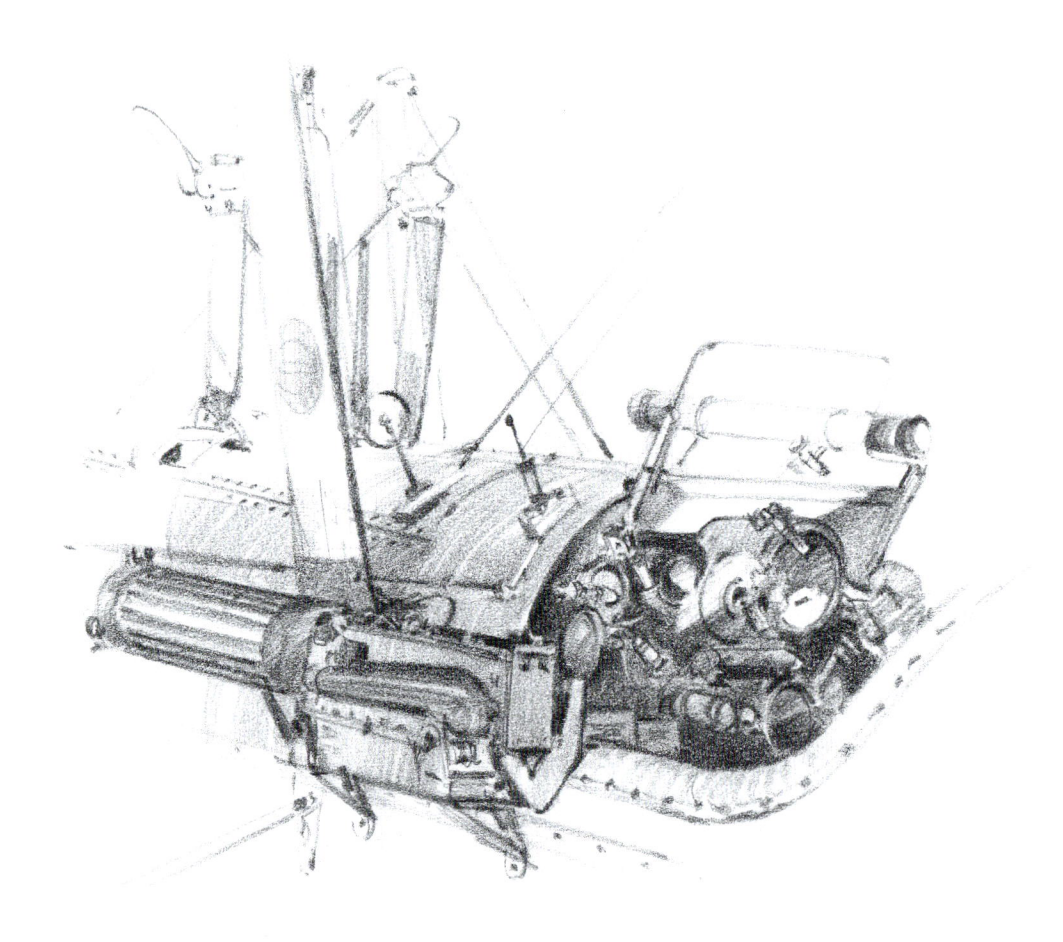

Despite inadequate maintenance facilities and financial backing almost throughout its 'peacetime' years, the DH9a and its stoic crews successfully undertook a wide variety of operational roles.

While India and Iraq saw the biggest concentration of 'Ninak' operational employment, the aircraft did useful work in many other areas. In Africa a handful helped pioneer the vogue for long distance proving flights; while in Britain from 1925, DH9a's formed the initial equipment of several squadrons of the freshly-created Auxiliary Air Force. Like all old soldiers the 'Ninak' faded away from RAF service and by 1932 few were in evidence.

Essentially a military aeroplane - hardworking, dependable - and displaying real fortitude when called upon to operate in conditions above and beyond the call of duty; the DH9a was a stalwart of the RAF's adolescence, and will always be remembered with affection by those who flew and maintained them.

de Havilland 9a A flight of DH9as on patrol against dissident tribesmen in Mesopotamia (now Iraq) in 1926. The DH9 was an 'improvement' on the DH4, but in fact was inferior because of its less powerful engine - the 9a (the 'Nine-Ack' or 'Ninak') had the more powerful liberty engine.

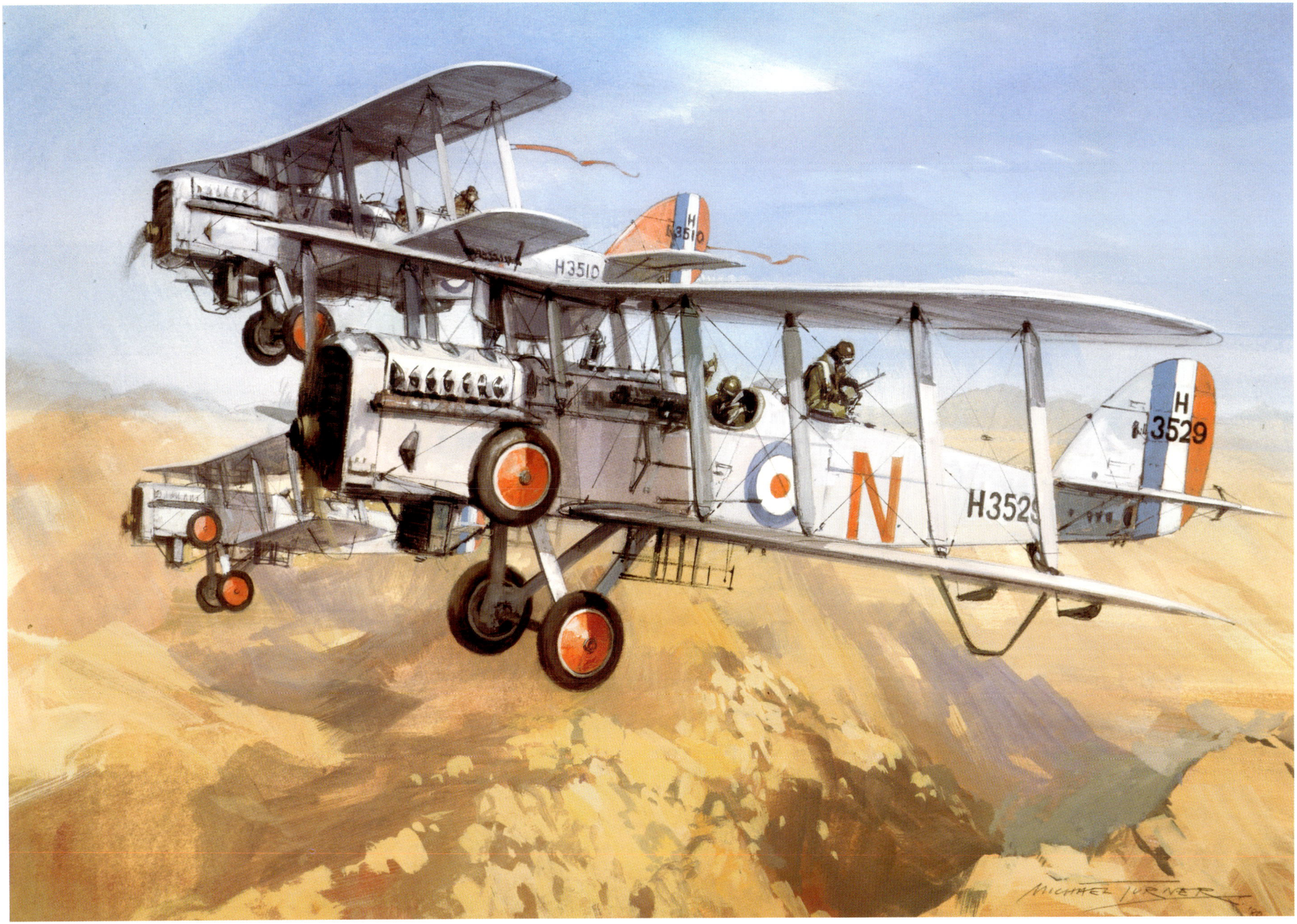
H
3510
H3510
H
3529
N
H3529
MICHAEL TURNER

Supermarine Southampton

The immediate post-1918 years saw the tiny RAF's coastal protection units equipped mainly with wartime-designed flying- boats and other seaplanes, and it was not until 1925 that a post-war design of flying boat began to re-equip the squadrons. This was the Supermarine Southampton, designed by R J Mitchell who later was to 'father' the Spitfire prototype. The Southampton was to set a pattern for future RAF flying-boats and served for some ten years in first-line use - hence its nickname 'Old Faithful' by its crews. Early versions of the Southampton had wooden-constructed hulls, but these were eventually replaced by metal-hulled Mark II versions which eliminated the natural impediment of some 400lb added weight of sea-water soakage in the wooden-hulled types. Southampton crews pioneered many of the long range cruises of the late 1920s, testing endurance and in-flight maintenance, and virtually fostered the self-dependent character thereafter associated with all RAF flying boat crews.

The most publicised exploit by Southampton crews began in October 1927, when four aircraft of the Far East Flight set out from Britain and eventually completed some 24,000 miles of flying to Singapore, Australia and around the China Sea without serious mishap - an event heralded in the contemporary press as 'the greatest flight in history'. Various attempts to modify and extend the life of the

Supermarine Southampton *Supermarine Southamptons of the Far East Flight, which became No 205 Squadron, after their epic 27,000-mile cruise to India, Australia, Hong Kong and Singapore.*

Southampton were modestly successful, but after nearly ten years of faithful service the Southampton was finally retired from the RAF - a longevity all the more remarkable when it is realised that an all-Mark production of the type only amounted to 78 aircraft.

G. E. Livock, who was one of the pilots on the Far East Flight, wrote about some of the problems they encountered en route: *"The selection of refuelling places took a great deal of working out on account of the limited range of the aircraft - about 500 sea miles was a safe maximum in still air. On a few occasions we had to make do with very unsatisfactory mooring sites. It was well known that most of the danger to flying-boats occurs when they are on the water. They are then vulnerable not only to bad weather, but also to attacks by sight-seeing motor boats, drifting native river craft and, of course, refuelling boats.*

Our first real test came on the leg from Alexandretta in Syria across the desert to Baghdad, a distance of 480 sea miles. Owing to a strong downdraught, we had difficulty with our full petrol load, in climbing over the cloud-covered mountains. Once over the desert we were met by an increasing headwind with alternative dust and rain storms, which reduced visibility in places to a few hundred yards. After more than eight hours in the air we ran into a thunderstorm and, as it was clear that we did not have enough fuel to reach Baghdad, we landed on the River Euphrates at Ramadi and anchored for the night. There was a store of petrol at the local RAF emergency landing ground and we took 30 gallons for each boat, which we brought off in our rubber dinghies. The night was made miserable by thunderstorms, howling jackals on the banks and the boats swinging wildly as first the 5-knot current and then the 20-knot wind took charge.

We stayed for three weeks at Karachi to enable the base party to carry out a thorough inspection of the aircraft, which were hauled up on to a beach. After Karachi we were not to see another RAF station until we landed at Hong Kong a year later."

32

Fairey III

With successive variations and modifications, the Fairey III series of land and floatplanes served in the RAF and the air services of several other countries. Originating from two 1917 experimental Fairey designs, the first Fairey IIIAs saw brief service in 1918 and were steadily improved until the first IIID appeared in August 1920. Simply constructed, tough and reliable, the IIID was extraordinarily versatile and may be regarded as Fairey's most successful aircraft in general terms. Convertible from landplane to floatplane configuration easily, the IIID saw extensive use with the RAF and the Fleet Air Arm in many guises, and is particularly remembered for its many long distance proving flights in the Middle East and African zones; pioneering routes which were later to become standard flightpaths for Imperial Airways and its successors.

One pilot who flew IIIDs described them as: *"Large, heavy and clumsy"* and went on to say: *"It had been designed as a seaplane and, naturally enough, it made a better seaplane than a landplane. It carried two passengers in addition to the pilot, had a maximum speed of about 120mph, and an*

Fairey III *Fairey IIID floatplanes of No 202 Squadron fly over Marsaxlokk Bay, Malta in 1929. Over 200 IIIDs were manufactured and they were widely deployed: this included service with the carriers HMS Argus and Vindictive (in the inter-war period the RAF operated the Fleet Air Arm aircraft).*

Fairey III *No 47 Squadron's Fairey IIIF floatplanes operating from the Nile at Khartoum.*

endurance of four and a half hours. The Napier Lion engine gave very little trouble except for cooling system water leaks, and in four years' flying from RAF Leuchars we only had one forced landing directly due to engine failure, and that could have, and should have been avoided. The IIID was the despair of pilots who liked to do 'pretty' landings, for it had a gliding angle rather like that of a brick, and then 'fell out of your hand' without any warning. However, it was so strongly built that it was difficult to damage it."

The pilot G. E. Livock gave the following account of using the Fairey IIID on reconnaissance in Malaya in the mid-1920s: *"Each morning the duty seaplane was wheeled out of the hangar and prepared for take-off. One of the cranes on each side of the hangar doors was swung inwards, and the patent slip hooked on to the wire slings on top of the centre section of the fuselage. If the weather conditions appeared favourable the order was given to hoist out. The engine was started and the pilot and observer climbed on board. After testing his engine, the pilot indicated that he was ready, and the RAF duty officer, standing on deck with a small flag in each hand, signalled to the crane driver for the plane to be hoisted a few feet off its trolley. The crane was then swung outboard until the aircraft was clear of the ship's side. When the signal was given, the seaplane was slowly lowered until the floats were just touching the water. The duty officer then signalled 'slip' to the observer, who was standing on top of the fuselage. The observer jerked the quick release. The seaplane dropped gently into the water and taxied away for take-off. In two or three minutes the aircraft was in the air and climbing gently towards the area chosen for the day's photographs. About half an hour later, at 10,000ft, the observer began to give instructions to the pilot.*

A minute or so before passing over the starting point the observer said: 'Steady as you go. Starting camera in one minute.' The pilot concentrated hard on maintaining his height at exactly 10,000ft, and adjusted the trim of the aircraft so that it kept absolutely level and on a steady course. During the run along the strip the observer gave the pilot any minor alterations to his direction, and kept an eye on the camera to see that it was working properly. It was not easy flying, for we had none of the delicate instruments one has today, but just the standard sluggish old 'clocks'. However, we had plenty of practice and eventually became very expert. After completing two or three strips our time was up: we would then have been in the air for one and a half to two hours. The throttle was eased gently back and we began the long slow glide towards the ship.

It was necessary to come down very slowly to prevent condensation forming in the camera and film boxes due to the great variation in temperature. It was wonderfully cool at ten thousand feet and one was quite happy to be wearing a flying-coat and scarf. For the first few thousand feet of the descent there was only a slight rise in temperature, but at about two or three thousand feet the hot pungent smell of the jungle suddenly enveloped the aircraft. Off came the scarf and the flying-coat was unbuttoned and opened wide. By the time one flattened out to land the heat seemed intolerable, and prickly heat, which had been dormant in the cold, burst out again."

Blackburn Iris

After two years in the making, the first Iris was launched in June 1926 with a wooden hull, but the following year was converted to the Iris II by having its superstructure refitted to a new metal hull. Only eight other examples were built thereafter, but one of these (S1593) was eventually redesigned as the prototype RB3a Perth - the ultimate

Blackburn Iris *A Blackburn Iris III flying-boat of No 209 Squadron taxis out from RAF Calshot, Hampshire for an evening return-flight to its base at RAF Mount Batten, Plymouth.*

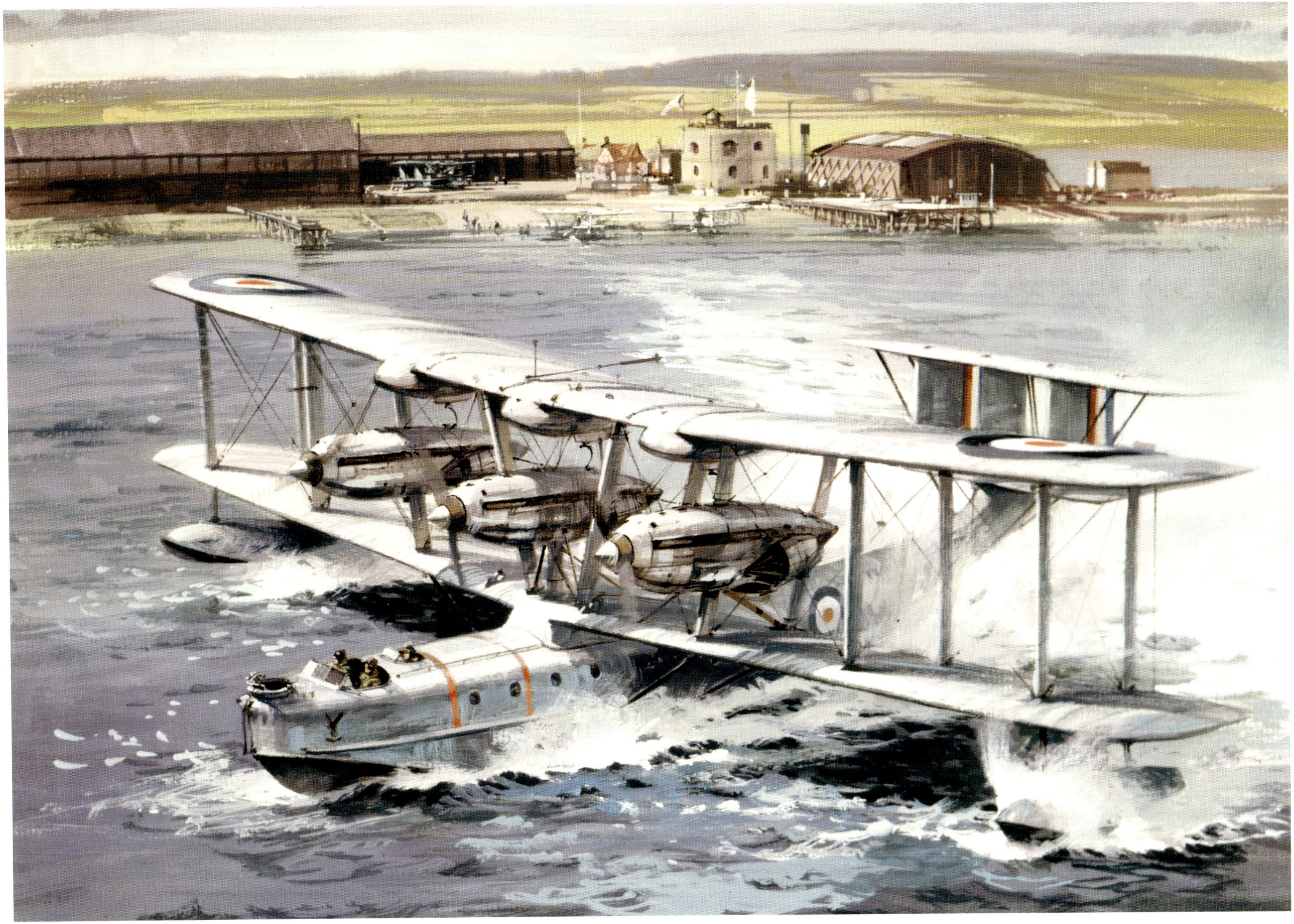

Iris development and the largest biplane flying boat ever used by the RAF. Of sound design and extremely strong construction, the Iris came to be used for a number of very long range flights around the world, and various modifications were made progressively both to improve the basic design and to increase crew self-sufficiency, including the provision of an 80lb five-man duralumin dinghy carried inverted on the lower centre section. Remaining in service until the early 1930s, the various versions of the Iris was subjected to a bewildering variety of technical improvements, many of these on a testing basis for future flying-boat requirements. In particular, S1593, titled Zephyrus, which was delivered to No 209 Squadron in July 1931, had its bow compartment enlarged to accommodate a 37mm Coventry Ordnance Works (COW) cannon - an unwieldy form of armament which quickly became dubbed the 'Flying Battleship' in the popular press of the period.

Often referred to as the Iris VI, the Blackburn Perth development differed externally from its 'parent' design by having enclosed pilots' cockpits. Only four examples were constructed and these staying in RAF service until 1936 before being relegated to experimental use. The success of the Iris, Blackburn's first venture into flying boat design, led to construction in 1930 of the Blackburn Sydney, which was a high-wing monoplane flying boat. Its hull was patently derived from the Iris, and though the Sydney was never awarded a production order, it was the first British military monoplane flying-boat of the heavyweight type.

Wing Commander F. L. Petch flew on all 245 sorties of the Blackburn Iris S1263:

"His Majesty's Flying Boat, Iris III, Service No S1263 was built by the Blackburn Aircraft Company Limited at Brough, East Yorkshire in 1929. It was the first production model from the design of Major Rennie and was destined for service with No 209 (Flying-Boat) Squadron which reformed at RAF Mount Batten, Plymouth in January 1930.

The Iris was designed as a long range, ocean-going aircraft to augment the coastal patrol services so ably fulfiled hitherto by the squadrons of Supermarine Southamptons. It was powered by three Rolls-Royce Condor engines, each of 675hp. Only the one squadron was equipped with Iris aircraft, first with the Mark III which later, by modification, became the Mark V and ultimately with what might well have been a later mark, but was, in fact, designated the 'Perth'.

The armament of the Iris consisted of Lewis guns in bow and midship positions with a third one at the tail end of the hull which, however, had only limited arc of fire. In the bow position, a one-pounder gun, made by the Coventry Ordnance Works, and consequently known as the 'Cow' gun, could be mounted, and indeed was, once every year for demonstration purposes, thus providing the press with an annual opportunity to publish pictures of 'Britain's Aerial Battleship'.

S1263 was launched on 5 February 1930 and, after a trip only five minutes short of five hours, completed her maiden flight to her home base at RAF Mount Batten. From that day, for her life of nearly three years with No 209 Squadron, it performed those duties for which she was built, without any claim to fame, with few dramatic highlights and rarely achieving press mention beyond her own parish, until her last day's duty. Its total contribution to the defence of the shores of Britain could be statistically presented as 245 sorties, totalling 343 hours in the air."

Bristol Bulldog

The Bulldog represented the most successful of the earliest attempts by British manufacturers to produce a fast-climbing, fully aerobatic, interceptor fighter, and the prototype first flew in May 1927. Service examples first reached No 3 Squadron in May 1929, and within three years nine other squadrons were equipped with Bulldogs; thereby representing some two-thirds of the UK's contemporary home defences. Regarded by all pilots who flew them as probably the best aerobatic machines of the day, Bulldogs featured largely in the annual air displays at Hendon; performing highly accurate formation flying, trailing coloured smoke and undertaking superb individual aerobatics. Bulldogs remained in RAF squadron use until 1937, though several two-seat variants were still flying two years later at 4 FTS, Egypt. The only Bulldogs to actually see war operations were 17 machines sold to Finland in early 1935, which saw brief action during the Winter War of 1939.

Frank Tredrey's impressions of his first flight in a Bulldog reflect the esoteric delight experienced by most pilots of those pre-1939 days of RAF flying: *"Four of them were being warmed up by the fitters as we walked over, line abreast heading into wind, their fat short little bodies hugging the ground, their thick and stubby airscrews making the dust fly as they tore around and pulled the wheels against the chocks. Green and silver backs and yellow wheel-shields, airscrew spinners and cowling gun channels. Cockpits fairly crowded with instruments and levers and direction plates.*

In the Bulldog you half lie back. The straps are tight over your shoulders, your legs straddled out to reach the rudder bar, your right fist on the spade grip and your left closed round the big throttle lever. You taxi out bumping and rocking vilely, your toes ready to stab on the footbrakes if it won't stop swinging in the wind. After (Avro) Tutors it fairly leaps off the ground, and climbs at a rate of knots. In level flight the airspeed needle sticks around the 130 mark, well throttled back to cruising revs."

Bristol Bulldog *Bristol Bulldogs from No 19 Squadron in formation at the 1934 Hendon Air Display, led by Flight Lieutenant (Later ACM) Harry Broadhurst. This aircraft, which was the RAF's standard fighter in the early 1930s, had an immensely strong steel frame that enabled the aircraft to withstand a great deal of stress; other advantages included a forward-placed cockpit that gave the pilot a good field of vision and easy changing of fuel tanks in the upper wing.*

38

Avro 504N

The 1918 Avro 504K trainer received a virtual new lease of Service life in 1927, when the last major variant of that doyen of RAF instructional aircraft was re-engined with a Lynx radial (in lieu of a rotary) engine and fitted with a new form of undercarriage. The resulting 504N remained in production until 1933, and thereafter, on being sold off to a variety of civil companies, was responsible for giving many thousands of people their baptism of the air on joy-rides. Within the RAF it helped to pioneer instrument flying instruction ('blind flying') from late 1931. It gave splendid service in the RAF, AAF, and overseas at 4 FTS, Abu Sueir, Egypt.

It gave staunch service at the Flying Training Schools and with the University Air Squadrons for over a decade. Retaining the rugged oleo-pneumatic undercarriage, twin-fuel tanks beneath the upper main plane, it had additional stringers rounding out the fuselage sides. Early models of the 504N had a wooden fuselage and tapered ailerons. Later, Frise ailerons of rectangular shape were substituted and the fuselage was of welded steel construction.

A total of 590 was built. At RAF Wittering with the CFS, six 504Ns of 'E' Flight pioneered instrument flying in the RAF, the first course starting in September 1931.

Though eventually replaced by its stable-mate the Avro Tutor, by 1934, seven civil 504Ns were recalled for duty with the RAF in 1940, to form a Special Duty Flight at RAF Christchurch.

Allen Wheeler, who flew Avro 504Ns at RAF Henlow in 1927-28, recalled:

"Like its predecessor, the Lynx Avro, as it came to be called, was quite impressive in aerobatics, being able to do almost everything that other aeroplanes could do, and indeed one manoeuvre which most other aeroplanes could not do; this manoeuvre we called the 'Bunt'. It involved pushing the aeroplane over into a dive and then further over until it was flying level but inverted. It was possible to trim the Avro 504N in a glide, with the engine just above idling power, and it should land itself without the pilot doing anything. The landing was, of course, a bit untidy but safe enough: one could taxi in after it anyhow. They were excellent for recreational flying of all kinds - even visiting friends in the neighbourhood, since they could be landed in any reasonable field and left idling for a long time."

Avro 504N An Avro 504N from Cambridge University Air Squadron flies over Stonehenge. This was the last of innumerable variants of the 504, and was also known as the Lynx Avro after its Lynx radial engine.

Hawker Fury

The sleek Hawker Fury I, which first equipped No 43 Squadron at Tangmere in mid-1931, gave the RAF its first fighter in squadron service able to exceed 200mph with a full warload. Highly aerobatic, powered by a 640hp Rolls-Royce Kestrel VI the Fury was also at least 30mph faster than any contemporary RAF fighter; whilst its performance and control response was summed by one ex-No 25 Squadron pilot as *"...perfectly delightful"*. Epitomising the elegant Fury's manoeuvrability and instant response were the four Furies of No 1 Squadron's aerobatic team, which gave many superlative exhibitions of formation flying at the annual Hendon Displays of the late 1930s.

Fury Is eventually equipped just three squadrons - Nos 1, 25 and 43 - but remained in frontline use until the outbreak of World War Two.

The Fury II became a standard fighter in the RAF. A total of 122 was built and entered service with No 25 Squadron at RAF Hawkinge in 1935. Within a year four more squadrons received Fury IIs, and nearly 100 examples were built, but their Service life was brief, being gradually replaced by 1938. With its uprated Kestrel engine, and spatted wheels, the Fury II showed a 20% increase in speed, and 34% improvement in rate of climb over its predecessor. Nearly 50 were still used for training at the outbreak of war.

The late Owen Thetford in his book Aircraft of the Royal Air Force since 1918 remarked: *"...it was*

Hawker Fury *Hawker Fury IIs from No 27 Squadron taxi forward ready for take-off. The Fury was faster than larger contemporary fighters and had an excellent rate of climb. It was an ideal single-seater interceptor.*

light and sensitive on the controls, had a fast climb, and was quite unsurpassed for aerobatic prowess". A Fury pilot said: *"That it was the most beautiful biplane and the most perfect fighter that could be built"*.

Handley Page Heyford

The Heyford will always be remembered primarily as the last biplane heavy bomber to enter RAF squadron service - the ultimate 'cloth bomber'. The first prototype made its first test flight in June 1930, and commenced its Service life with No 99 Squadron at, appropriately, RAF Upper Heyford in late 1933; one of the new designs to assist the early stages of RAF expansion from the 1920s' doldrums. Its distinctive configuration included such novel features as the 'shoulder' upper wing attachment to the long slender fuselage, the much-lowered bottom wing in which a thickened centre-section accommodated its bomb load, and the ventral 'dustbin' gun cupola for under-tail defence. Eleven squadrons were eventually equipped with Heyfords, and although replacement designs began to arrive in these units from 1937, Heyfords still lingered on several units until late 1939, and the Heyford was not officially declared as obsolete until mid-1941.

Heyford pilots generally liked the huge biplane; it was sturdy, agile - more than one Heyford was actually looped without mishap - while the ground crews found the aeroplane relatively simple to

Handley Page Heyford *Handley Page Heyford bombers of 'B' Flight, No 10 Squadron, on a training flight during the summer of 1936.*

maintain and arm. In February 1935, one Heyford (K6902) was the RAE test vehicle for radar experiments, and later that year air-tested the first airborne radar transmitter conceived by Dr Robert Watson-Watt and his colleagues. The last 'active' Heyford was still airworthy at RAF Cardington as late as August 1944; but the most vivid memory of the 'Jolly Green Giant' for most contemporary people was the immaculate formations of Heyfords which flew at pre-1939 Hendon Displays, and especially the Royal Review of the RAF by HM King George V in July 1935 at RAF Mildenhall and RAF Duxford.

A No 99 Squadron pilot quoted: *"For their time they seemed huge, especially if you sat in the open cockpit or in the exposed front gunners' position. The arrangement of the fuselage abutting under the surface of the top wing gave the crew a field of vision hitherto unknown in a bomber".*

Westland Wapiti

The Wapiti was in effect a compromise between official desire for a replacement for the ageing DH9a and Bristol F2b equipping most overseas squadrons of the RAF, and the need for strict economy in the contemporary parsimonious annual budgets for the RAF. From seven other contenders for an official contract, the Wapiti found favour because of its utilisation of certain DH9a components and spares readily available in the RAF's 'larder' at that time. As a two-seat 'general purpose' aircraft it could be fitted with wheels, floats or skis.

The first units to receive Wapitis were squadrons in Iraq in 1928-30, while the first Wapiti squadrons to arrive in India were Nos 11 and 39 in October 1928. By early 1932 all eight India-based squadrons were operating the type. In all-round comfort and performance the Wapiti was a great improvement on is predecessors, and for the next ten years the Wapiti bore the brunt of operations among the mountains and hills of India's North-West Frontier (now Pakistan). Moreover, Wapitis formed the equipment of the first Indian Air Force unit when this service was inaugurated in April 1933; while in Britain Wapitis were flown extensively by several AAF squadrons.

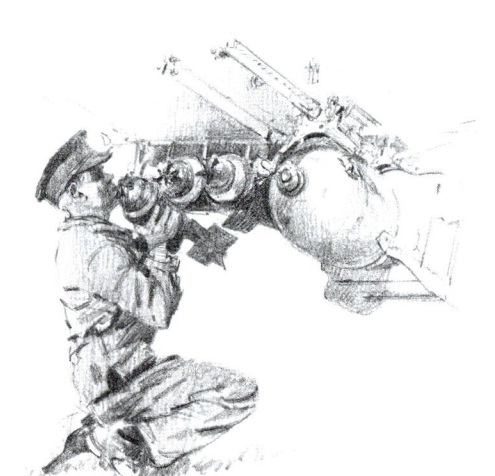

From a pure flying viewpoint pilots found the Wapiti to be strong and thoroughly stable, responding easily to controls and, if required, fully aerobatic. One of the design's few vices was a permanent tendency to swing strongly on take-off and, especially, landing, thereby requiring 'Stick right back and fully stalled if you wanted a neat three-pointer' - a characteristic which, in view of the lack of brakes, often led to 'expensive' landings. The Wapiti remained on active service in India until 1940 with the RAF, but continued in squadron use with the Indian Air Force for a further two years before being phased out.

Major Laurence Openshaw took the Wapiti for its maiden flight in the spring of 1927 and wrote: *"Again, it was*

Westland Wapiti *A Wapiti of No 30 Squadron sets off on patrol over Iraq in 1932, on policing duties for the League of Nations.*

43

Sunday morning and many employees came to watch. All felt this was a crucial day affecting their continued employment. We knew that five rival firms were competing for orders with their own versions of aircraft to the same specification. I climbed aboard with clinking parachute which the firm had at last purchased. With a commonplace machine there could be trouble - and there was! The rudder hardly worked at all! On investigation it was discovered that the fuselage had been drawn two feet shorter than intended. When rectified, we sent the machine to Martlesham so that the Air Ministry's RAF pilots could decide whether it was good enough. Fortunately it won."

Supermarine Scapa

Initially titled Southampton IV, the Scapa was basically a re-engined, all-metal version of its parent design which entered RAF service in mid-1935 until 1938. A total of 14 machines was built for the RAF, serving with Nos 202 and 204 Squadrons.

Although the Scapa had the same overall dimensions and basic lay-out as the Southampton, the detailed changes were considerable - including an all-metal hull and wings. Twin fins and rudders were used instead of three. The two pilots, instead of sitting in open cockpits one behind the other, were accommodated side-by-side in an enclosed cockpit. Instead of engines mounted mid-way between the

Supermarine Scapa *One of No 204 Squadron's Supermarine Scapa flying-boats over the harbour and lighthouse at Alexandria.*

upper and lower mainplanes amidst a complicated array of bracing wires, the Scapa had its two 525hp Rolls-Royce Kestrel IIIMS engines faired smoothly into the upper wings.

A redesigned hull, with straighter sides, gave more internal capacity. Of the 14 Scapas built for the RAF, with the final delivery in July 1936, most were deployed to Kalafrana in Malta with No 202 Squadron and Alexandra in Egypt with No 204 Squadron. They were employed on anti-submarine patrols in the Mediterranean during the Spanish Civil War to protect neutral shipping.

Saro London flying-boats replaced the Scapa in 1937.

Hawker Hart

Graceful and elegant in appearance, the Hart was also efficient. It proved to be one of the most adaptable biplanes ever to enter service with the RAF and some 415 examples were delivered. On equipping No 33 Squadron at RAF Eastchurch in January 1930, it promptly outpaced every contemporary RAF fighter. Yet the Hart's greatest claim to fame was its extreme versatility and adaptability, being the 'father' to a long and prodigious variety of Hart derivatives in subsequent years. From March 1933 onwards it entered service with the Auxiliary Air Force squadrons, where it remained until 1938. In home-based squadrons the Hart was eventually superseded by its stablemate, the Hind in 1936. It continued to serve on the North-West frontier of India until the Blenheim arrived in 1939.

In September 1939, the RAF still held more than 1,600 Harts and variants on charge overall - a sixth of the service's grand total of aircraft. Even after war was declared Harts continued active operational duties in India until 1942, while the many Harts relegated to training roles during the 1930s virtually trained the bulk of Bomber Command's crews of the early war years.

Group Captain Frank Tredrey recorded his first flights in a Hart in his delightful book Pilot's Summer as follows:

"It had a tendency to swing to the left as you took-off, which had to be firmly counteracted with right rudder... and you could see a frightful lot of ground ahead over the tapered nose when you were in flying position... climb seemed rather steep after Tutors because it was much more powerful... straight and level flight, once more you could see a lot of ground ahead, and until you had watched the altimeter for a time and noticed that it did not register a change, could swear that you were diving it... turned very nice, with a Hart you could rip into a turn and out again as smoothly as slipping down a water-shoot... spinning, nice and slow. Needed full opposite rudder to make it come out. Aerobatics? Far easier than Avro 504N, Tutor or Atlas. Plenty of loading in rolls off a loop... Landings a little bit tricky. On a windy day you had to get the stick back that last little bit in double quick time

46

Hawker Hart *Hawker Harts from No 11 Squadron in flight over the Himalayas during a patrol along India's North-West Frontier. This two-seater single-bay biplane bomber was so successful a design that it gave rise to a long line of derivatives.*

or else it dropped on to a nice springy undercarriage and to go up like a lift to about five feet, half bouncing and half ballooning with the wind under the wings... give her a touch of throttle as she sank it would stay down all right the second time... I gave it a good fat burst and it sat down like a two-year-old."

Vickers Virginia

Although the Vimy of 1917 was Vickers' first successful venture in heavy bomber design, the Virginia of 1922 et seq is usually regarded as the real 'father' to the line of large Vickers biplane bombers and transports which were to give some 20 years service to the RAF. Built on strictly utilitarian lines, the 'Ginnie' served its masters well, seeing RAF service mainly from 1924 until 1937, with a few examples even soldiering on in minor capacities until as late as 1941. It was progressively modified and developed throughout its long life, and provided an embryo bomber force's crews with their basic experience.

Its ultra-steadiness on bombing runs is exemplified by the Ginnies of No 7 Squadron which captured the annual Lawrence Minot Trophy for bombing no less than eight times against all

Vickers Virginia *Among its other roles, the Virginia was used for parachute training in the mid-1930s, by which date it was reaching the end of its operational life as a bomber. For this purpose parachute jump-off platforms were fitted behind the wing-tip struts.*

opposition. Its regular appearances at each RAF Display from 1925 to 1937 made it a particular favourite with the public; while its years of acting as a platform for parachute training of air and ground crews will be well recalled by hundreds of ex-RAF men.

In view of its outstanding Service longevity it is perhaps surprising to note that, fully loaded, a Virginia could seldom exceed 100mph in flight; while its nominal 3,000 lb bomb load and ever-open crew cockpits were direct throwbacks to 1914-18 vintage designs. Notwithstanding its ancient charisma, the Virginia was beloved by its four-man crews; a dependable, rugged packhorse which seldom failed them.

Group Captain Sawyer flew Vickers Virginias in 1934 and remembers them with affection:

"I had graduated from Cranwell in 1933 and joined No 7 Squadron which flew Virginias. To a keen young airman of those days it was something of a joke. It looked like a great big flying bird-cage in which were a crew of four: pilot, second pilot who also navigated, wireless operator who also worked the front gun and a rear gunner. The Virginia was very easy to fly, but fully loaded it could only trundle along at 80mph, which was slower than many First World War aircraft.

The Virginia also resembled First World War aircraft in that it had an open cockpit, or rather three as the rear gunner operated a Lewis gun mounted at the back in what was known as the 'dustbin' and the wireless operator had to crawl forward to another front open cockpit to use the front Lewis gun. The rear gunner could not get up to the main cockpit, but simply climbed into the dustbin and stayed there throughout the flight. His only method of communication to the pilot was the speaking tube, or 'Gosport tube'.

The Virginia was very steady on bombing runs, but its slow speed could mean that air currents greatly affected it and this particularly affected the rear gunner. I remember that one fine summer's day I moved into the dustbin on a photographic trip. Sitting there, I realised that even very gentle manoeuvres by the pilot would yaw the tail around horribly, and that the slightest movements caused by air currents would be greatly exaggerated for the rear gunner. I don't know how they endured it.

These comments may seem highly critical of the Virginia. In fact I and most of my contemporaries felt a lot of affection for the aeroplane, but by this time it had been in service for over a decade, and it did seem terribly old-fashioned."

Handley Page Hinaidi

The Hinaidi was a re-engined development of the HP Hyderabad with later production Hinaidis being of metal construction. The lighter weight 440hp Bristol Jupiter VIII engines made it necessary for the Hinaidi's wings to be slightly swept by some two-and-a half degrees. It first flew on 26 March 1927. Three Lewis guns, in nose, dorsal and ventral positions and the bomb load was 1,448lb. From late 1929, Hinaidis replaced Hyderabads in four squadrons, ie Nos 10, 90, 502 and 503. A total of 12 Hanaidi Is and 33 IIs were delivered before production ceased in 1932. Some Hyderabads were subsequently converted to Hinaidis. The Hinaidi served until 1934 before being gradually replaced.

Rendered obsolete by the HP Heyford, the Hinaidi remained the equipment of a Special Reserve Squadron, No 503 at RAF Waddington, until it converted to Wallace light bombers in October 1936.

The prototype Hinaidi, which was silver-painted, supported Victorias of No 70 Squadron at the evacuation of Kabul in December 1928.

A wood-constructed troop carrier version, initially titled Chitral but later named Clive, was first flown in February 1928 and one example gave several years service in India.

Handley Page Hinaidi *Handley Page Hinaidis of No 99 Squadron, operating from their base at RAF Upper Heyford in 1933.*

Avro Tutor

By the late 1920s, the RAF's need for a modern replacement for its ageing Avro 504 training aeroplanes resulted in the Avro firm producing a new, two-seat biplane with welded steel structure, the Avro 621, initially merely titled trainer but soon relabelled as Tutor. Under the latter name the type was adopted by the RAF in June 1932 as the Service's standard 'ab initio' instructional machine, which it remained until 1939 with nearly 800 Tutors being built and delivered.

Its non-corroding superstructure, albeit fabric-covered, made the Tutor suitable for use in most climates, and the type became a familiar sight not only in Britain but also at the RAF's chief training school, 4 FTS at Abu Sueir, Egypt. Usually doped in a bright yellow colouring - a warning to all other aircraft that its occupants were almost certainly student pilots - Tutors were highly aerobatic; a facet superbly exploited by some of the Central Flying School instructors of the 1930s, whose inverted formation aerobatics in Tutors were a highlight of the Hendon Displays.

One pilot's initial reaction to flying his first Tutor was succinct: *"Gentlemanly little things from the flying point of view. Nicely balanced controls, light and smooth to handle, beautiful for all manoeuvres, no tricks or vices, sweet glide at seventy, and as easy to land as buttoning up your coat. Neat instrument board, excellent hidden and yet easily accessible arrangement of controls, hand-lever wheel brakes, and the usual slots."*

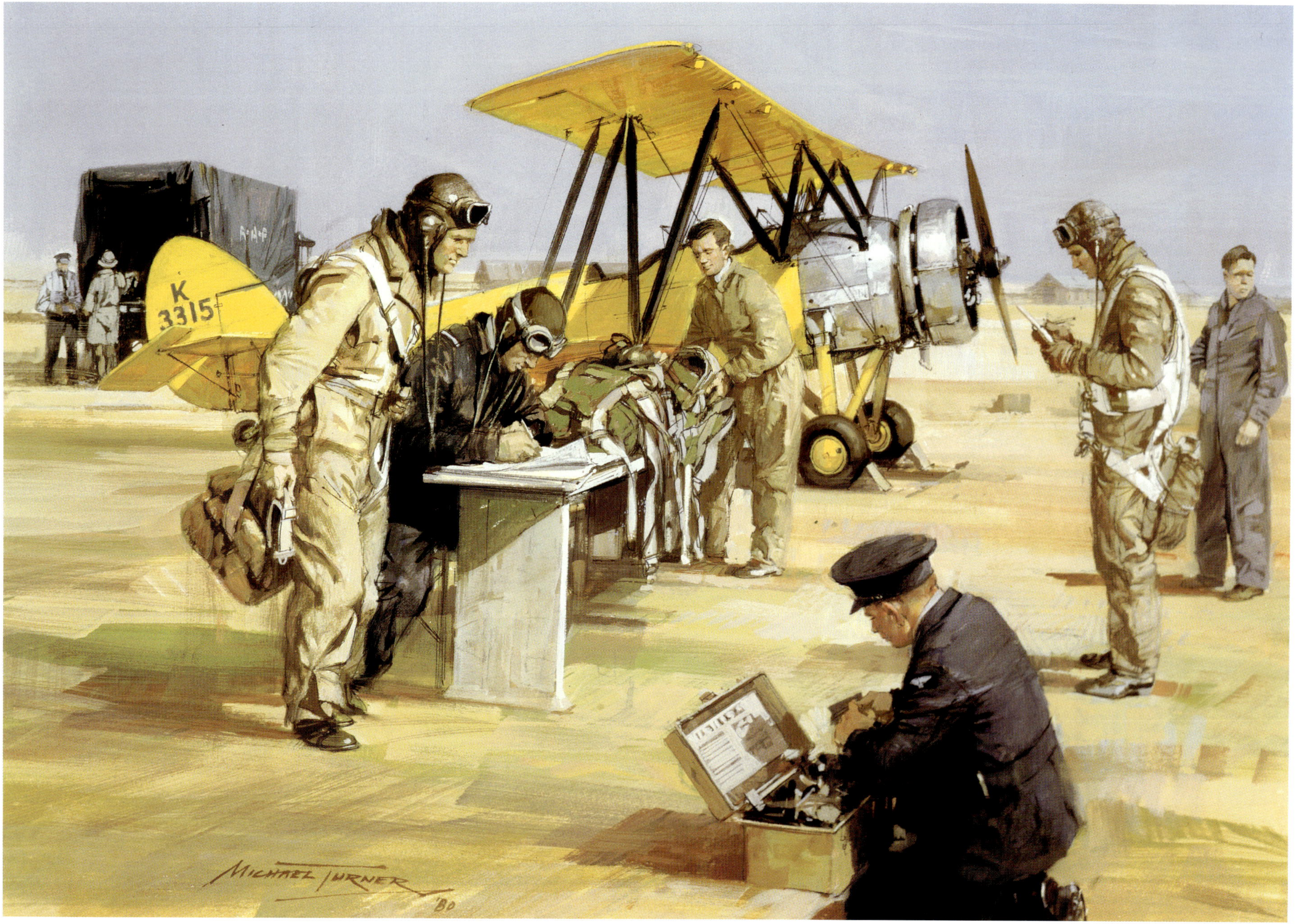
K
3315
MICHAEL TURNER
'80

Avro Tutor *An Avro Tutor stands ready, as student pilots prepare for a day's flying at 4 Flying Training School, Abu Sueir, Egypt in 1938.*

The present generation may still witness the neat flying always associated with Tutors by virtue of the sole airworthy example existing in Britain, K3215, at present owned and regularly exhibited by the Shuttleworth Collection at Old Warden aerodrome in Bedfordshire.

Hawker Demon

On its introduction the speedy Hart bomber was able to outstrip all contemporary fighters with such ease that Hawkers immediately set about designing a fighter version - in Sydney Camm's reported phrasing: *"Let's set a Hart to catch a Hart."* Modifying the first production Hart J9933, the new two-seat variant was initially titled the Hart Fighter, but soon after was renamed Demon. In this guise it revived the 1918 concept of a two-seat fighter - the first such for the RAF since that war. In view of the Demon's top speed of nearly 200 mph, however, serious thought was given to protection of the rear gunner from the effects of slipstream, and commencing with J9933 a number of Demons were fitted with a Frazer-Nash 'lobster-back' folding metal cupola over the rear cockpit. This armadillo type of screen hardly solved the problems of hand-wielding a Lewis gun in high speed combat, but at least afforded a degree of pure physical comfort to the wretched gunner.

The first Demon squadrons began receiving their aircraft in 1933-34, but in September 1938 when the Munich crisis erupted seven of Fighter Command's full strength of 28 squadrons (including the AAF units) were still flying Demons. Had war with Germany resulted at that time it is difficult to imagine how their crews would have fared against the Luftwaffe's latest fighters. By the following September no Demons remained in

Hawker Demon *A Hawker Demon from No 600 (City of London) Squadron practices dive-bombing off the Chesil Beach in Dorset during summer camp in August 1938. The Demon was a variant of the Hawker Hart bomber (see page 45), and was the first two-seater fighter to be ordered by the RAF since World War One.*

squadron front-line service, though almost 140 were still on RAF charge in various locations. At least 64 Demons were delivered to Australia, the first batch of 18 forming the new equipment of No 1 Squadron RAAF, though these were used for army co-operation and bombing roles in addition to their intended fighter task.

Vickers Vincent

The Vincent was merely one of several little-publicised, hardworking aeroplanes used operationally by the RAF. A direct variant of its stablemate the Vildebeest torpedo-bomber, the Vincent carried an extended range fuel tank between its undercarriage legs, plus all the military paraphernalia commonly associated with army co-operation aircraft of the period serving in overseas commands. Joining its first squadron in late 1934, the Vincent equipped 11 squadrons in all - each unit being based in the Middle East zones. An ungainly design, with few concessions to streamlining or other aerodynamic refinements, the Vincent proved very reliable and enormously tough while operating in conditions of extreme heat and primitive landing grounds. They were still in front-line squadron use when World War Two began, and saw plentiful action in East Africa during 1940-41 and in Iraq in 1941.

In the context of pure progression in engineering techniques, it might be noted that the Vincent was Vickers' last design constructed by the traditional metal-frame, tubular fuselage *et al.* After the Vincent the firm turned to using the geodetic airframe construction patterns conceived by the eminent inventor and designer Barnes Wallis.

Philip Middlehurst flew as a passenger in one of the last operational Vincents:

"After two years based in the UK and No 78 Squadron, Bomber Command, I had been posted to Aden, and found myself in charge of a group of Arab-manned radio outstations scattered around the mountains and deserts of the protectorate, and which provided communications for the Government Colonial Administration Service. In most cases flying by Vincent was the only convenient way to reach them.

The gap left by the demise of the Vincents was never adequately covered. Their replacements, Fairey Albacores, might have looked vaguely similar and could take-off and land in the same tight corners, but they were no match when it came to carrying awkward-shaped freight. Then again, after all that fresh-air flying in old Vincents they were just that wee bit on the civilised side."

Vickers Vincent *A Vickers Vincent from No 55 Squadron circles over the Iraq Command Boat Club sheds at Habbaniya, its home base in 1938. This three-seater 'general purpose' aircraft served throughout the Middle East and Africa until 1942 and saw action against the Italians in East Africa.*

53

Vickers Valentia

In 1920, when the Vickers firm was already engaged in planning what was to become its Virginia bomber, the firm was also asked to tender for the design of a troop-carrying military transport aircraft. The first outcome was a design later called the Victoria, and this initiated a family tree of developed variants which gave birth to the Valentia. This was in essence a more powerfully engined Victoria with wheel brakes and a tail wheel to replace the tail skids on its predecessors. Additional strengthening of the structure meant greater weight-carrying capability.

Entering squadron service in May 1934, Valentias operated in most overseas theatres and accumulated an impressive number of flying hours over deserts and mountains in Iraq, Egypt and India. Patient, plodding workhorses, the Valentias carried troops or freight over the barren wastelands with

Vickers Valentia *A Vickers Valentia military transport of No 31 Squadron, which in 1938 was engaged in troop-carrying operations in India.*

Handley Page Harrow and Fairey Hendon *A No 115 Squadron Handley Page Harrow runs up its engines prior to a flight from RAF Marham, Norfolk, while a Fairey Hendon from No 38 Squadron passes overhead.*

steady regularity.

The outbreak of war in 1939 merely accentuated the importance of air transportation, particularly in the overseas theatres of war, and the outdated Valentias continued to give trojan service in the Middle East, but especially in India, where No 31 Squadron's Valentias continued to operate until well into 1942. Even as late as 1943 a few examples were still in use as pure communications 'hacks'; while the last-known Valentia to survive, K3600, was sold to the Indian government in July 1944. The Valentia, with its forebears the Victoria and Vernon, founded what was eventually to blossom into RAF Transport Command, and in addition were instrumental in pioneering many of the overseas civil air routes around the Far East.

Handley Page Harrow and Fairey Hendon

The urgent need for expansion of the RAF set into motion in the early 1930s coincided with a period in British aircraft design when emphasis on the monoplane configuration was mounting. In 1935 the Air Ministry ordered 100 Handley Page Harrows as troop carriers but by early 1937, when the first Harrow reached its squadron, the design had become a bomber. Within that year five squadrons became Harrow-equipped. Of simple yet impressive outline the Harrows served as 'interim' heavy bombers until 1939, when most reverted to their original intended role as transport vehicles. In the latter role Harrow Transports - usually nicknamed 'Sparrows' - provided sterling service in several war theatres.

Another monoplane bomber, of much earlier conception, was the Fairey Hendon. Built to the same 1927 specification as the biplane Heyford bomber, the Hendon was literally ahead of its time. Procrastination by the Air Ministry meant that this successful 1927 project was not actually awarded a contract until 1934, despite the Hendon's obvious superiority over its biplane contemporaries. In the event the Hendon - the RAF's first all-metal constructed, low-wing, cantilever monoplane heavy bomber - did not enter squadron service until November 1936, and then only fully equipped one unit, No 38 Squadron, based at Mildenhall and, later, Marham. Capable of carrying some 2,500lb of bombs on internally accommodated racks, enclosed by automatic doors, and with wings spanning just over 100 feet, the Hendon presaged a much later generation of heavy bombers. Only 14 Hendons were built, and the final 11 were withdrawn in July 1939.

Hawker Audax

During World War One the prime function of the Royal Flying Corps had been close liaison with the Army's ground forces; a role which was continued by certain RAF squadrons thereafter. Specifically designed to fulfil this role, the Audax, which first flew on 29 December 1931, was almost identical in engine, armament and general appearance to its stablemate, the Hawker Hart day bomber. It could be readily recognised by a message-collecting arm pivoted to the cross-section of the Audax's undercarriage and long exhaust pipe. This arm, fitted with a rod and hook attachment, could retrieve message bags from a suspended wire standing about six feet from the ground. This technique required precise flying by the pilot.

The Audax was chosen as a replacement for the Armstrong Whitworth Atlas and for the re-equipping of two Wapiti squadrons on the North West Frontier of India. The first RAF squadron was No 4 at RAF Farnborough in February 1932, and demonstrated at the RAF display in summer 1933. It was later used as an advanced trainer with FTS at home and overseas.

In home-based Army Co-operation squadrons the Audax was supplanted by the Hawker Hector in 1937-38, but overseas they saw service during the early stages of the war, operating in the East African campaign with No 237 (Rhodesian) Squadron and at RAF Habbaniya during the Iraqi rebellion of May 1941. A handful served as glider tugs in the UK, towing GAL Hotspurs until 1942.

In addition the Audax carried wireless equipment for direct communication with ground forces. Eventually equipping a total of 25 squadrons, the Audax was finally replaced in the UK by purpose-built designs, such as the Westland Lysander for army co-operation duties.

Hawker Audax A Hawker Audax from No 4 (AC) Squadron, picks up a message during Air Exercises in 1934.

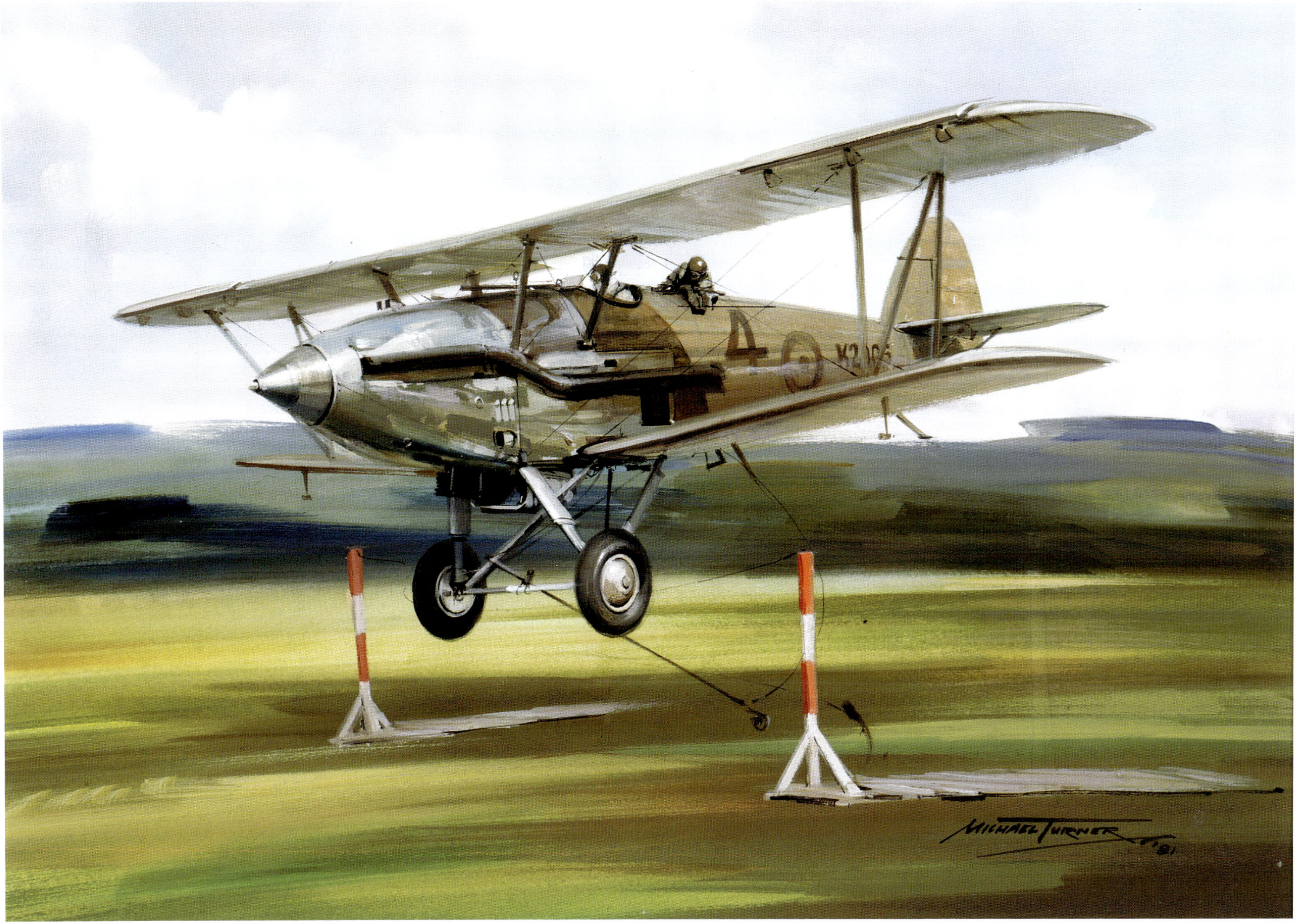
4
MICHAEL TURNER
'81

Armourers load a Short Stirling

Aircraft of World War Two

The hasty resurgence in rearmament from the mid-1930s brought with it a flood of fresh designs from which emerged the age of the metal monoplanes, replacing the canvas-skinned biplanes of long and faithful service. Twin-engined monoplane bombers such as the Hampden, Blenheim, Whitley and Wellington began to reach RAF squadrons in the late 1930s, while open-cockpit Gauntlets and Furies began to be replaced by eight-gun Hurricanes and Spitfires.

More significantly, a decision was taken to equip a future Bomber Command with a fresh generation of four-engined, strategic, heavy bombers, ultimately exemplified by the Stirling, Halifax and Lancaster.

When war came in 1939, however, the RAF was still at a transitory stage of modernisation, with all Commands still equipped with a mixture of biplanes and monoplanes. It was to remain so for at least two years of war before finally gathering sufficient strength of strike power to begin a true air offensive against Germany. In the interim several new aircraft came into service - most significant of which was the radical all-wood constructed de Havilland Mosquito bomber which in subsequent years was to be seen in most operational forms.

Even as such new designs reached squadron service the jet-engined aeroplane was being secretly developed. The first examples in RAF service were Gloster Meteors in 1944 - harbingers of a new era in RAF aircraft.

Supermarine Spitfire I

Vickers Wellesley

If for no other reason, the Wellesley has a particular niche in RAF history for being the first aeroplane to introduce the unique Barnes Wallis geodetic, or 'basket-weave', style of construction to operational service. Its active service record, however, added honours to the Wellesley and its crews. The first production aircraft were delivered to the RAF from March 1937 to No 76 Squadron at RAF Finningley, the first unit to be fully equipped with the type.

Eventually a total of ten squadrons were to fly Wellesleys; while in January 1938 the RAF's Long-Range Development Unit (LRDU) was formed with Wellesleys at RAF Upper Heyford especially to investigate the associated problems of ultra-long range flying. Here the design's overload Service range (normal) of well over 2,000 miles was to be surpassed when two of an original flight of three LRDU Wellesleys left Ismailia, Egypt on 5 November 1938 and arrived non-stop at Darwin, Australia in the early hours of November 7 - a total of 7158 miles, and a new world distance record set to last seven years.

In a personal letter to Vickers' sales manager, then Tommy Broome, the former test pilot, Sqn Ldr R. Kellett who commanded the epic long distance flight wrote: *"The planes are in awfully good shape, the fabric bare and torn in places from rain, otherwise as new and very clean. Two broken valve springs the only engine defect found, apart from routine adjustments. The automatics (the three-axes automatic pilot control system as first developed by the RAE) behaved splendidly in all three aircraft."*

Vickers Wellesley *Vickers Wellesleys from No 14 Squadron fly over the Pyramids. This two-seater bomber was in action well into 1942.*

The outbreak of World War Two saw all Wellesleys in Bomber Command already replaced by newer aircraft types, but three units already based in the Middle East, Nos 14, 47 and 223 Squadrons, flew their Wellesleys on highly active operations throughout the East African campaign and the opening rounds of the desert war in north Africa.

By mid-1941 some would argue that the monoplane's worthy front-line roles were over, but the design remains as one of the best interim aircraft flown by the RAF during its changeover from 'cloth' biplanes to metal monoplanes. Its undisputed 'proving' of the superiority of geodetic construction over more conventional structuring was to bear even more fruitful results with its stablemate, the classic Vickers Wellington bomber of revered memory.

Fairey Battle

The Battle was unfortunate in many ways. A clean, aesthetically-appealing monoplane bomber which, at the time of its conception, out-performed most of its rivals in most departments, the Battle was nevertheless under-powered and under-armed defensively for the daylight bombing role thrust upon its gallant crews in the first year of World War Two. The inevitable result was an appalling casualty rate - and, a partly undeserved evil reputation fostered by many latter-day historians resulted.

Stemming from a 1932 specification, Battles first equipped No 63 Squadron in early 1937 and were then over-produced in 'shadow' factories - mainly for quasi-political reasons - with the result that by September 1939 Battles were being flown by no less than 15 squadrons of Bomber Command's total of 53 squadrons. Ten of those units comprised the whole equipment of No 1 Group and all 160 Battles of this Group were despatched to France on 2 September 1939.

From the first clashes with the Luftwaffe it was clear to all but the obtuse that the design was totally inadequate for modern warfare, while the German *blitzkrieg* of May-June 1940 saw the Battle crews being massacred daily as they valiantly tried unescorted daylight bombing sorties against vastly superior opposition. Indeed, the first two airmen awarded Victoria Crosses in 1939-45 belonged to No 12 (Battle) Squadron - both were posthumous awards. After withdrawal to England in mid-June 1940, the exhausted survivors were dispersed and the Battle faded rapidly from the operational scene.

Many hundreds of Battles were sold overseas, going to Australia, Belgium, Turkey, Greece and South Africa, but the largest quantity - almost half of all Battles built - were sent to Canada to implement the Commonwealth Air Training Plan.

Squadron Leader D. H. Clarke DFC, AFC is outspoken in his dislike of the plane: *"It was born too late; it died early - but not early enough! Before it died it killed far too many damn good, fully-trained aircrew. After it died nobody regretted, nobody wept - nobody even noticed. Only those who flew it on ops - and survived - heaved a sigh of relief, but they were flying bigger and better bombers by then and couldn't care less.*

And, let's face it - almost any bomber was better than the hideously ugly Fairey Battle which was neither nice to fly nor nice for ops. It lumbered and wallowed behind its

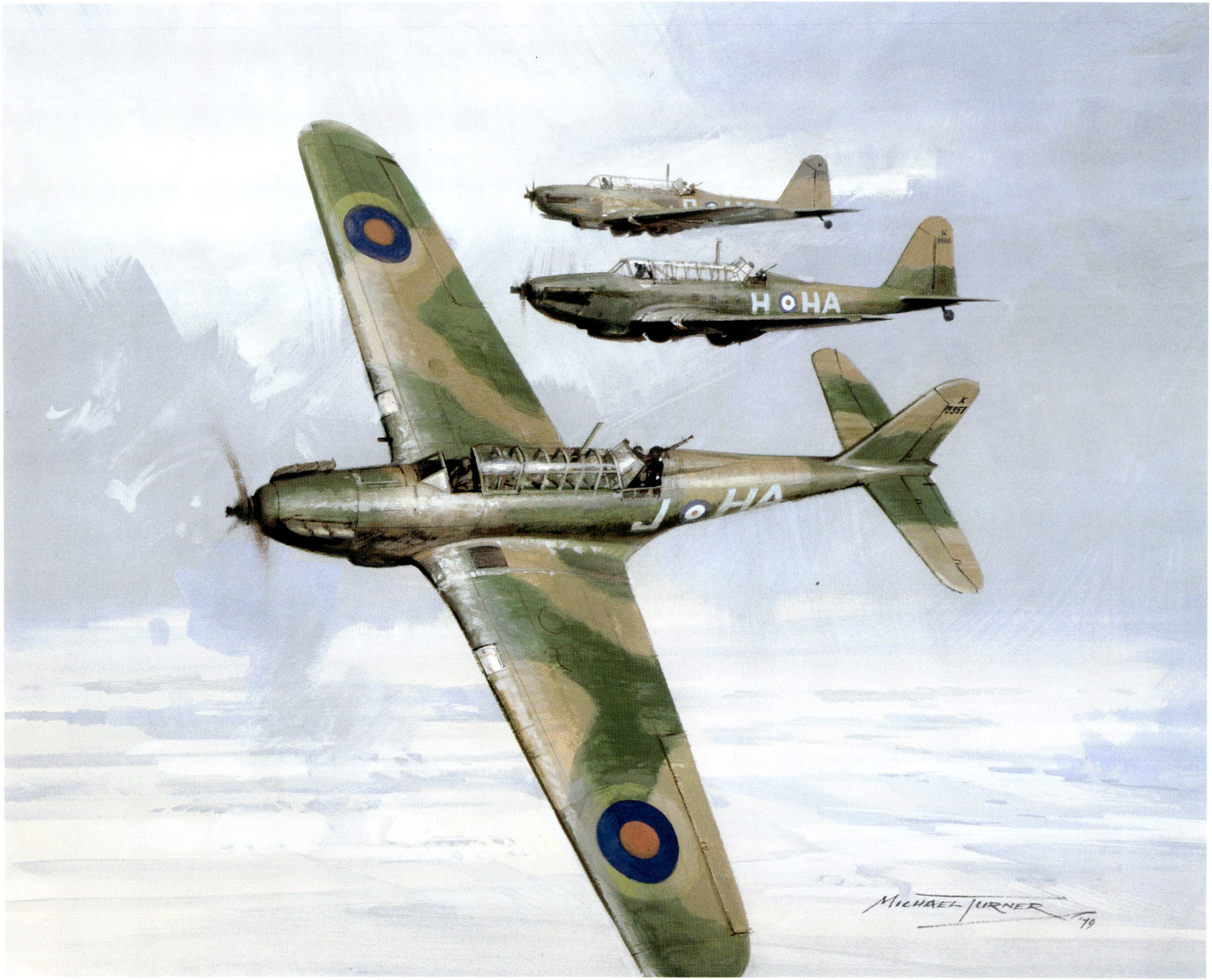
H HA
J HA
MICHAEL TURNER '79

Fairey Battle *A flight of Fairey Battles of No 218 Squadron on patrol over the snow-covered French countryside in January 1940. This plane lacked the performance and fire-power necessary to combat the German fighters and was quickly withdrawn from service.*

spinnerless v.p. airscrew, incapable of reaching its designed top speed - in fact doubt was often expressed as to whether the darned thing had been designed, or whether the pre-war Hitler panics had caused the Air Ministry to rush into an order for one. I can only describe this ill-named aircraft thus: it was no fairy, and it just couldn't battle - except hopelessly."

Hawker Hurricane I

No list of the world's greatest fighter aircraft could fail to include the ubiquitous Hurricane. The world's first eight-gun operational fighter, and the RAF's first squadron aeroplane able to exceed 300mph with full warload; the Hurricane bore the brunt of the first nine months of the war in France where it gave the much-vaunted Luftwaffe its first taste of RAF opposition.

In the Battle of Britain a total of 1,715 Hurricanes was flown in combat at some period, more than the total of all other aircraft employed, and Hurricane pilots claimed almost 80% of all claimed victories by the RAF. In the following years 1941-45

Hawker Hurricane I *Hawker Hurricane Is of No 85 Squadron 'scramble' from an airfield at Merville in May 1940 at the height of the war in France.*

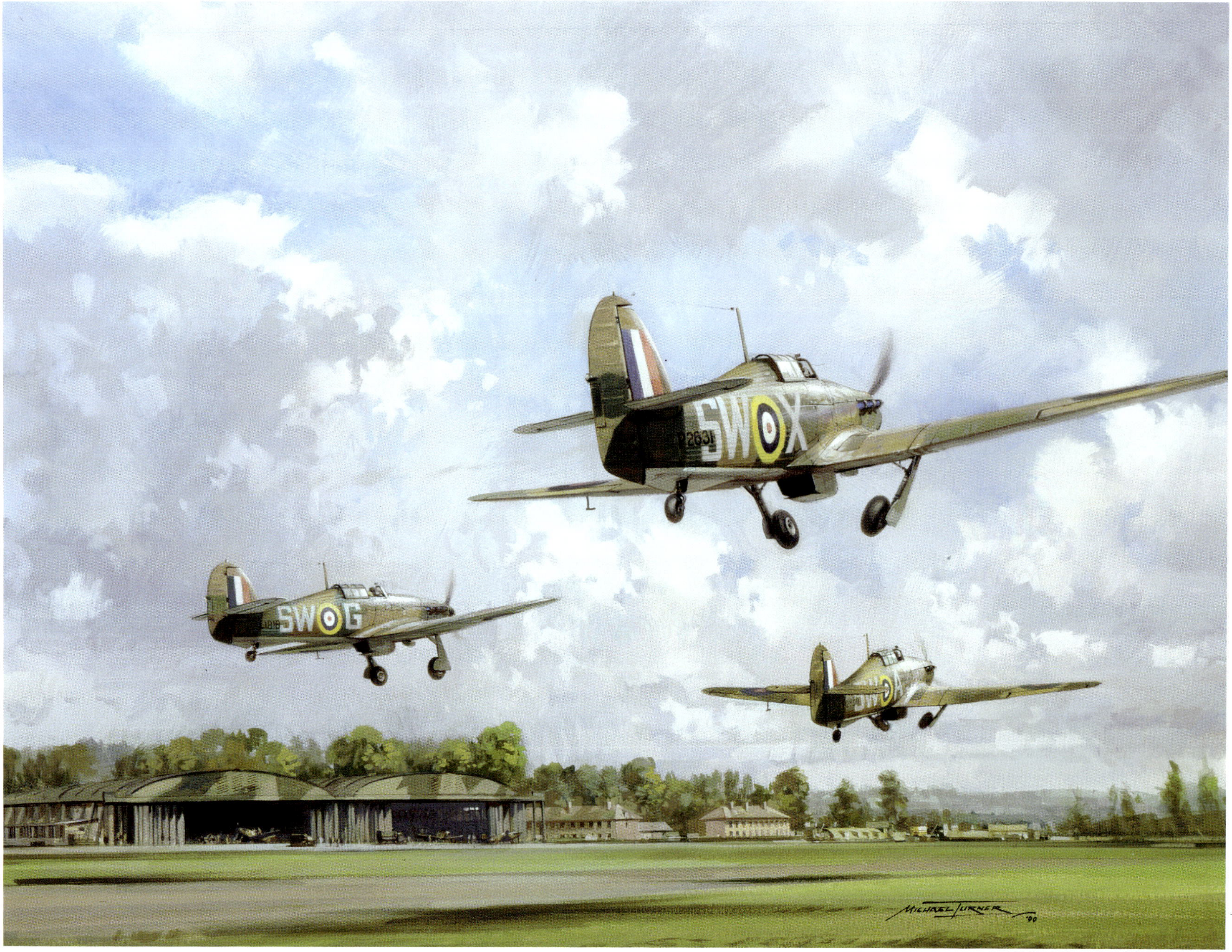
SW X
P2631
SW G
SW A
MICHAEL TURNER '90

Hawker Hurricane I *A flight of No 253 Squadron Hurricanes taking off from Kenley in August 1940 at the height of the Battle of Britain led by Sqn Ldr Tom Gleave.*

Hurricanes of later marks gave splendid service on operations throughout the world, and in virtually every role possible for a single-engined fighter. Its battle honours included every theatre of war and facet of operations.

One of the men who faced the numerically superior Luftwaffe from a Hurricane's cockpit throughout 1939-40 was Wing Command Roland Beamont, CBE, OBE, DSO, who served on No 87 Squadron in France. His view of the Hurricane came from hard experience:

"In the spring and summer of 1940, although without the elegance and high altitude performance of the Spitfire, the Hurricane was a machine of its time, and many of us would not have changed it for any other mount. We knew it as a rugged, stable, forgiving aeroplane which was tolerant of our clumsiness and the worst that the weather could do. It absorbed legendary amounts of enemy fire and kept flying. We could hit the target well with its eight guns and when in trouble we felt able to outfly the enemy's best. The Hurricane and the Spitfire made a great turn, but I never regretted my posting to a Hurricane squadron in that fateful time.

The Hurricane I with constant speed airscrew was a magnificent fighting machine, with excellent qualities of gun-platform stability, manoeuvrability up to 20,000ft, ruggedness and ease of control on take-off and landing. In climb and level speed it was slightly slower than the Messerschmitt Bf 109, but no more than 20-30mph, which meant it was not always easy to get away from a 109 - but that was not the object of the exercise. Once in combat the Hurricane could easily out-manoeuvre the 109. Above 20,000 feet the 109 was better; but when correctly employed against the bomber formations and close escorts below 20,000 feet the Hurricane was magnificent for the task.

When in September 1940 there was talk in my squadron (No 87) of replacement by Spitfires there was nearly a riot - if our Hurricanes were 'inferior', no one had told us about it! This tremendous spirit and confidence in their aircraft was typical of Hurricane squadrons at that time. In direct comparison I found that the Hurricane could out-turn the Spitfires I and II at low and medium altitude, and could very easily do this to the Bf 109."

Bristol Blenheim I

A military version of the Bristol Type 142 Britain first presented to the nation by Lord Rothermere, the Blenheim I medium bomber first equipped No 114 Squadron at RAF Wyton in early 1937. Its immediate ability to outpace any contemporary fighter established the 'short-nose' Blenheim as the RAF's fastest bomber of the pre-war years. Though soon to be replaced in UK-based squadrons by its development, the Mk IV 'long-nose' version, the Mk I Blenheim continued its operational service in the Middle East and India for several years; while converted Mk Is with four-gun packs added under the belly were flown operationally as night fighters during 1938-41.

This latter variant helped to pioneer airborne radar and achieved a modicum of success against German night raiders during 1940-41. During the early stages of the Middle East campaigns, particularly in the Greek débâcle, Blenheim I bomber crews played a significant part in the Allies' desperate defences against greatly superior odds and in relatively primitive maintenance and operating circumstances.

Overall, no less than 54 RAF squadrons operated Blenheim Is at some period, apart from its operational use by several other foreign countries.

An ex-Blenheim I pilot summed his feelings about operating the type as a bomber: *"On the surface it was pleasant to fly, was certainly very manoeuvrable, and had few technical vices. Initial reaction - coming from Hind biplane bomber cockpits - was a feeling akin to a cramped goldfish, with all those window-frames surrounding one up front, but the pilot's view forwards, sideways and down was excellent in relation to take-offs or landings. One-engine landings could be dicey, but provided one remembered to maintain or increase critical speed limits a simple, steady circuit with the good engine on the inside of the turn usually produced a safe landing. The Blenheim's most evil characteristic - and it appeared to apply to all marks - was the minimal chances for pilot survival should he need to take to his brolly (parachute). I personally knew of three men who were forced to bale out, and each one was chopped up by the propellers."*

Bristol Blenheim I *A Bristol Blenheim I from No 211 Squadron attacks Italian troops at Klisura, Albania during the Greek campaign of late 1940.*

Lockheed Hudson *A Hudson from No 206 Squadron at RAF Bircham Newton on patrol over the beaches at Dunkirk during the evacuation of the Allied Expeditionary Force in May 1940. Although primarily a long-range reconnaissance aircraft in Coastal Command, the Hudson performed many other duties.*

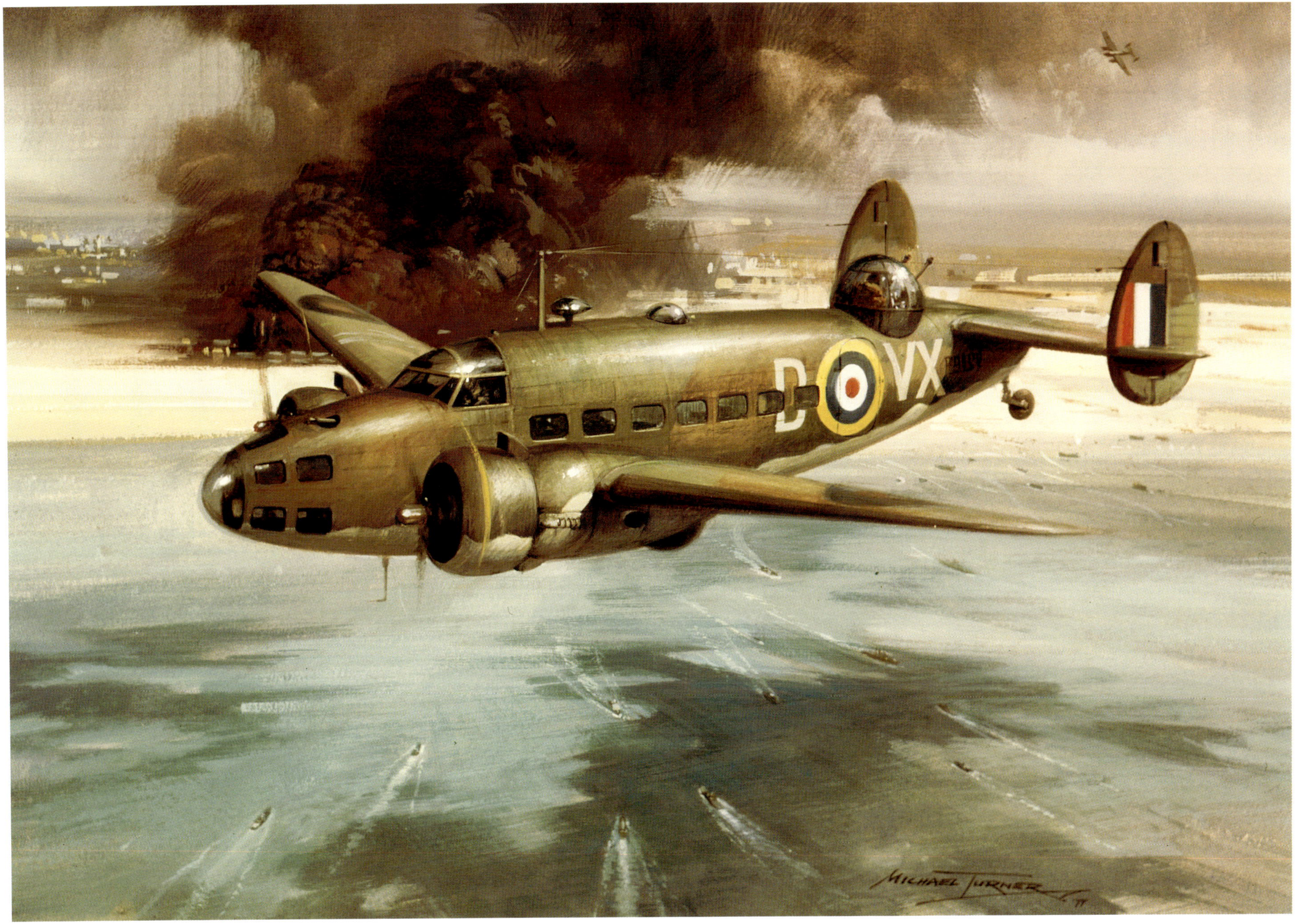
D VX
MICHAEL TURNER

Lockheed Hudson

With the distinct possibility of war with Germany looming large in 1938, and mindful of the RAF's genuine need for advanced designs of aircraft in real quantities; Britain turned to the USA for possible sources of production aircraft. An original British Purchasing Commission (later retitled Mission) went to America in April 1938, and one of its purchases was a block order for 200 militarised variants of the Lockheed civil Model 14-F62 (to be named Hudson I for the RAF) as navigational trainers and eventual replacements for Avro Ansons.

The first Hudsons for RAF operational use equipped No 224 Squadron at RAF Leuchars in mid-1939 initially, and a total of 27 squadrons plus numerous other units ultimately. Their prime role was with Coastal Command during the opening war years, in which they excelled relative to other twin-engined designs with similar duties. In later years Hudsons became festooned with radar antennae, rockets and other fitments as such items came into general use.

To RAF-trained pilots the American cockpit instrumentation appeared highly complicated with numerous knobs, levers and hand-operated devices scattered around the 'front office'. This produced near-mesmerisation as was possibly summarised by H A Taylor, describing his first Hudson landing on a ferry trip:

"While my right hand fluttered over the various levers on the throttle pedestal (a baker's dozen of them, in fact, not counting those for undercarriage and flaps) I tried to remember all that I'd been told, rightly or wrongly, about this formidable aeroplane. Never use full flap...never trim it right back on the approach...motor it in to a wheeler...don't try to three-point it. These and other things (which escaped my memory) they had said. As the grass came up, instinct forced me to haul back on the control column in a valiant effort to make a 'proper' landing. The main wheels touched rather heavily...I pushed the control column hard towards the dashboard and waited. After an agonising second or two the wheels touched again, and then again - and stayed on the ground. Not my idea of a landing, but it seemed that the Hudson had, in its own way, duly arrived."

Ex-Aircraftman Fred Adkin recalls the Hudson:

"The Hudson was a distinctive aircraft, having a large girth, twin fins and rudders, an a two-gun turret mounted very close to the tail unit. In accordance with my usual practice I took the opportunity to have a flip in one. The visibility was amazing from the turret, where it seemed as though one was perched high on top of the fuselage. The aeroplane was quite good to service, displaying the typical American flair for tidy and compact lay-out of services, compared with the British method of putting items as afterthoughts in any odd space available.

These aircraft were prone to an irritating and dangerous snag, that of excessive tailwheel shimmy, which sometimes caused them to swing off during the landing run. I remember one Hudson night-landing at Kaldy when the aeroplane swung off, its undercarriage collapsed and the crew were out and running before the aircraft had come to rest, shouting 'Keep clear. DC's aboard'. There was a resultant departure of all hands to all points of the compass. Fortunately the depth charges did not go off and were later rendered safe. This undercarriage weakness resulted in the Met losing all its Hudsons within a few months."

de Havilland Tiger Moth

From 1932 until 1947 the 'Tiger' was primarily responsible for elementary flying instruction of virtually all RAF air crews, and was also the last biplane 'ab initio' trainer used by the RAF. It was a cold, draughty machine in which to fly; it had no brakes but an efficient, forgiving undercarriage which saved countless would-be pilots' pride and was surprisingly tough in view of the rough handling meted out to it by ham-fisted student 'drivers'. In the air the Tiger was fully aerobatic and could be 'wrung out' with complete confidence in its inherent strength of construction; though for reasons still not fully explainable, slow rolls were always difficult to achieve neatly. Indeed it was said: *"If you can roll a Tiger, you can roll anything."*

By the outbreak of war in 1939, over 1,000 Tiger Moths had been delivered to the RAF, most of them serving with the Elementary and Reserve Flying Training Schools. The basic design remained virtually unaltered throughout its long, patient service, though many Tigers flown in Canada were provided with an enclosed canopy for their open cockpits to combat the icy temperatures of the Canadian winters.

Slightly more than 8,800 Tigers were eventually built, and many privately-owned examples are still in evidence today - living tributes to a fine aircraft and to the affection in which the type is still held by those who prefer 'real' flying. The last Tiger

de Havilland Tiger Moth *A de Havilland Tiger Moth ready to start-up at an Elementary Flying Training School in the summer of 1942. This was the last biplane trainer to be used by the RAF. Over 8,800 Tiger Moths were built and many can still be seen flying today.*

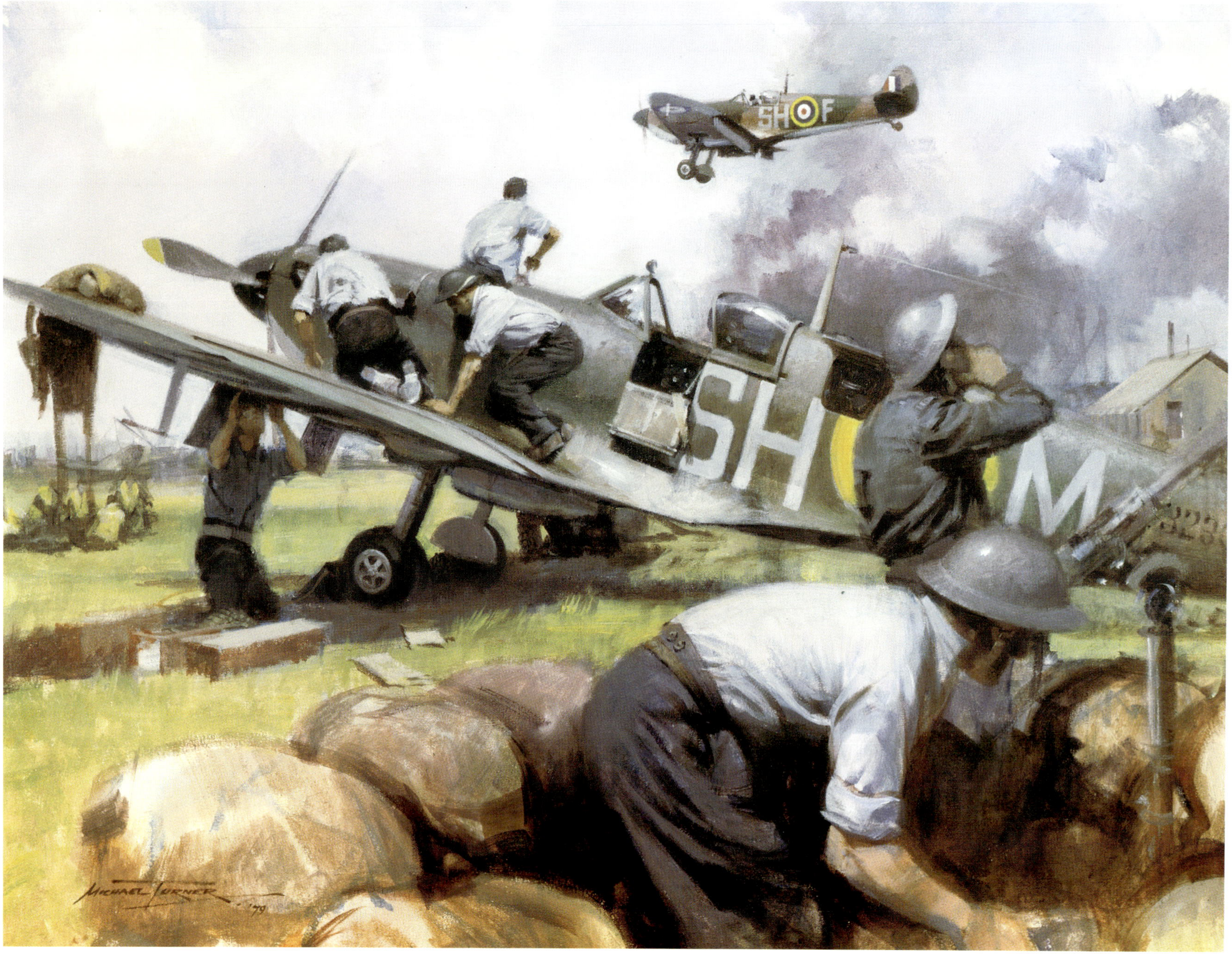
SH F
SH M

Moth in RAF service flew with a UAS in February 1955.

Squadron Leader Dick Smeardon who instructed on the aircraft recalled: *"The Tiger Moth was the aircraft on which I learned to fly, was trained as a flying instructor and on which I instructed, for a total of 500 hours. It is difficult not to become nostalgic, but the Tiger had endearing qualities. Though a simple aircraft to fly, it was not easy to fly well, with ailerons on the lower mainplanes only. It was very much more comfortable to fly from the front cockpit - less slipstream, better view and in the tropics more shaded from the sun. The Tiger was such a good trainer that I had little difficulty converting to the Harvard."*

Les Leetham, who went solo in 1943 wrote: *"I soloed after 11 hours dual instruction and will never forget the one thing the instructor failed to mention, and could never demonstrate - the amazing difference in performance without his weight aboard. It seemed like a rocket, and at the required height for a turn, I was over the boundary instead of well upwind and this threw the whole circuit out."*

Supermarine Spitfire I

The Spitfire is now an international legend. Created by Reginald J. Mitchell and his Supermarine design team in the 1930s, it was the only Allied fighter to remain in full production from pre-1939 until after 1945. During those years more than 40 major versions and a host of minor variants came into being; an indication of the superb development potential of Mitchell's original brainchild.

The prototype first flew in March 1936, and No 19 Squadron became the RAF's first Spitfire unit at Duxford in August 1938. The change from obsolete biplanes to this sleek metal monoplane was summed by Adolph 'Sailor' Malan, DSO, DFC, who was with 74 Squadron then: *"It was like changing over from Noah's Ark to the Queen Mary. The Spitfire had style and was obviously a killer. Moreover, she was a perfect lady. She had no vices. She was beautifully positive. You could dive till your eyes were popping out of your head, but the wings would still be there - till your inside melted, and she would still answer to a touch."*

Malan was referring to the Spitfire I, and it was this version which equipped Fighter Command throughout the Battle of Britain of 1940. Here its superior rate of climb and higher altitude performance made it an ideal partner to the more rugged Hurricane when tackling the armadas of Luftwaffe bombers and fighters attacking Britain. The confidence felt in their aircraft by

Supermarine Spitfire I *Spitfires of No 64 Squadron return to their burning airfield at RAF Kenley to refuel and re-arm at the height of the Battle of Britain.*

all Spitfire pilots of 1940 was encapsulated in the words of the late D M Crook, DFC, who flew the 'Spit' in the 1940 battles: *"Practically everybody who has flown a Spitfire thinks it is the most marvellous aircraft ever built, and I am no exception to the general rule. I grew to like it more than any other machine I have flown. It is so small and compact and neat, yet it possesses devastating fire power, and it is still probably the best, fastest fighter in the world."*

Group Captain J H Hill commanded a fighter squadron at the height of the Battle of Britain:

"By mid-1940 I had spent several months in France as an Air Controller before being seconded to a Hurricane squadron to command it. I had only about five hours flying time on Hurricanes and unfortunately was shot down very early on, but managed to bale out and after returning via Dunkirk and a period in hospital, I had a quick refresher course on Spitfires and was sent to command No 222 Squadron, then equipped with the Spitfire I. Although I had hardly seen a Spitfire before, in a fortnight we were in RAF Hornchurch in the thick of the battle, but by that time I had flown about 15 hours and was quite happy as the Spitfire was a beautiful aeroplane to convert on to.

One of the most extraordinary features of the Mark I was the undercarriage lever on the right-hand side of the cockpit. It was a large piece of equipment resembling iron piping; when the aircraft took off the pilot selected 'undercarriage up' and had to pump this piece of ironmongery with the right hand. However, the Spitfire had extremely sensitive elevators. Consequently, when we took off in squadron formation, as we normally did, the planes would be seen to be 'porpoising' up and down - an effect of pulling and pushing the lever with the right hand while trying to keep the aeroplane steady with the left hand which normally controlled the throttle making quite an amusing sight. But the sensitivity of the elevators and the ailerons made it a beautiful aeroplane to fly. Having flown both the Hurricane and the Spitfire, I feel it is true to say that one could not have had two better aeroplanes for their respective roles. The Hurricane was a slightly sturdier aeroplane and a more stable gun-platform whose role was to attack the bombers; the Spitfire was a dog-fighter that would get as high as possible as quickly as possible to keep the German fighters from attacking the Hurricanes lower down."

Avro Anson

'Faithful Annie' was the universal and affectionate nickname for one of the RAF's hardest-working and long-lived aircraft. Just as its ancestor the Avro 504 had 'taught a nation to fly', so the Anson carried on the tradition by providing basic airborne instruction for a later generation of air crews. Entering service with No 48 Squadron at RAF Manston in March 1936 as a coastal reconnaissance aircraft, the Anson was the first RAF aeroplane to incorporate a retractable undercarriage in first-line use. At the outbreak of World War Two a total of 301 Ansons

Avro Anson An Avro Anson, on Air-Sea Rescue duties with No 278 Squadron, liaises with an RAF launch off the East Anglian coast.

was with Coastal Command - representing exactly two-thirds of the command's aircraft strength.

By the close of 1941, however, all Ansons had been replaced at squadron level, and the design reverted to what proved to be its greatest contribution to the RAF - as a training or communications machine. Chosen as a standard instructional aircraft for the Commonwealth Air Training Plan, the Anson trained many hundreds of bomber crew members; while in its 'hack' transport role, the 'Annie' flew with most RAF units and in particular the Air Transport Auxiliary. More than 11,000 machines were built, and the Anson was officially retired from RAF service in June 1968 - the close of 32 years of faithful service.

The Anson's reputation among experienced pilots was once summed succinctly by an ATA pilot: *"It is virtually as easy to fly as a Tiger Moth, and just about as viceless. In fact, a pilot would really have to try to kill his passengers in an Anson which is just one of the many good reasons why it is such a good machine. Others are its ease of maintenance and extreme economy, its astonishing reliability, and the fantastic loads it will carry. Add to all of which it can be flown in and out of the tiniest aerodromes... Undoubtedly the Anson is one of the most wonderful aeroplanes that has ever been built."*

H A Taylor flew the Anson many times:
"Myths are built up around nearly every aeroplane. For the Anson the myth was one of reliability and harmlessness. Annie, the Old Lady of Woodford, could never, never turn and bite you; her Cheetah engines never stopped; and any fool could handle her.

In fact, the Anson could, like any other aeroplane ever built, turn and bite; the Cheetahs did sometimes (though very rarely) stop before the cutout wire had been pulled; and it was not particularly easy to fly. But it was a forgiving old thing.

Of course, the Anson was sometimes treated too carelessly by people who had not yet learned that all aeroplanes are, by the nature of the laws of Sir Isaac Newton, intrinsically dangerous.

Once, while making a final approach in an Anson, I noticed some surprising and variable changes in the fore-and-aft trim. The landing was completed without incident, but I was surprised that my test-pilot passengers were so insistent that there would be no need to put in a report to the unit's chief technical officer. It transpired that these over-healthy young men - on a test-flying 'rest' between operational tours - had been 'playing harps' with the bare wires running through the fuselage.

For me, there is one reason why the Anson is an exclusive aeroplane. In it I learned to fly with my left hand while doing all kinds of other things with the one which had been originally taught most of the tricks."

Westland Lysander

Conceived in World War One, the role of army co-operation was considered essential enough to justify a series of aeroplanes specifically designed for this task in the following two decades, and for the RAF to

Westland Lysander *A No 208 Squadron Westland Lysander, patrolling the Suez Canal in 1939, circles the Gebel-Mariam monument.*

designate complete squadrons to such duties. Westland's high-wing Lysander - or 'Lizzie' as it was commonly called - was the first monoplane in RAF service to undertake the role, and in the event the last to be designed solely for such a purpose.

First issued to No 16 Squadron at RAF Old Sarum in June 1938, Lizzies eventually equipped more than 30 squadrons and other special units. Seeing brief but gallant action in France and the North African campaigns of 1940-41, the Lysander was then relegated to more mundane but no less vital roles such as target-tugs, air-sea rescue, and general communications liaison.

Specially adapted versions, however, played a secret 'cloak and dagger' role from 1941 to 1944, transporting and retrieving Allied secret agents to and from Occupied Europe.

Bearing in mind its original design conception, the Lysander was admirably suited to its role. Pilots sat high with an excellent all-round downward field of vision, while the aircraft's slow speed characteristics offered landing runs said to be no longer than a cricket pitch. A heavy landing was occasionally known to shake loose the weighty Mercury engine from its holding bolts, but when treated with average respect a Lysander was considered a pleasant, restful machine to operate.

Group Captain Vaughan-Fowler flew the Lysander extensively:

"My first introduction to the Lysander was in November, 1941 at RAF Old Sarum where the Army Co-Operation Operational Training Unit was based. Having finished my advanced training on Hurricanes I

Westland Lysander *A Lysander prepares to take off from a field in Occupied France. The aircraft entered service as a two-seater army co-operation aeroplane, but during the war was given a multitude of tasks.*

75

was not looking forward to regressing to some aircraft that looked as though the Science Museum was clearing out its old stock. How wrong my original thoughts were. Some three years and 800 hours later I had - and still have - a tremendous affection for an aircraft which had taken me and not a few passengers in and out of some fairly odd places.

One's first approach to the aircraft was slightly daunting. To get into it required two steps to reach the top of one of the wheels and then a rather complicated climb up the wing strut and into the cockpit which sat some ten feet above the ground. From this vantage point a very good downwards view was obtained. The main difference in the controls from other aircraft of the time was the elevator trimmer. This changed the angle of incidence of the tail plane and could be lethal if the aircraft was taken off with the landing incidence still selected; this was achieved by winding a wheel on the left of the seat. Another similar wheel on the right of the seat raised and lowered the seat. This could also cause embarrassment at times; if dive bombing was being carried out and the seat was not in the fully up position you found yourself plummeting to the bottom of the cockpit when high G-forces were applied.

I was able to fly the Mark I, II, III and IIIA. They were all very similar except for the engines. The Mark I had the Bristol Mercury XV rated at 15,000ft and with only a two speed propeller it had to be throttled back above 10,000ft so as not to exceed engine speed limitations. The Mark II had the Bristol Perseus, a sleeve-valved engine; not too successful and not many were built. The Mark III had the derated XX and XXX Bristol Mercurys and the aircraft used for special operations also had the Rotol variable pitch propeller allowing for more economical operation.

My main connection with the Lysander was over two years on special operations operating into France from the UK and into Greece, Yugoslavia and France from Italy and Corsica. If I describe one of the more difficult trips it will, perhaps, best underline the sterling qualities of the aircraft. Squadron Leader Hugh Verity (author of We Landed by Moonlight*) and I were detailed for an operation (code-named* Floride*) near Chateroux in the middle of France. Cloud base was 200 feet and raining when we left Tangmere on the night of 21/22 July 1943 and remained thick and low for virtually the whole trip. By that time in our tour of operations we were fairly experienced and we had to fly on instruments most of the time breaking cloud just before coming to our major check points like the French coast, the River Loire and the target area where there were a number of easily recognised water land marks. The return was similar and about $6^{1/2}$ hours later we arrived back at Tangmere with seven passengers including a mother and her two children. I noted at the time that we were the only two aircraft to leave the UK on operations that night. It would have been impossible for any other aircraft to manoeuvre in such poor visibility and low cloud base let alone land in a 600-yard field. One of the more bizarre episodes of this period was a landing on a flare-path of three candles! The Gestapo had surprised the reception party the day before and they were unable to replace the torches that had been abandoned."*

Gloster Gladiator

Gloster Gladiator *Malta's famous Gladiators, which formed the nucleus of No 261 Squadron's defence of the island.*

The Gladiator was the last biplane fighter to be used by the RAF's operational units, and though regarded by many as a 'peacetime' aircraft in fact Gladiators saw highly active service, first as fighters and later in 'backwater' roles throughout World War Two. Their true fighting heyday was from 1939 to 1941, during which period Gladiator pilots claimed at least 250 combat victories over such diversified war zones as France, Norway, East Africa, Egypt, Libya, Greece, Crete and Malta. Indeed, the highest-scoring Allied fighter pilot of the war, Sqn Ldr M. St J Pattle, DFC, gained almost half of his 40-plus victories from a Gladiator cockpit.

Entering service with No 72 Squadron at RAF Church Fenton in early 1937, Gladiators formed the equipment of more than 30 squadrons or other front-line units both at home and, particularly, overseas.

To one pilot who had spent several years flying open-cockpit fighters the Gladiator made a great impression: *"The claustrophobic feeling of being surrounded by a greenhouse canopy took some time to disperse. With the lid shut one felt like a goldfish. In flight the Gladiator was astonishingly easy to fly; very manoeuvrable and tight on the controls, with instant positive response. Admittedly, I had a good rigger to look after my kite, but I think most Gladiator pilots would probably say the same. The knowledge of having four instead of two machine guns was oddly comforting when we first took on the*

Luftwaffe, but despite the type's good speed and aerobatic qualities, we knew we were well outclassed by most opponents. As one officer put it, we were fighting World War Two with World War One equipment."

Flight Lieutenant W.J. Woods described an early combat mission in Malta GC: *"During the day there were constant raids. The Italian bombers continued to fly over at high altitudes, in faultless formation and the accuracy of their high-level bombing earned grudging respect. Our Gladiators, Faith, Hope and Charity took off from Hal Far to fight greatly superior numbers. People in the streets cheered us and our photographs appeared in shop windows, but we were only three against all the Regia Aeronautica in Sicily. I sighted a formation of five S.79 enemy aircraft approaching Valetta at 15,000ft. I delivered an attack from astern, and got a good burst at a range of approximately 200yds. He went down in a steep dive with black smoke pouring from his tail! I could not follow him down, but he appeared to go into the sea. I then broke away and returned over the island at 11,000ft south of Grand Harbour."*

Armstrong Whitworth Whitley *Whitley Vs of No 51 Squadron from RAF Dishforth drop propaganda leaflets over Germany in 1940. This five-seater heavy bomber had a maximum bomb load of 7000 lb, and was one of the mainstays of Bomber Command at the outbreak of war.*

Armstrong Whitworth Whitley

Unspectacular in design, performance and operations, the Whitley was a particularly rugged packhorse for the RAF from its introduction in 1937 until 1945. Despite its ungainly appearance - and due to the angle of its huge, thick wings, the Whitley always seemed to be flying with its nose well down - it shared with the Wellington and Hampden in spearheading Bomber Command's night offensive over Germany during the first three years of World War Two. Nevertheless, the bomber that many did not want, exceeded most expectations.

Thereafter it served in many roles; coastal reconnaissance, glider-tug, paratroop carrier and trainer. Individual OTU Whitleys were still flying occasional bombing sorties over France as late as 1944. Many outstanding bomber captains in the latter years of the war cut their teeth on Whitleys, and the aeroplane established many firsts in Bomber Command annals during 1939-41.

Its hefty construction absorbed astonishing damage on occasion, yet Whitleys suffered the lowest casualty rate among their contemporaries on operations.

From a pilot's viewpoint the Whitley was, as one put it: *"A strange device for the uninitiated. Requiring very firm handling generally, it was nevertheless very stable. On take-off or landing it had a tendency to 'float' for lengthy periods, a trait which - combined with the unusual wing angle in relation to the fuselage - gave many inexperienced pilots some unnerving moments during first flights. Once its idiosyncrasies were understood, the Whitley offered dependable, patient qualities well appreciated by most of its early bomber crews."*

A No 10 Squadron pilot operating from RAF Dishforth leading an attack on Turin in Italy involving a 1,350 mile trip over the Alps said of the raid: *"I got my heavily laden Whitley to 17,500ft over the Alps flying blind on instruments. We knew we were crossing them because of the bumps which the aircraft felt every time it crossed a peak. On we went until I judged we were in the murk over Turin. Then I let go a flare which lit up the middle of the city. I ran in at 5,000ft, dropped two bombs, one of which burst on the Fiat building, the other on the railway sidings beside it. The Italian gunners were detonating their shells about a mile above our heads expecting us to be flying at 10,000ft."*

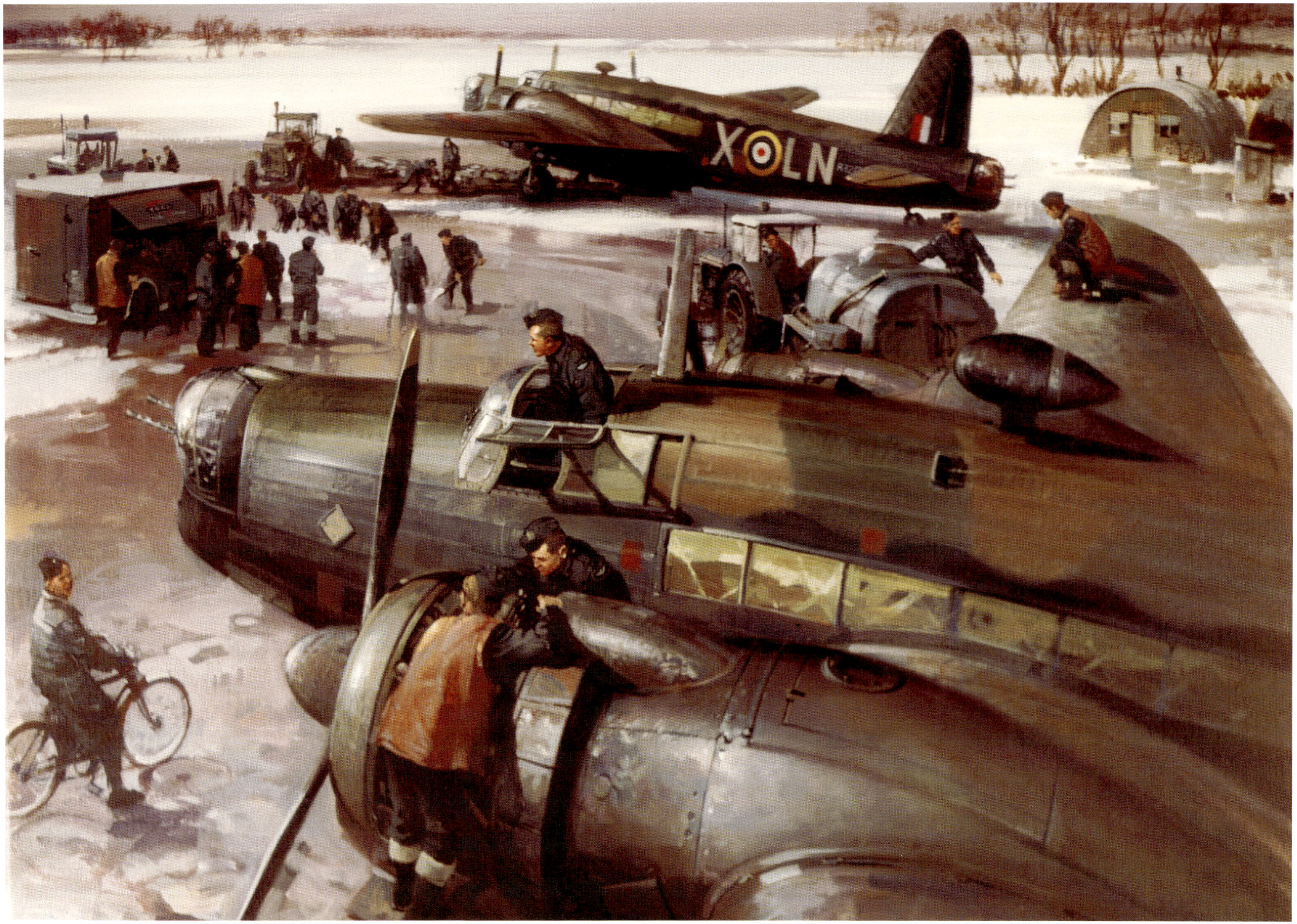
X LN

Vickers Wellington

The 'Wimpy' - its universal nickname which derived from a pre-1939 newspaper Popeye strip cartoon featuring a chubby, hamburger-eating trencherman named J. Wellington Wimpy - was the real mainstay of Bomber Command during 1939-42, and remained on active operations throughout the war. As with its predecessor, the Wellesley, the Wellington framework was of lattice-work geodetic construction, fabric-covered, and this offered surprising strength. It also permitted somewhat alarming flexing of both wing and fuselage to pilots fresh to the design. Having accumulated a prodigious record as a bomber by 1942, the Wimpy was then to give great service with Coastal Command in the unceasing war against German U-boats, and by 1945 maritime Wellington crews had sunk or at least seriously damaged a total of 51 enemy submarines. Outside the European war zones, other Wellingtons gave trojan service in the Middle and Far East theatres.

In flight a Wellington was never exactly placid; wings and tails seemed to have a strong desire to flap, controls tended to wander of their own accord in the cockpit, and wing fabric ballooned alarmingly with decreasing air pressure at altitude. Nevertheless, on becoming accustomed to a Wimpy's inherent quirks, pilots found them pleasant, forgiving machines to fly, with relatively good powers of manoeuvrability if made to undertake mild aerobatics. Extensive development was attempted with the Wellington, including a drastically revised Mark VI version which had a pressurised cabin for the pilot and a separate pressurised cocoon for the tail gunner.

The following are extracts of correspondence we have had with Group Captain W. S. O. Randle, former Keeper of the Battle of Britain Museum:

"No-one can question that the Wellington ranks amongst the great aircraft of all time. For my part, I was one of the fortunate many who can look back with affection on the Wimpy, as most of us called her, which occupied the first seven years of my flying career. It was also my good fortune to see at close quarters the first Wellington, the B9/32 prototype, K4049, rightly regarded as the most advanced design of its day, in the New Types Park at the Hendon Air Display in 1936. When working at the Royal Air Force Museum, I could daily visit MF628, the sole survivor of the thousands of Wellingtons which served the Royal Air Force.

After training, my crew and I joined No 150 Squadron at RAF Snaith, which was equipped with the new Mark III, with its more powerful Hercules engine and wooden fully-feathering propellers. We arrived there on 8 July 1942 and on 23 July in X3313 my crew and I went on our first trip, to Duisburg.

Most of our flying was at night and a considerable proportion of it in cloud; I found the Wellington relatively easy to fly accurately on instruments and by no means tiring. It was also manoeuvrable for a bomber and could corkscrew under certain circumstances well within the turning circle of an approaching fighter. Her durability was renowned and No 150 Squadron had its full share of aircraft returning with damage which in another type would probably have meant loss or destruction.

I last flew a Wellington in August 1948, and the aircraft disappeared from service soon after. MF628, at RAFM Hendon, is the sole survivor of the 11,461 built."

Vickers Wellington Ground crews from No 99 Squadron at RAF Newmarket, prepare Wellington Mark IC bombers for a night operation in the winter of 1940. This Mark had a range of 2200 miles, a ceiling of 22,000 feet, a bomb-load of 4,500 lb and a maximum speed of 235 mph.

North American Harvard

From 1938 to 1955 the noisy Harvard was a standard instructional vehicle for the RAF, and was responsible for conveying the art of 'real' flying to thousands of embryo air crews. Usually nicknamed the 'Yellow Peril' - a reference to its normally all-yellow training livery - the Harvard was always immediately recognisable in the air by its harsh, rasping tone akin to dry linoleum being torn hastily. Though not unstable, the Harvard needed constant flying from take-off to landing; a valuable asset in that it ensured total concentration by student pilots while airborne. The layout of the controls was distinctly American, with a daunting array of instrumentation facing the new 'driver' on his first Harvard solo. Its long 'glasshouse' perspex canopy offered excellent vision fields, while its manoeuvrability permitted instruction in aerobatics to a high degree; a necessary adjunct to any advanced trainer.

As H A Taylor said: *"Things had to be done properly and in the right order. A 'drill' was required and its routine flying and handling had necessarily to be left largely to pre-trained reflex action. It was for the Harvard that we were taught one of the school's most valuable tricks - a kind of mnemonic for the cockpit drill. Throughout six years of war, while flying maybe 50 or so different aircraft types, this mnemonic worked. With a few modifications and additions it could be used successfully even for monsters like the*

North American Harvard *A pupil pilot under instruction bring a Harvard in to land after a training flight at 2FTS, RAF Brize Norton in the summer of 1940. As for all instructional aircraft, the Harvard was painted bright yellow on its undersides to ensure maximum visibility.*

B-24 Liberator bomber."

Squadron Leader Clarke was familiar with the Harvard during the last years of the war:

"The comfortable front cockpit, not too roomy, not too small, with sufficient knobs, instruments and gadgets to make you feel that you were pretty clued up knowing what they all did. The rear, instructor's, cockpit was perhaps more stark and the visibility not nearly so good, but you soon got used to splay-eyed hold-offs instead of the old fashioned hang-your-head-over-the-port-side method of landing. The instructor was comfortable enough in the back, but the real enjoyment came when he was solo - in the front.

The formidable and characteristic external blare of the Pratt & Whitney Wasp was a muted sewing machine to the pilot's ears, yet it gave a reasonable punch in the back for take-off and had enough reserve to make continuous aerobatics possible without losing height. Ailerons, rudder or elevators; stalling, high-speed stalling or spinning; flaps, undercart or pitch - whatever you used or did, in or with the Harvard, it was positive, easy and emphatically safe. Apart from the steerable tailwheel which pupils sometimes, somehow, managed to unlock by ruddering over forty-five degrees whilst landing (which inevitably resulted in a ground loop, but with no more damage than a dented wingtip), the Harvard was more snag-free than any other kite of equivalent or better performance - and a good deal better than the majority of slower aircraft!

So...I practised for hours to take the Harvard to the limits of its wide safety margins - partly because I enjoyed practising, partly because I had to do some special work, partly because I rather fancied myself as an aerobatic pilot in 1945.

The special work was using a Harvard virtually as a helicopter. As CI of the OTU at Fayid I took it upon myself to be responsible for rescuing any 'red-on-black', 'forget-to-switch-over-tanks' or 'started-pinpointing-when-the-ETA-was-up' pupils. There were plenty of 'em - quite apart from the more excusable, but just as frequent reason when our war- and OTU-weary Spits and Kitty's gave up the ghost on the Course triangular across country or at any other time - generally the most inconvenient. Then, everybody (and by that I mean Instructors, not - Allah preserve us! - pupils) got airborne and square searched the vastness of sand until the unfortunate pranger was located.

Desert landings on soft sand, hard sand, rock, small plateaux or wriggling wadis taught me that a Harvard, if pressed, could take off in 50 yards and land in 55 - that is, with an average windspeed of ten mph. Undoubtedly this sounds like a line, but I expect that there are still a few bods who will remember the occasions when I used to land on the compass base at Fayid, touching down and stopping inside the marked circle of cardinal points. The whole secret was to descend near-vertically with the stick back, stalled (fifty-five on the clock); then, undershooting and just before touching down, slamming the throttle wide open for a couple of seconds to check the fall. The result was spectacular, dangerous for one's rank in the event of the engine missing even for a second (the undercart would have gone straight up through the wings, and my superiors through their respective ceilings), but very necessary to pick up those pupils who might otherwise have had to wait sometimes for days before being rescued."

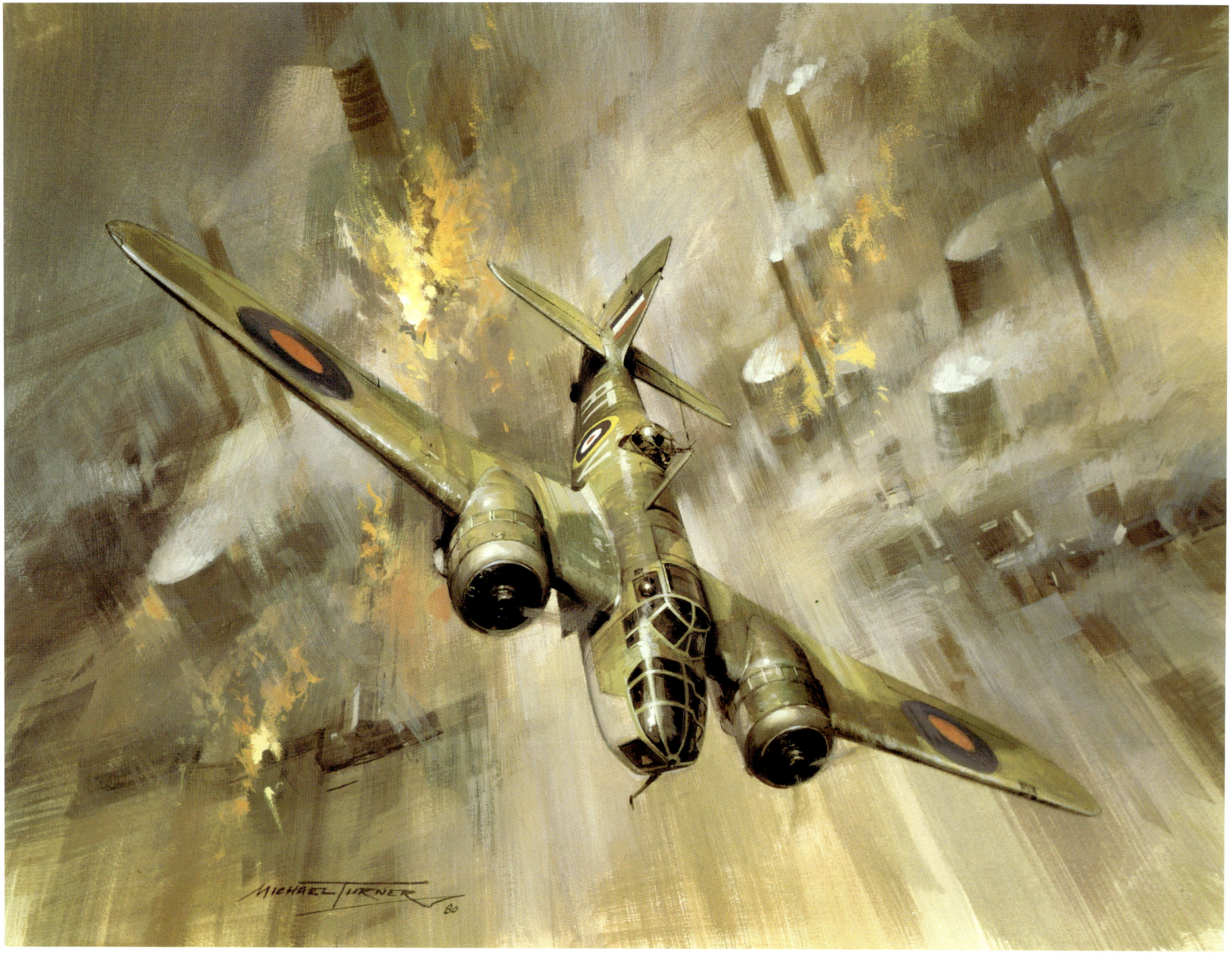
MICHAEL TURNER
80

Bristol Blenheim IV

The first RAF aircraft to penetrate German skies in World War Two was a Blenheim IV (N6215) of No 139 Squadron, on a reconnaissance sortie from RAF Wyton on 3 September 1939; the next day Blenheim IVs of Nos 107 and 110 Squadrons carried out the RAF's first bombing sortie by attacking German ships in the Schillig Roads. In effect a 'stretched' Blenheim I, having extended nose accommodation for the observer/navigator/bomb aimer, the Blenheim IV saw a high degree of operational use during the years 1939-42 in most theatres of war. Usually operating by day, the Blenheim IV crews of No 2 Group, Bomber command are particularly remembered for their dauntless courage in returning to the fray almost daily during 1941-42, despite appalling casualties. More than 60 RAF squadrons flew the type at some period until being superseded by more modern designs.

The many hydraulic and other engine controls in a Blenheim - mostly esoterically designed and located by its makers including their own design of the mid-upper power-operated turret - could be frustrating to a fresh pilot; particularly the many similar-looking plungers and handles, and the two-pitch propeller controls which were placed behind the pilot's seat location. Once airborne, however, the aircraft was easy to operate, with few real vices. Surprisingly compact for a bomber, the Blenheim IV could lift a bomb load of some 1,320 lb over a range of 1,300 to 1,400 miles. Defensive armament - as with so many other pre-1939 designs - was inadequate for daylight operations; comprising merely two guns in the dorsal turret and, inexplicably, a single fixed forward gun for the pilot.

Richard Passmore, a Blenheim air gunner wrote: *"In the early days of the war, Blenheims were sent over the Channel on solo raids, and usually in daylight. It was my duty to fend off any attacking fighters from my turret on top of the fuselage. I did this in the knowledge that the range of my gun was inadequate, and that it was me most likely to be killed. So the pilots invariably tried to stay out of sight in cloud. But invariably the cloud rolled back a few miles north of the French coast, leaving a dangerously blue sky."*

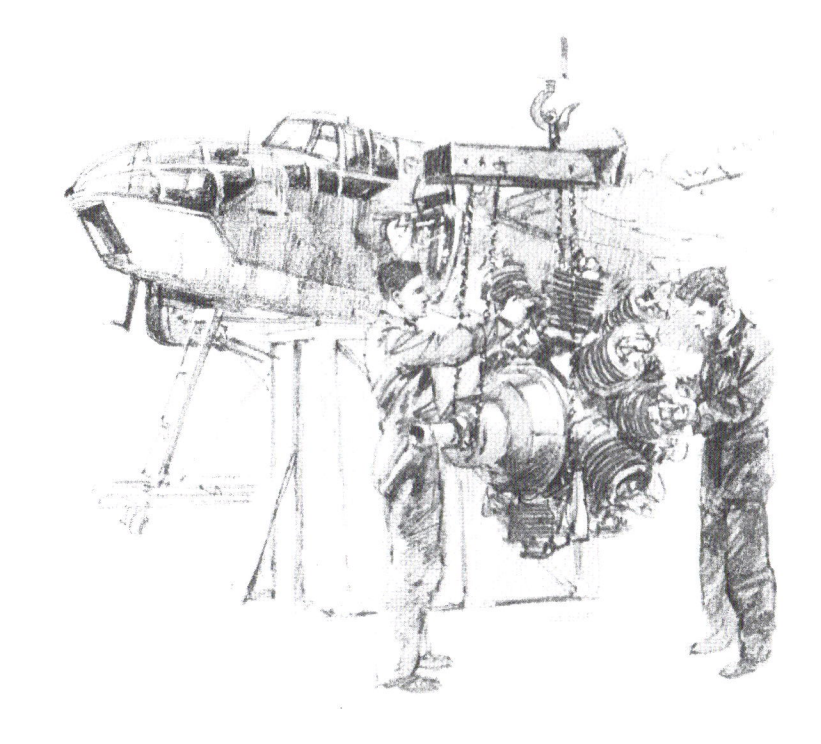

Bristol Blenheim IV *A Blenheim IV of No 114 Squadron, flown by Sgt (later ACM) Ivor Broome, on a low-level bombing run over the power station at Knapsack, Cologne in 1941.*

Handley Page Hampden

Six years old in concept, and incapable of significant development, the Hampden stood worthily alongside the Whitley and Wellington as the spine of Bomber Command at the outbreak of war in 1939. And until the advent of bigger, four-engined bombers in 1941-42, the Hampden soldiered on valiantly, maintaining the RAF's main offensive capability against Germany despite its patent obsolescence and totally inadequate defensive armament. Even then, after being replaced in the bomber role, Hampdens continued operations with Coastal Command as torpedo bombers until late 1943.

Cramped crew accommodation - the internal fuselage width was a mere three feet - increased crew fatigue over any extended sortie; yet the 'Flying Suitcase' was ever popular. To an astonishing speed range from 73mph landing to 260mph maximum, was added extreme ease in handling and fluid manoeuvrability. Sitting high, with an unmatched field of vision, a Hampden pilot could handle his bomber almost like a fighter. As one pilot expressed his own experience: *"It was a delightful aeroplane to fly. The aileron control was brisk and tight turns were a special pleasure...and if you were prepared to take a little trouble with the business of landing, it offered the kind of landing that made one's day."*

The 'wring-out' capabilities of a Hampden is

Handley Page Hampden The Handley Page Hampdens of No 408 'Goose' Squadron of the Royal Canadian Air Force are prepared for a night-time mine-laying mission. The 'Flying Suitcase' was fast and manoeuvrable, but had inadequate armament.

perhaps exemplified by the occasion when the late Grahame Ross, DFC, at Aston Down OTU in 1940, engaged two Spitfires in a friendly dogfight with surprising results for them: *"Both Spit pilots were amazed at my Hampden's aerobatics and had to pull out all the stops, and even then had great difficulty in getting even a passing sightline on me."*

Boulton Paul Defiant

The ill-starred Defiant was unique on its introduction to the RAF as being the Service's first fighter fitted with a power-operated gun turret as its sole armament. Its design conception envisaged its use for attacking enemy bomber formations from the beam, but in early 1940 when Defiants first flew into combat, it was used as a normal fighter - with disastrous results. Despite early optimistic claims of combat successes, the Defiant crews soon suffered devastating casualties, and by August 1940 the type was relegated to night-fighting duties. Fitted with early Airborne Interception (AI) radar, the night Defiants proved relatively successful during the German night blitz of 1940-41, but were superseded in the role by Beaufighters thereafter. For the rest of the war Defiants served as training target-tugs, while a number gave valuable service with the newly-created Air Sea Rescue organisation.

Pilots generally liked the Defiant from a pure

Boulton Paul Defiant *A Boulton Paul Defiant night-fighter from No 255 Squadron, based at RAF Kirton-in-Lindsey, searches the moonlit sky. The Defiant was outclassed as a daytime fighter but was a capable night-fighter; the observer in his power-operated turret could constantly scan the upper sky and shoot down bombers from below or beam-on.*

flying viewpoint. The front cockpit was relatively roomy, and visibility forward better than in most in-line engined aircraft of the time. In the air it tended towards heaviness on the controls. As one pilot explained. *"It was as solid as a rock in a dive, built up a lot of reserve speed through her weight, and was nice near the ground. If anything it handled rather more like a bomber than a fighter."* Another ex-Defiant crew member has recorded: *"The Defiant was well liked for its reliability, good handling qualities, lack of vices and simplicity for flying and landing at night."*

Squadron Leader Clarke expressed the general combination of satisfaction and frustration that pilots felt about the Defiant:

"There were two rear-gun fighters in World War Two: the Blackburn Roc and the Boulton Paul Defiant. They were both armed with the same Boulton Paul turret which fired four .303 Brownings, which rotates through 360 degrees (they automatically cut out in the appropriate places so that the gunner could not shoot off the prop, tail or rudder!), and which was so accurate that the maker's expert could insert a pencil in one of the muzzles and sign on a piece of board held in front of the guns.

There was only one snag. Whoever invented the rear-gun fighter completely forgot to invent how it could attack anything! You just couldn't attack unless you ran away - and if you ran away how could you possibly call the thing a fighter?

From the pilot's point of view the Defiant was a reasonable enough aircraft. Heavy perhaps, with a very definite relationship towards the Hawker Hurricane - so much so that the one outstanding victory achieved by Defiants was when a gaggle of Bf 109s jumped 12 of them from out of the sun and ran into the concentrated fire of forty-eight .303s - but without inheriting the rather poor top speed of that over-praised fighter and most certainly without approaching its manoeuvrability. The Defiant handled more like a bomber than a fighter.

The cockpit was roomy enough and as well equipped as most British wartime fighters; in other words the pilot soon realised that 'things had been added', and nine times out of ten they had been put in the worst possible place. Still, the visibility forward was better than average for an in-line engine, and it was obvious that the rear gunner could warn the pilot about the E/A coming up astern.

The rear gunner was really the most important person on board, and if the Defiant had made the grade there is no doubt that PBOs would have re-created the importance they justly earned in World War One. But apart from that one glorious massacre they did not have a chance, and the Defiant became a jack-of-all-trades."

Miles Master

Developed from the Miles Kestrel projected trainer, the Master offered an excellent vehicle for interim-stage conversion of elementary-trained air crews to the fast monoplanes in squadron use by 1939. Production of Master Is began in 1938 and seven aircraft were on RAF strength by September 1939. A total of 900 Master Is was eventually produced for the RAF, while an overall total of 3,450 machines of all Marks had been built.

The Master was of wooden construction and plywood covered. Initially it was an elegant private venture type which aroused much interest in the RAF. It first flew in 1938, fitted with a 715hp Rolls-Royce Kestrel XXX engine. First deliveries to the RAF were made in May 1939, most being used by FTS at Sealand, Montrose and Hullavington.

The Master II, with a 870hp Bristol Mercury radial engine first flew in November 1939, and a total of 1,747 was built. The final version was the Mark III, with a 825hp Pratt & Whitney Wasp Junior and first flew in 1940.

Major user of the II and III was No 5 (Pilot) Advanced Flying School at RAF Ternhill from 1942 onwards. Some Masters were still in service in 1950.

Miles Master *A Miles Master I advanced trainer gets airborne, with the instructors rear seat raised to increase forward visibility.*

Supermarine Walrus

A 'Shagbat' is, according to Service legend, an ancient Egyptian bird able to fly in ever-decreasing circles - with a logical conclusion to its flightpath. It was also the nickname for the Walrus amphibian. Originally a private venture design by the 'father' of the immortal Spitfire, R. J. Mitchell, the Seagull V - its original title - was adopted as the Walrus from 1935 by the Fleet Air Arm as a spotter-reconnaissance aircraft able to operate from land, aircraft carriers or, via a catapult, from individual ships of the Fleet. For the next ten years the Shagbat served its masters faithfully, accepting a myriad of unlikely tasks in a bewildering variety of circumstances and climates around the globe - and never failing to uphold its

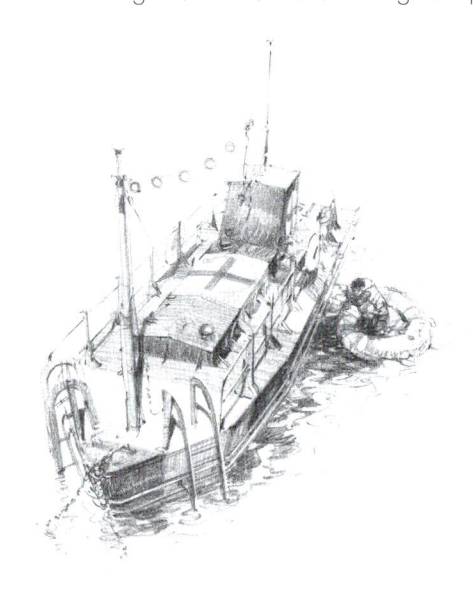

***Supermarine Walrus** A Supermarine Walrus Air-Sea Rescue amphibian picks up a ditched pilot from the English Channel in 1941. This was a development of the Supermarine Seagull and was a very angular single-engined biplane. The slab-sided fuselage hull was made from sheet aluminium alloy.*

ubiquitous roles as a naval jack-of-all-trades.

At one and the same time Supermarine earned the distinction of supplying the RAF with its slowest front-line type, the Walrus, and with its fastest, the Spitfire. The Walrus caused no recognition problems as its biplane configuration, with its engine driving a pusher airscrew, and wing tip floats were very distinguishable. Its heroic work in the ASR role involved seven UK-based and four Middle Eastern squadrons, while also being used for mine spotting and, on one memorable occasion, dive bombing duties!

By 1945, its prodigious Service record had earned it the unofficial Service motto: 'Where there's a war, there's a Walrus'. Apart from its outstanding maritime honours, the pusher-engined Walrus became from 1941 an increasingly welcome sight to many hundreds of RAF and USAAF crews forced to ditch in the sea. Its use for air-sea rescue duties gave birth to many mini-epics of cool courage by Shagbat crews as they alighted in mine-infested waters to retrieve Allied airmen.

A noisy, underpowered anachronism on the aerial scene of 1939-45, nevertheless the Walrus was always regarded by those who flew in it with high affection. Indeed one FAA pilot, B J Hurren declared: *"Excepting possibly the Swordfish, one may doubt whether any aeroplane in any Service in the world has a record in war which can match the old Shagbat."*

Short Sunderland

For over a 21 year period after the Sunderland flying-boats had entered service with the RAF in June 1938 (with Nos 210 and 230 Squadrons), they were still on first-line duties in the Far East. No other operational RAF aircraft could then claim such a long period in its original role in such duties.

The Sunderland, built by Short Brothers alongside the similar, civilian, Empire flying-boats was a four-engined monoplane aircraft to supplant the time-honoured biplane boats, which had reigned supreme in the RAF since the famous Felixstowe boats of World War One. Its high wing allowed the four radial engines and propellers to be reasonably clear of spray, and the fixed wing-tip floats provided stability on the water.

At the outbreak of war in 1939 four RAF squadrons were equipped with the Sunderland, the only long-distance aircraft available to Coastal Command.

'The Battle of the Atlantic was the dominating factor all through the war', wrote Sir Winston Churchill - and it was in that battle against enemy U-boats that the Sunderland, with its twelve hours duration, may best be remembered. The first U-boat kill came in January 1940, and by mid-1942 new depth charges coming into service with Coastal Command, provided Sunderland crews with a more effective weapon against submarines.

Flight Lieutenant E. R. Baker, skipper of a Sunderland of No 210 Squadron based at RAF Pembroke Dock, South Wales, recalled a convoy protection sortie on 16 August 1940: *"We were concerned about the atrocious weather conditions with driving rain and a cloud base hardly higher than 400ft. Six hours later the weather had hardly improved when the second pilot shouted 'Sub', and I immediately sounded the Klaxon. The crew jumped to their action stations. The U-boat was on the surface but started a crash dive when it saw us. I was diving low over it to drop a depth charge. The whole surface of the sea seemed to shudder for yards around and then suddenly blew up. In the middle of the boiling sea the submarine emerged with its deck awash, and then U-51 sank rather like a brick. Then great globs of oil began to spread. I signalled a destroyer and circled for an hour."* Baker received a DFC for the episode.

The Twin-Wasp engined Sunderland V continued in use after 1945, notching up impressive sortie totals in the transport role during the Korean War, the Berlin Airlift

92

Short Sunderland *A Short Sunderland I of No 210 Squadron at RAF Pembroke Dock undergoes maintenance while at its moorings. This was arguably the best flying-boat of World War Two.*

(operating from the city's lakes) and the 1951-54 Greenland Expedition. The last Sunderland, an MR5 of No 205 Squadron, retired on 15 May 1959.

Supermarine Spitfire V

The Mark V versions of the Spitfire not only predominated in Fighter Command's squadrons' equipment in 1941, but were built in greater quantity - a total of 6,479, or almost 30% of all Spitfires ever constructed - than any other Spitfire variant. The Mark V offered three main forms of armament. The Va carried eight .303in Browning machine guns; the Vb a mixture of two 20mm Hispano cannons and four .303 Brownings; while the Vc could be fitted with either of these 'batteries' or alternatively be fitted with four 20mm cannons plus carriage of a 500lb bomb under the fuselage. All Mark V versions had a more powerful engine than their Mark II predecessors, and were able to engage the newly-introduced Messerschmitt Bf 109F of 1941 on roughly equal standing.

Many, though by no means all, Spitfire Vs were instantly recognisable by having 'clipped' wingtips; though later variants also employed this

Short Sunderland *A Short Sunderland III from No 461 Squadron R.A.A.F. circles low over an Atlantic convoy.*

particular modification for low altitude roles.

The introduction by the Luftwaffe of its Focke-Wulf Fw 190 fighter by mid-1941 came as a shock to Allied air authorities, and the new German fighter quickly proved itself well superior in most facets of combat performance to the Spitfire V. The result was the introduction of the Spitfire IX, built in quantities only second to the Mark V in the Spitfire story. The Mark V was also the first Spitfire type to be tropicalised, and served in the North African campaign and other Mediterranean zones of operations. It remained in production for some two years supplying several hundreds of examples to the Royal Navy and to Australia.

Flying Officer M Feric was one of the Polish pilots of No 303 Squadron based at RAF Northolt. This is an account of one of his first dogfights in a Spitfire:

"Kellett's flight split up and each of them selected one Messerschmitt Bf 109. What about us? We did not have to wait long for a job. Another flight of three Bf 109s, flying much higher than the first, came to the rescue of their comrades. They dived down and were passing in front of us, as we were some 300 yards behind our first flight. That was lucky, especially as one of the Huns was already firing at Sergeant Karubin, who was busy with the Bf 109 ahead of him. Wunsche took him on. I went after the other, putting on full throttle. I caught up with him easily, he grew in my sights until his fuselage occupied the whole luminous circle. It was certainly time for firing. I did it quite calmly and I was not even excited, rather puzzled and surprised to see that it was so easy,

Supermarine Spitfire V *Spitfire Vbs of No 303 (Polish) Squadron take off from RAF Northolt to make a sweep across the Channel in 1942.*

quite different from Poland when you had to scrape and try until you were in a sweat, and then instead of getting him, he got you."

Westland Whirlwind

The Westland Whirlwind was designed to perform the two duties of long-range escort and night fighter and first flew on 11 October 1938. It possessed an extremely heavy offensive capability with four 20mm cannon mounted in the nose, and entered service in June 1940.

It was not only the first Westland fighter ever used by the RAF it was also the first single-seat twin-engined fighter to see service. Its existence was a closely guarded secret in the early days of the war.

However, the aircraft suffered from serious defects. The Whirlwind's two Rolls-Royce Peregrine engines (used by no other types) were both unreliable and low-powered, and in addition the aircraft had a very high landing speed of 80 mph that made it impossible to use on grass airfields. Performance fell off at altitude but was fast low down. Eventually a mere 112 Whirlwinds were built and were used only on Nos 137 and 263 Squadrons.

From 1942, modified as fighter bombers, to which the Whirlwind indulged in low-level cross-Channel sorties, attacking shipping, locomotives, bridges and harbour installations. It was withdrawn from service in November 1943 and declared obsolete in June 1944.

Westland Whirlwind *Westland Whirlwinds of No 263 Squadron, operating from RAF Filton, on patrol near Bristol early in 1941.*

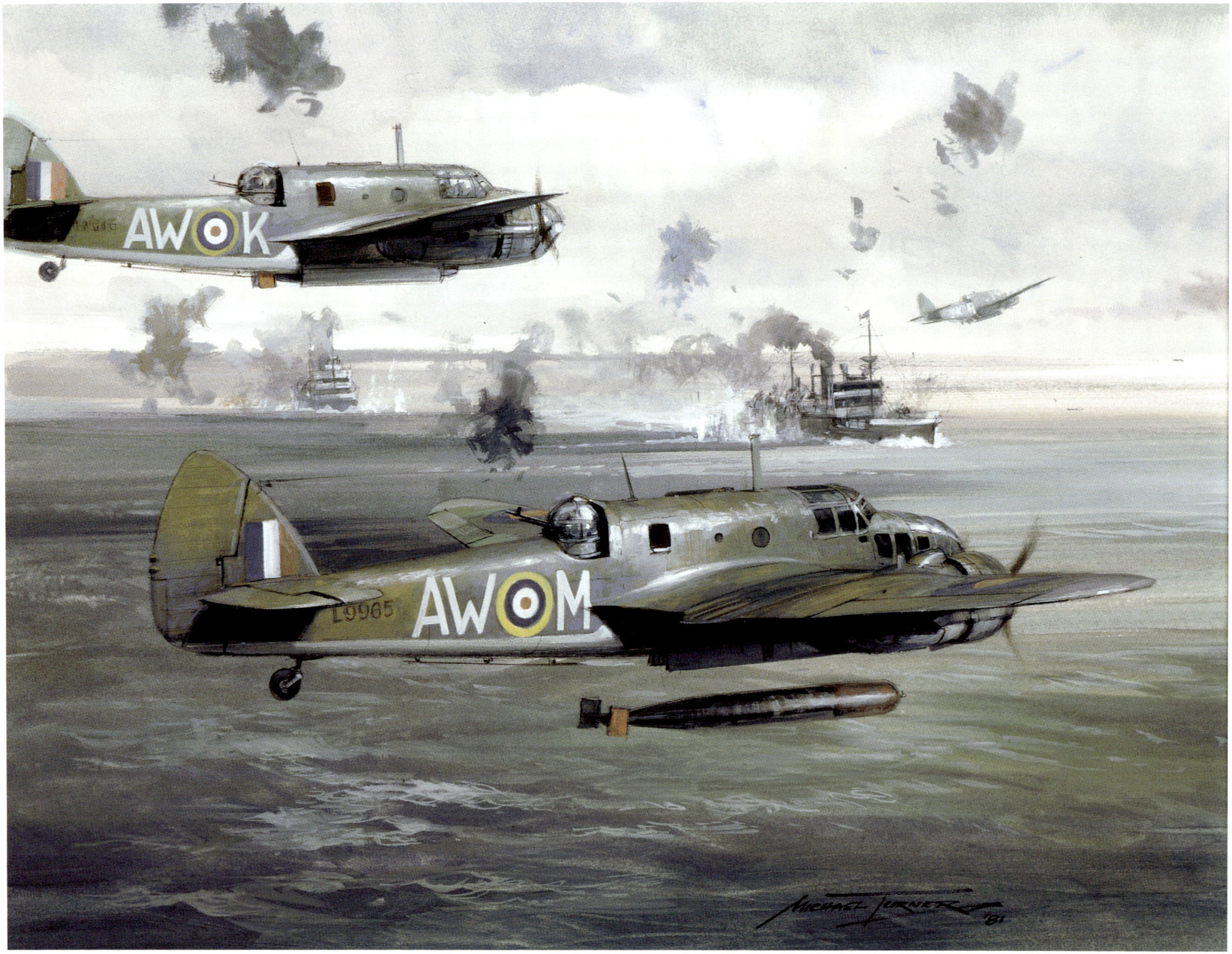
AW K
AW M
L9965
MICHAEL TURNER '81

Bristol Beaufort

Pilots' reactions to the ungainly Beaufort torpedo bomber varied. Peter Geldart, undergoing a conversion course to Beaufighters, had no great opinion of the type: *"The Beaufort I with two 1,010hp Bristol Taurus engines was an underpowered aeroplane, incapable of maintaining a straight and level flight on one engine. However, how they flew these machines on operations with an 18-inch torpedo slung underneath her I shall never know - I only know I'm pleased I was not asked to do it."* Pat Gibbs, DSO, DFC, possibly the leading torpedo specialist of the RAF then, was less scathing but no less respectful of the Beaufort's characteristics: *"The Beaufort, although completely without vices, was something of a handful and demanded respect...it was not docile and demanded constant and vigilant supervision. This first impression that a Beaufort required always to be consciously flown and never left to its own devices, particularly near the ground, is one which I have never since found reason to modify. The aircraft had to be flown right from the start of the take-off until it had actually stopped running at the end of the landing run. To enter a shallow dive was to see the needle of the airspeed indicator rapidly cover the 200-knot scale, pass the 300 mark, and still continue upwards."*

First entering service with No 22 Squadron at RAF Thorney Island in November 1939, the Beaufort became the RAF's standard torpedo bomber until 1943, albeit being used more as a day bomber. Ten squadrons were eventually equipped with the type, operating mainly in European or Mediterranean waters; but some 700 machines were built in Australia and operated over the Pacific with RAAF units.

Roy C. Nesbitt flew Bristol Beauforts on No 217 Squadron, Coastal Command from January 1941 to March 1942:

"I joined the RAFVR in September 1939 and trained as an air navigator, being commissioned when aged 19 in January 1941 when I joined No 217 Squadron and began flying on Bristol Beauforts. There were only three Beaufort Squadrons at that time; Nos 22, 42 and 217. I completed 49 operational flights, 217 Squadron being based successively at RAF St Eval in Cornwall, Thorney Island in Hampshire, and Wick in Caithness. During my operational service, the squadron lost 24 Beauforts, the normal operational strength being no more than ten. I left the RAF as a Flight Lieutenant in 1946.

Originally designed as a torpedo bomber for Coastal Command, the Bristol Beaufort also fulfilled a variety of other roles, such as dive bombing warships and merchantmen, low level attacks on ports, mine-laying and anti-submarine and other patrols. These sorties could vary from fairly safe to suicidally dangerous.

The Beaufort was an immensely strong aircraft, but it was heavy and difficult to fly and there were many accidents on training and operational work. Even after modification of the early Taurus engine, only a very skilful pilot could maintain height on one engine. Later, the Pratt & Whitney Wasp engine proved far more reliable, for if one engine was hit during an attack the pilot could feather the propeller and reduce the risk of fire, whilst there was a good chance of getting home on one engine.

Although the Beaufort achieved some success as a torpedo and dive bomber, losses could be extremely heavy when flying at low level in the face of intense flak, and Beaufort crews were often considered to have the highest mortality rate in the RAF."

Bristol Beaufort *The Bristol Beauforts of No 42 Squadron, Coastal Command, launch a torpedo attack on an enemy convoy in 1941. The Beaufort was a four-seater torpedo bomber that was derived from the Blenheim (page 85) and in turn gave rise to the Beaufighter (page 104).*

de Havilland Mosquito

With the golden advantage of hindsight, it could be said that the superb Mosquito - always 'Mossie' to its crews - came into being despite the Air Ministry. Conceived in 1938 as a private venture, its all-wood construction and lack of defensive armament - the latter in deference to the design's high speed for evading attack - was officially considered too unorthodox for Service use. Delays in official sponsorship meant that the first prototype did not fly until November 1940, but by mid-1941 the aircraft's superlative performance earned it full-scale production orders.

The Mosquito relied for defence on its ability to outpace any intercepting fighter. With two powerful Rolls-Royce Merlin engines, extreme aerodynamic cleanliness and a high power-to-weight ratio, the performance of the 'Wooden Wonder' surpassed that of any other operational aircraft. Aesthetically, the Mosquito was one of the most appealing combat designs of World War 2 and it possessed delightful flying characteristics.

The 'Mossie' filled almost every front-line requirement in all theatres of war. It became the RAF's premier long-range photo reconnaissance aircraft - in 1943 alone, No 1 PRU at RAF Benson despatched

de Havilland Mosquito *Mosquitos of No 105 Squadron carry out a low-level raid on the marshalling yards at Ehrang on 1 April 1943. 7,781 Mosquitos were made before production ended in November 1950.*

de Havilland Mosquito PRU *Mosquito flying down the Tromso Fjord, Norway, looking for the* Tirpitz.

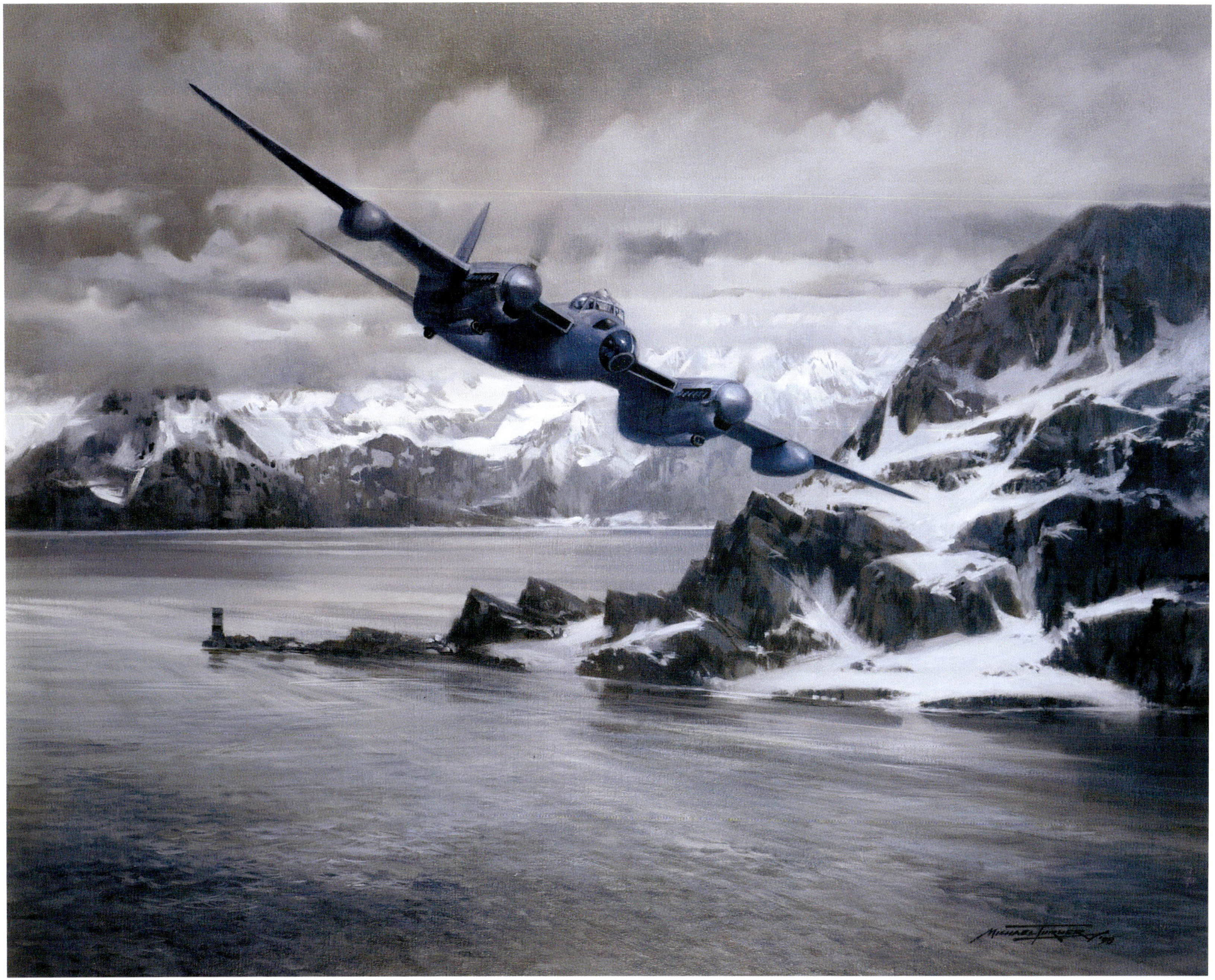

some 3,000 sorties all over Europe, and the type continued in the role well after the war. Subsequently, alongside night bomber operations, 'Mossies' became the mainstay of the light night Pathfinder Force.

Considering that one of the earliest Mosquito bombers, with full load, outpaced a Spitfire V which was using emergency boost, it is worthy of speculation as to what effect on the overall bomber offensive of 1941-45 might have been created had the Mosquito been accepted for full bomber production from its inception in 1938. Post-war statistics indicate that Mosquito crews flew roughly four times the number of sorties per aircraft loss than the equivalent ratio in Lancasters.

Few RAF aircraft have escaped condemnation from some quarter on their introduction - but the Mosquito was certainly one. From 1941 to 1945 Mossies undertook many roles: reconnaissance, bomber, fighter, anti-shipping scourge and submarine hunter and destroyer. All were facets of the Mosquito's versatility. Whatever its role it retained a fighter-like performance, an aerobat's fluid agility, and a ruggedness which absorbed terrifying damage, yet still delivered live crews from the wreckage.

Syd Clayton, DSO, DFC, DFM, who flew 145 sorties as both navigator and then pilot, said of the 'Wooden Wonder': *"I'm obviously biased regarding the 'Mossie' but as a pilot I found it a wonderful aircraft which would take a severe hammering and still fly on one engine."* Frank Ruskell, DFC, a navigator, summed up his feelings: *"The Mosquito was a good-looking aeroplane of high performance. It seldom let you down - you could not help loving it and went to war in it with every confidence."*

As Wing Commander Anderson, OBE, DFC, AFC said in his book *Pathfinders*: whereas *"a Lancaster taking off gives the impression of tremendous power hauling a ponderous weight triumphantly into the air, a Mosquito taking off rather suggests a bundle of ferocious energy that the pilot has to fight to keep down on to the runway. The place to watch is from the end just where the Mossie gets airborne. You see it starting towards you along the flarepath, just a red and green wingtip light. Soon you can distinguish its shape, slim and somehow evil, suddenly she is screaming towards you just like a gigantic cat. A moment later she is past and 30 feet up in the air."*

Group Captain Leonard Cheshire VC recalled the target marking for No 617 Squadron in his Mosquito: *"It was 14 June 1944 and the invasion was going well. Nevertheless, the Allies had no great desire to allow German E-boats to sink the supply ships, so the the pens were to be attacked. As I reached the French coast, I pushed the Mosquito down and hurtled through a curtain of ack-ack to the heart of the harbour, and there tied up in the neat concrete bays, were 15 E-boats. No amount of ground fire could deter me now, not with a target like this. Down, deadly accurate went my red marker flares. Overhead, in the gloaming, protected by Spitfires, our massive Lancasters droned in. Then tallboy after tallboy smashed down on those twinkling spots of red that were my flares."*

Avro Lancaster

This was, indisputably, the finest heavy night bomber of World War Two - some would even argue it was the best bomber of those years. Originally projected in 1939 as the Avro Manchester III, the Lancaster began arriving in Bomber Command in late 1941, and from 1943 was the RAF's principal heavy bomber. A total of 7,377 was built, and some 56 squadrons flew the type at some period.

Bomber Command created No 5 Group entirely equipped with Lancasters. It achieved many feats - it was the first aircraft type to fly Pathfinder missions (August 1942); the first to carry 3,636kg (8,000lb) bombs (April 1943); the first to carry a 5,455kg (12,000lb) bomb (September 1943) and the 5,455kg (12,000lb) 'Tallboy' deep penetration bomb (July 1944), and the mammoth 10,000kg (22,000lb) bomb (March 1945). They flew 156,318 sorties and dropped 608,613 tons of bombs but 3,345 were lost in action.

Avro Lancaster Lancaster Pathfinders have dropped their colour-coded markers (green in this case) to pinpoint the target, and the Lancs of No 57 Squadron follow them in to release their bomb-loads. The golden trails are fire from automatic weapons, but these rarely reached as high as the Lancasters.

With rare exception all men who flew in Lancasters praised the aircraft, while its increasing adaptability for heavier and more complex warloads as the war progressed became a byword. Excluding No 100 Group, Bomber Command's strength in April 1945 showed approximately 67% were Lancaster-equipped units.

Perhaps the most famous of all Lancaster raids were carried out by No 617 Squadron on the Möhne and Eder Dams - Operation *Chastise* - in May 1943. The 'Lanc' achieved further fame by the sinking of the *Tirpitz* in November 1944 and playing the major part in the raid on the German experimental rocket base at Peenemunde in August 1943. Of the 32 VCs awarded to RAF personnel during World War 2, ten were given to Lancaster aircrew.

Sqn Ldr Jack Currie, who flew Lancasters on operations with No 12 Squadron, said of the aircraft: *"The Lancaster looked good because everything was well-shaped and in proportion and it had a good flying attitude, and in between take-off and landing the 'Lanc' flew herself. It was a dream aeroplane."* Another veteran bomber pilot who completed two tours of operations recalled: *"My first tour of ops was on Hampdens and how I survived unscathed I will never know. Yet when I was posted to a Lancaster squadron for my second bite of the cherry, I felt no apprehension. The 'Lanc's' reputation was already spreading round the aircrews, and after my first test flight in it I knew that I would survive - such was the confidence this beautiful bomber inspired. Throughout 30 sorties it never once failed me - despite several distinctly hairy trips when flak*

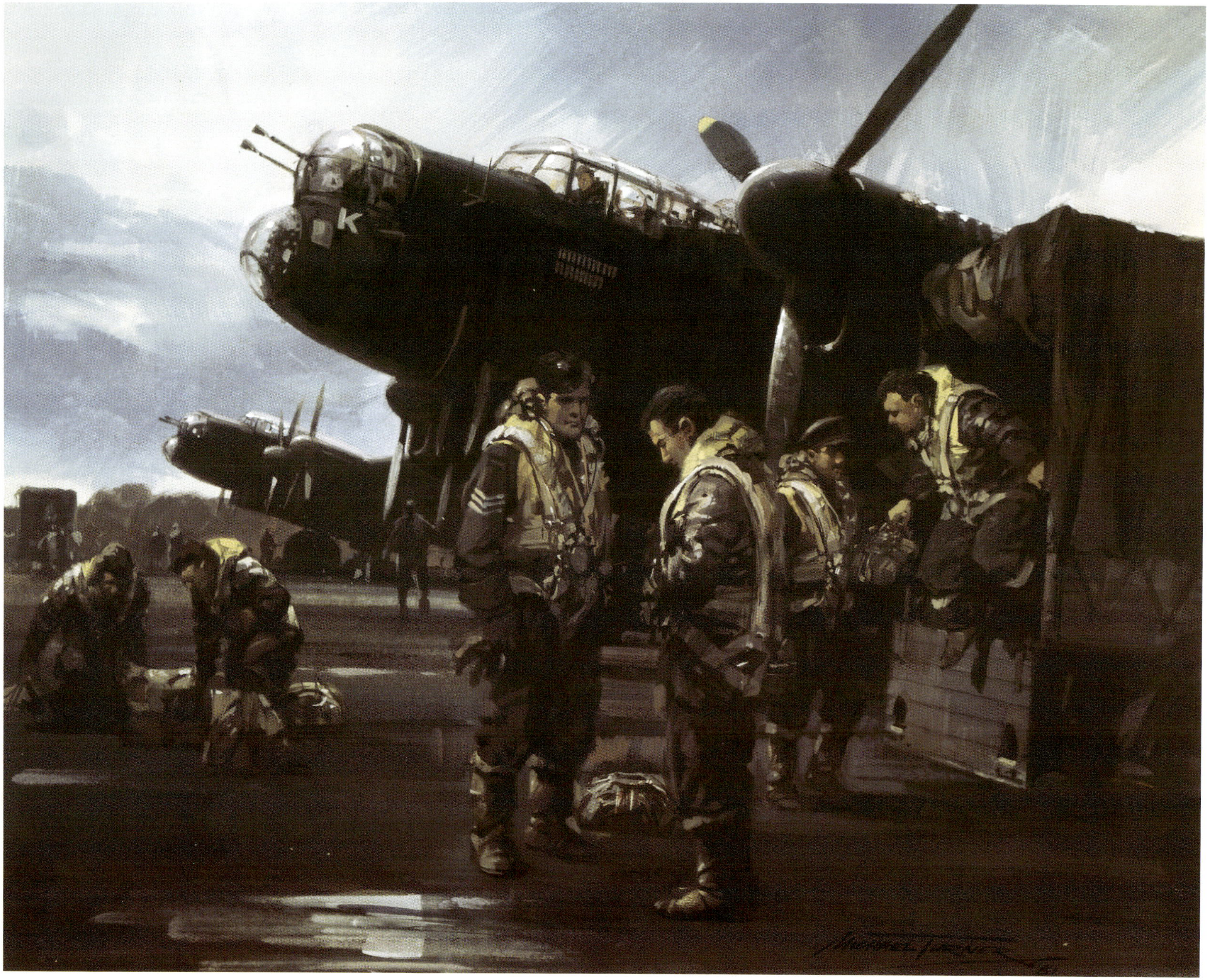

and 'Jerry' fighters punctured it liberally - and the Merlin engines always functioned perfectly. If one can love a hunk of metal, I certainly loved the Lancaster."

Group Captain Leonard Cheshire VC extolled the virtues of Lancasters of No 617 Squadron: *"We have now achieved an accuracy with the Lancaster such that, from 20,000ft we can guarantee two direct hits on any target, fifteen per cent of their bombs within 25 yards of the centre of the target, and seventy-five per cent of their bombs within 80 yards of it. This is precision undreamed of in the past."*

By mid-1942 the Lancaster was in full production and beginning to replace the outmoded pre-1939 designed bombers in the ranks of Bomber Command. In August 1942 a new specialised bomber formation came into being - the Path Finder Force (PFF) - equipped initially with four squadrons of mixed types of aircraft, with No 83 Squadron as the only Lancaster unit of this founder-members' quartet. The PFF was to act as the spearhead for future night raids over Germany, providing accurate marking of the target for a following main force to destroy, and ensuring the highest degree of navigation to and from any objective. PFF air crews were, with rare exceptions, already veterans of the bombing offensive before transferring to the force. By 1944 the PFF was equipped solely with Lancasters for the heavy bomber role, plus Mosquitos for pin-point marking and bombing support in the PFF tasks. A measure of the hazards voluntarily undertaken by the crews of the PFF during its three years' war was the final tally of casualties suffered - a total of 3,727 air crew members killed, or the rough equivalent of the air crew strength of 20 Lancaster squadrons, representing a sixth of Bomber Command's overall casualty figures for the whole war. Wing Commander Anderson has described the problems of pinpoint bombing at night:

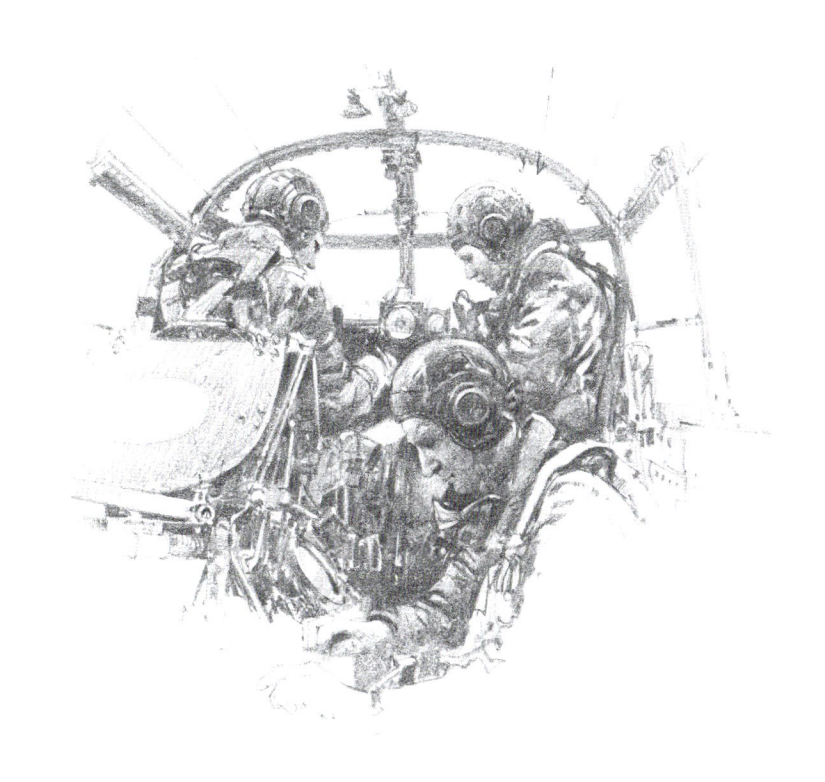

"Bombing an area from 20,000ft is one thing. Attacking a small factory or a vital marshalling yard tucked away in the middle of a French town is quite another. So a method of very careful target control was introduced and the Master-bomber came into his own. Markers were dropped as before, but no bombs were dropped until these markers had been checked and if necessary corrected by further target indicators. Crews were then told exactly where to aim. So now it was possible to follow the whole progress of a raid from an operation room in England, and to hear the Master-bomber calling from somewhere in the Paris area, 'Hallo, Main Force, hallo Main Force, overshoot the yellows by two seconds'. And if smoke covered the markers or it was too hazy to see, the boys would be told to go home. Then they would have to jettison a few bombs just off the French coast as the loads were far too heavy for happy landings! It is believed one night that a very clever German tried to send our boys home by pretending to be a Master-bomber. Unfortunately we had omitted to give him the code-word!

Avro Lancaster *Air crew at dispersal points make final preparations before climbing aboard their Lancasters. The height of this very large plane can be clearly seen - it stood over 20ft off the ground - as can the two 0.303in Browning machine guns in the nose turret.*

Bristol Beaufighter

They called it 'Whispering Death' in Burma, while in Britain and the Mediterranean theatres the Beaufighter was renowned for its brute-like strength and ultra-lethal punch of four 20 mm cannons and six Browning machine guns - the heaviest armament battery fitted to any RAF fighter of World War Two. A brilliant adaptation of its stablemate the Beaufort, the first Beaufighters were issued to the RAF's nightfighter units in 1940 and 1941, but in time the aircraft came to be used in many other roles.

In the Middle East its low-level performance as a ground-strafer was put to good effect, and in Coastal Command 'Beaus' formed the original strike squadrons for the vital anti-shipping offensive role. In the latter task the 'Beau' was soon adapted to carry torpedoes, rocket projectiles and/or bombs in addition to cannon or gun armament. From October 1942 Beaufighters began to arrive in the Far East and remained on operations there until several years after the war.

George McLannahan flew Beaufighters and said of them: *"I found the Mark I a strong and powerful machine but very tiring to fly on patrol at night, or on instruments, as it was completely unstable fore and aft. This was virtually cured on the Mark VI. I came onto the Mark VI after flying Mosquitos and it was like handling a battleship after being used to a destroyer. On this aspect an American on No 153 Squadron who had joined the RCAF early on to get into the war commented that he felt completely at home in a*

Bristol Beaufighter Bristol Beaufighters of No 254 Squadron from RAF North Coates, Coastal Command, attack enemy flak ships with cannon and torpedoes. The aeroplane shown is a 'Torbeau' that has dropped its torpedo and has continued over the enemy ship. The forward pair of shackles that carry the torpedo can be seen under the pilot's cockpit.

'Beau' as he'd previously been a truck driver! Rather unfair on the 'Beau' as it was a very fine, solid aircraft. For just one example, landing it in a cross-wind was never a problem; once placed properly on the ground it sat there and defied any deviations."

One of the most effective roles of the Bristol Beaufighter during World War II was against enemy shipping. Group Captain R. E. Burns, CBE, DFC and bar, commanded No 254 Squadron and earlier in the war the Aircraft Torpedo Development Unit. He was extensively involved in these operations and in the technical advances in the aircraft torpedo with which the anti-shipping variant of the Beaufighter - known as the Torbeau - was equipped:

"The first entry of the Beaufighter into Coastal Command was to counter the German long-range aircraft which were attacking our convoys in the North Atlantic. Focke-Wulf 200 Condors were four-engined aircraft that both attacked our merchant shipping and provided reconnaissance for the positioning of German U-boats. The Beaufighter had long range and endurance and terrific fire power and could knock these rather slow aeroplanes out of the sky, but it clearly had potential for other roles within the Command.

The appearance of a very much improved aircraft torpedo equipped with a gyroscopically controlled tail - the MAT Mark IV - that controlled the flight of the torpedo in pitch and roll after release, offered a useful weapon which was fully commensurate with the speed, performance and flexibility of the Beaufighter enabling these characteristics to be fully exploited in the anti-shipping role. This combination of aircraft and weapon produced the Torbeau.

Supermarine Spitfire IX *The Spitfires of 127 Wing led by Wing Command Johnnie Johnson strafe an enemy airfield during a sweep over Northern France in 1943. This was in essence a Mark Vc with a more powerful engine.*

Supermarine Spitfire IX

The début of the Luftwaffe's Focke-Wulf Fw 190 in mid-1941 and its patent superiority over the Spitfire V led to a hasty remedy by the RAF. The Spitfire VIII - a Mark VII with Merlin 61 engine - was already planned, but Fighter Command requested an interim variant which could be brought into service more quickly as an answer to the Fw 190. The resulting Mark IX was basically a Mark Vc, with a Merlin 61 engine, identifiable by its twin radiators and four-bladed propeller. The Mark IX first entered service in July 1942 with No 64 Squadron based at RAF Hornchurch, and was in combat before that month was out. It introduced a new combination of armament, having two 20mm cannons and two 0.50in machine guns, plus the capacity for carriage of up to 1,000lb of bombs. The Merlin 61 of 1,660 hp had a two-speed supercharger and raised the Mark IX's top speed to slightly more than 400mph. In the event the success of this supposedly interim variant led to its production in greater quantity (5,665 aircraft) than any other form of Spitfire except the Mark V, and the Mark IX remained in operational squadrons until 1945. More than 100 squadrons flew Spitfire IXs at some stage.

Hawker Hurricane II

While the Hurricane I bore the lion's share of the RAF's fighter campaigns from 1939-41, the quest for heavier armament and, if possible, better performance for the design commenced in late 1938. First thoughts included the installation of 12 Browning machine guns in the wings, up-rated Merlin engines, and fitments externally for extra fuel tankage to increase fighting range. This version, the Mark IIb, began to reach RAF squadrons in mid-1941; but a much more lethal armament of four 20 mm cannons followed in the Mark IIc. This was in turn followed by the IId, armed with twin 40 mm anti-tank guns under the wings; while other Mark IIs were introduced with under-wing rails for three-inch rocket projectiles and/or carrier-borne bombs.

All such variants had entered squadron service by the close of 1942, and many were destined to continue on operations until the end of the war serving in every war theatre in Europe, the Middle East and the Far East. Hurricane IIs were also given to Russia - nearly 3,000 in all - representing slightly more than a fifth of all Hurricanes ever built.

Fred Etchells, who flew Hurricanes for more than four years from Britain and in various Middle East campaigns, has summed up his own feelings:
"Although superbly manoeuvrable despite slightly heavy controls, we had to admit reluctantly that the Hurricane did lack speed, but I don't think I ever heard a word spoken against the aircraft. Somehow one loved the Hurricane without either realising or expressing it, and it was only after flying Spitfires with controls light enough for a five-year old to handle that one came to realise the strength required to throw a Hurricane about the sky."

By 1942 the Hurricane was patently outmoded for fighter operations in Europe, but its operational life was by no means ended. Many were despatched to the North African campaign and for the defence of besieged Malta, where they added considerable laurels to an already proud battle record. In the Far East Hurricanes were destined to figure largely in the early disastrous months of the Japanese onslaught in Malaya and Burma, but were then to provide a rock foundation for the long struggle which culminated in ultimate defeat of Japan in 1945. By June 1943 a total of 23 squadrons in India and Burma were equipped with Hurricanes, almost exclusively Mark IIs plus a few Mark IVs. Bearing clutches of bombs, rockets and cannons, Hurricanes proved to be deadly effective in their main role of close support over the battle areas for the jungle-bound infantry. By late 1944 most Hurricanes in Burma had been replaced by the seven-ton P-47 Thunderbolt for tactical back-up to the army, but on VJ-Day (15 August 1945) at least eleven squadrons, including the Indian Air Force, were still operating Hurricanes.

Appreciation of the Hurricanes' prodigious efforts are the words of a contemporary report: "The army displayed an enthusiasm for the Hurri-bombers as of no other combat aircraft in the India-Burma theatre. From the despatches of commanding generals to the private mail of the men fighting in the jungle, have come messages of praise for Hurri-bomber attacks pressed home at the appropriate moment. It is the proud boast of the pilots that they never failed to give prompt aid when called upon by their comrades fighting on the ground."

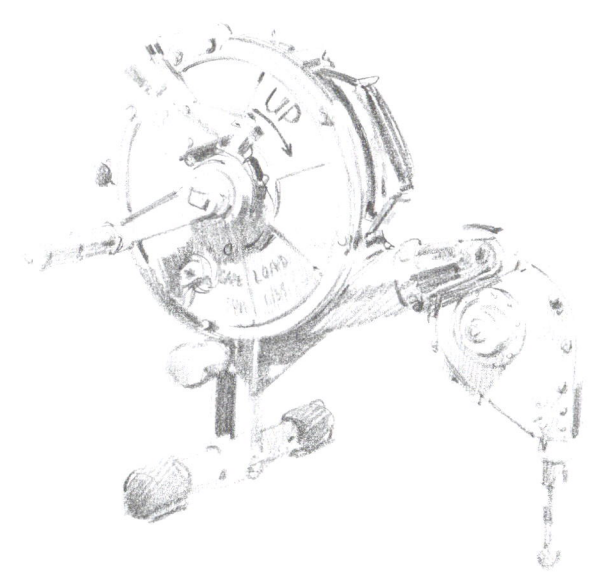

Hawker Hurricane IIc *fighter-bombers from No 274 Squadron take off from a desert airstrip in North Africa in 1942. In comparison to the Mark I (see pages 63-65) it had a more powerful engine (the 1,280 hp Merlin XX), a two-stage supercharger and heavier armament.*

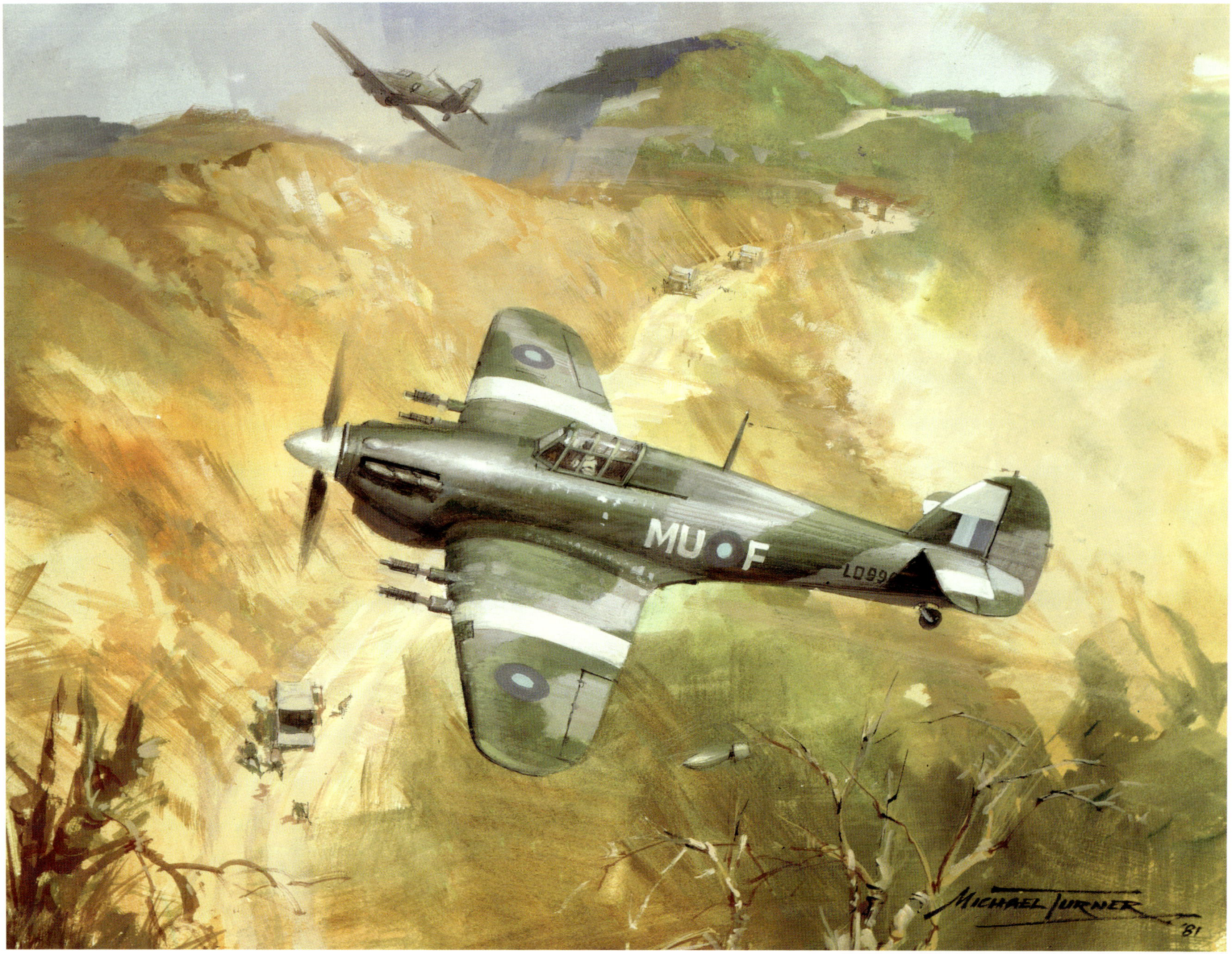
MU F
LD99
MICHAEL TURNER
'81

Curtiss Kittyhawk

A more powerful and better-armed development of the Curtiss Tomahawk, the Kittyhawk saw wide service with the American, Australian and New Zealand Air Forces in the Pacific theatre of operations. It served exclusively with the RAF in the Mediterranean campaigns, commencing in January 1942 and continuing in first-line squadrons until mid-1944. Its reputation as a tough, hard-hitting, low-level ground support aircraft was high. It had six 0.50 machine guns in the wings and provision for 1,000lb of bombs.

The remaining Desert Air Forces Kittyhawks in Italy were finally superseded by P-51 Mustangs when No 250 Squadron re-equipped in 1945. At the height of the desert battles, Kittyhawks were flying up to four sorties daily in answer to Army calls for close-support.

Over 3,000 Kittyhawks saw operational use with the RAF and its Allied forces. Wing Commander J. F. 'Stocky' Edwards, DFC, DFM, flew 195 sorties in Kittyhawks with Nos 94 and 260 Squadrons in North Africa: *"In diving and bombing the aircraft would pick up speed very quickly but had a tendency to roll to the right. One could trim this out reasonably well with the left hand, but even then when one pulled up it wanted to roll to the left quite violently. Although the Kitty provided a stable platform to fire from when flying straight and level at a given speed, it became a*

Hawker Hurricane IIc (Far East) *The Hurricanes of No 60 Squadron acting in support of the 11th East African Division bomb and strafe Japanese troops retreating along the Tamu Road in Burma.*

Curtiss Kittyhawk *Curtis Kittyhawks of No 112 Squadron providing support for Bren Gun Carriers of the British Army in North Africa during the Desert Campaign.*

monster in rapid diving and climbing. Reflector and gyro gunsights were used in our aircraft but they were a complete nuisance in a dogfight when speeds changed rapidly and the aircraft had a tendency to slip and skid."

North American Mitchell

Used in relatively small numbers by the RAF - only six squadrons within Bomber Command - the North American Mitchell was excellent for its purpose of day-bombing, which was its major role with No 2 Group and later 2nd Tactical Air Force (TAF). Relatively fast, well armed defensively, and able to lift bomb loads between four and six thousand pounds, the Mitchell came into squadron service from September 1942 and was still operational at the close of the European war. In American use the B-25 - its USAAF title - was built in greater numbers than any other twin-engined bomber, and its many variants gave sterling service in many war zones, particularly in the Pacific. Few crews found serious cause for complaint in the Mitchell. Docile to handle with good control responses, highly manoeuvrable for its size - its wing span was almost 68 feet - and with a dependable tricycle undercarriage; the Mitchell was popular as a war vehicle.

The main version supplied to the RAF was the Mk II, counterpart of the USAAF's B-25C and D of which 542 were received. Primary purpose of the

North American Mitchell *North American Mitchell IIs from No 180 Squadron at RAF Dunsfold on a daylight bombing mission over Northern France in 1943. Named after the American bombing pioneer Billy Mitchell, this light bomber was made in greater numbers than any other American twin-engined combat aircraft.*

Mitchell were the intruder Circus and Ramrod operations, with a secondary shipping attack role.

One pilot who flew Mitchells with No 98 Squadron RAF - the first RAF unit to receive the type - recalled: *"The Mitchell was my first three-wheeler and 'converting' to this seemingly frightening American monster with its new-fangled (to me) undercarriage gave me tummy tremors initially. On my first taxying-out to the runway, however, I was delighted with the tremendous amount of vision I was enjoying all round. Take-offs and landings soon proved uncomplicated, while in the air I quickly got used to the mass of instruments, levers, knobs and handles which (to me) seemed at first daunting. It was the first aircraft I had flown where I actually felt in real command of the aeroplane."*

In a critical assessment, test pilot Captain Eric 'Winkle' Brown, RN reported: *"My first impression of the B-25 was how functional and business-like it looked with its angular shape, gull wings, large engines, tricycle undercarriage and its bristling guns. The cockpit is surprisingly compact, with a fairly orderly layout and a reasonable view ahead. The take-off was perhaps the most exciting feature of the Mitchell, as the acceleration was so impressive. The elevators are very powerful in raising the nosewheel, and unstick takes place at 95mph in a very short distance. In my opinion the Mitchell was probably the most versatile medium bomber of the Second World War. It was not as fast as the Boston, but carried more bombs and was more heavily armed for its defence. However, for sheer flying exhilaration I preferred the Boston."*

Consolidated Catalina

The twin-engined PBY Catalina became the most numerous flying-boat of World War Two. The 'Killer Cat' served with nine RAF squadrons and sank or seriously damaged at least 45 U-boats, while two Catalina skippers were awarded VCs.

It first entered service with the US Navy in 1936 as the PBY-2. The success of the Catalina with the US Navy attracted the attention of the British Air Ministry and deliveries to the RAF began in early 1941, these being the equivalent of the PBY-5, but called Catalina in the UK. Not only did they serve in the Battle of the Atlantic, but also with the RAF in Singapore, Madagascar and Ceylon, patrolling the Indian Ocean. A total of 570 Catalinas was acquired by the RAF.

Though not of outstanding general performance, its long range of some 4,000 miles made the flying-boat an essential feature of the Atlantic air cover for Allied shipping. The Catalina enjoyed a better reliability record than the Sunderland, engine failure was almost unknown and it could alight in seas with waves of over six feet high. One remained in the air for more than 26 hours during the operations which ended in the sinking of the *Bismarck*. In winter and bad weather Catalinas often returned in darkness to base after an 18-hour patrol, and, finding it obscured by fog or low cloud, remained aloft all night until they could land in greater safety at dawn.

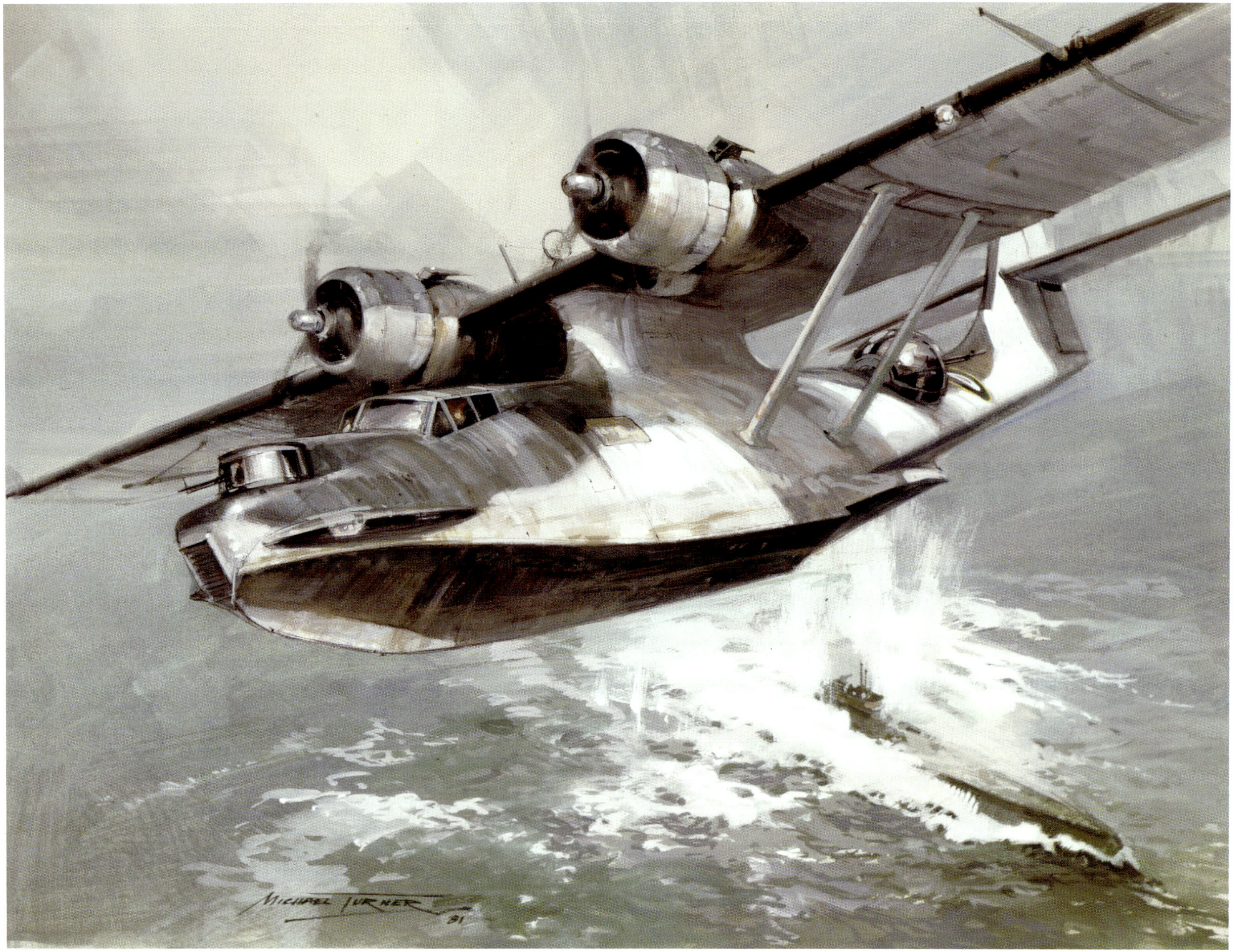
MICHAEL TURNER
81

Consolidated Catalina *A Consolidated Catalina of Coastal Command attacks a U-boat in the North Atlantic.*

Flight Lieutenant John Cruickshank of No 210 Squadron, the only Coastal Command VC to survive the war, recalled his mission in Catalina JV928 on 17 July 1944: *"We had an unidentified blip on the radar. I sighted the objective - a submarine, fully surfaced and running at about 20 knots. Pulling the Catalina into a turn around the U-boat, I began an attack run, descending from 1,000ft to 50ft. My nose gunner began splashing fire against the conning tower. Everybody ready? - in we go - we made a perfect run in at low level but when we were almost on top of the U-boat a shell burst in the aircraft, our navigator was killed and I was seriously wounded. The depth charges were released and it was a perfect straddle. The attack was accurate and U-347, on its second war patrol, was sunk."*

The 196th and final U-boat sunk by Coastal Command was destroyed by a Catalina of No 210 Squadron 120 miles north-east of Sullom Voe on 7 May 1945. The last Catalina in RAF service was a Mk IV with No 240 Squadron, which was disbanded in October 1945.

Handley Page Halifax

As the RAF's second four-engined 'heavy' to become operational in World War Two - it followed the Stirling closely but preceded the Lancaster - the Halifax initially did not acquire a good reputation among squadron crews and these lingered long after any such stigmatism was justified. By 1945, the Halifax's war record was a proud saga, rivalling that of the Lancaster in many respects. Successively modified and improved in the light of experience, the 'Hally' paired with the much-publicised Lancaster as the RAF's two principal weapons in the night offensive against Germany from 1942 to 1945.

Elsewhere the Halifax contributed significantly to Coastal Command's anti-submarine campaign, it fought in the North African struggle, acted as a glider-tug for the airborne invasions of Europe, ferried supplies and secret agents into enemy-held territory, and undertook a dozen other little-known yet vital roles.

The early variants' chief defect was an inability to maintain a safe operating altitude on operations, and the shape of the tail fins was changed to oblong. This was cured with the Mark III version with its Hercules radial engines.

Lettice Curtis, one of the many female pilots of the Air Transport Auxiliary (ATA) who ferried all types of aircraft to the squadrons, said of the Halifax: *"It was the heaviest of the three wartime four-engined bombers to handle - one could not afford to let it get out of trim - and application of aileron could call for a certain amount of brute force. RAF pilots who flew the Halifax were normally taught to make wheel landings, touching down on main wheels with tail wheel well off the ground. This reduced the chances of a heavy landing in difficult weather conditions, at night or when the aircraft was heavily loaded. ATA, however, were trained to make three-point landings which, in a Halifax, called for accurate judgment, since the change of incidence between flying and ground attitude was considerable, and full power was unlikely to help if the final hold-off was too high."*

Following one of the first missions using H2S radar, the pilot of Halifax W7851/N, Flight Lieutenant Brown reported: *"There was a thin stratoculumbus cloud over the target with tops at 5,000-8,000ft, as a result of which no ground cover could be seen. The target was identified, however, on special equipment and at 02:37 hours four red flares were dropped at 52 degrees North, ten degrees East from 21,000ft followed three minutes later by sixteen red/green star flares from the same height. Bombs were successfully dropped on the city."*

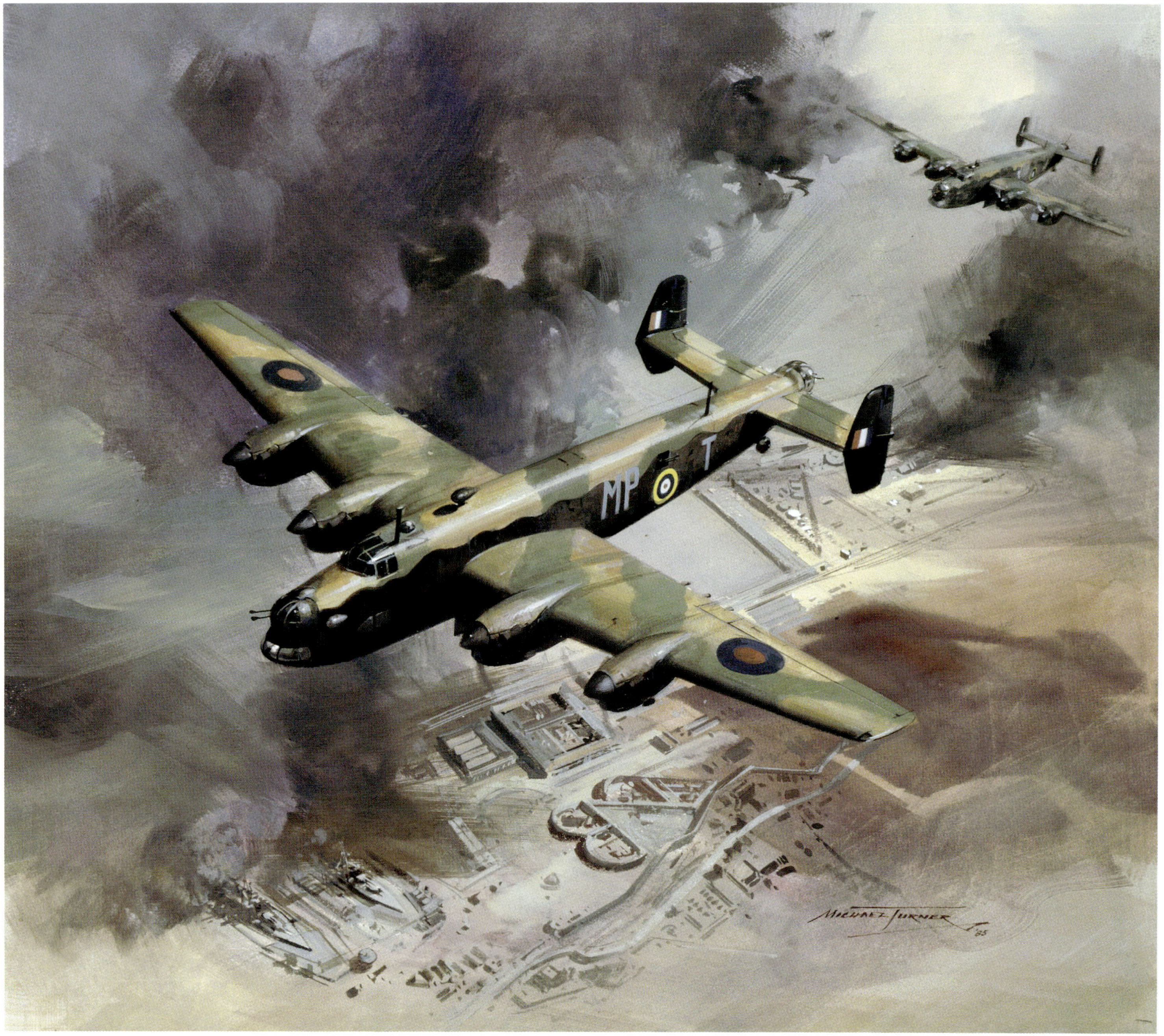
MP
T

***Handley Page Halifax** B1s of No 76 Squadron bomb the German pocket battleships Scharnhorst, Gneisenau and Prinz Eugen in the shipyards at Brest in December 1941.*

Short Stirling

'The most expensive contraption invented for the purpose of lifting an undercarriage into the air' - such was the view of one of the earliest operational captains of the huge Stirling bomber; other less kindly thoughts were expressed by some crews as they ran the gauntlet of anti-aircraft barrages due to the design's lack of a safe operating altitude on bombing operations. The massive Stirling will always be remembered as the RAF's first four-engined monoplane bomber of 1939-45, but the issue of the first example of No 7 Squadron in August 1940 was merely the beginning a long period of frustration and technical snags which delayed the operational use of this new bomber. Tentative sorties by a handful of Stirlings began in February 1941 but the bomber only began fairly regular operations from April that year.

It was to remain in first-line service until 1945, though by late 1943 the Stirling had been retired from bombing sorties, and was thereafter much modified to act as a glider-tug, airborne trooper and general transport machine. Of the 1759 Stirlings built as bombers, roughly one-third were lost in action.

H R Graham (later Air Vice-Marshal) who commanded No 7 Squadron at RAF Oakington in 1941, said of the aircraft: *"The Stirling, as originally produced, was a first rate aeroplane. However, it was not an easy aircraft to handle near the ground. The exceptionally long undercarriage gave it a steep ground angle and made a dangerous weathercock swing likely if you were not quick on the throttles. The true cause of the Stirling's disappointing operational performance lay in higher authority's insistence on overloading the machine by almost a third more than its intended all-up loaded weight; thereby making every take-off a marginal operation, and inevitably producing a crop of aerodrome accidents."*

The design with such unplanned overweight always failed to attain a safe operating altitude, thus inviting fighter attack and anti-aircraft fire. As in the case of so many other RAF aircraft, any successes achieved by the Stirling can mainly be attributed to the undaunted courage of its crews.

D. Murray Peden, QC, DFC flew one of the first of the four-engined bombers: *"The Stirling was a four-engined 'heavy' from the outset. Unfortunately, the Air Ministry stipulated that the wingspan of the new bomber must be less than 100 feet. It thus came in at one inch over 99 feet. This archaic criterion stemmed from a fact no more compelling than that the doors on the standard RAF hangars were only 100 feet wide. It posed near-insoluble problems. It meant, for all practical purposes, that a fully loaded Stirling would do its bombing around the 12,000 feet mark, an altitude well within the range of even light flak, many varieties of which could be hosed up in streams. Even this was often achieved only at the cost of an extra climb on the last leg into the target. With her four Hercules XVIs, a Mark III Stirling burned roughly 500 gallons per hour under climbing revs and boost; and on long trips every pilot was acutely conscious of those figures, and of how an extra climb would critically erode his fuel reserve.*

On the bombing run itself, those endless minutes suspended over the glare of the target, the strain of searchlights, flak, and fighters, was augmented for Stirling crews by the knowledge that, thousands of feet directly above them, bomb aimers in Lancasters and Halifaxes had opened gaping bomb bays and were already raining down bombs by the thousand. One strove to concentrate on the flaming target indicators far below, and on the tense note of one's own bomb aimer's voice in the headphones calling course corrections for the run-up. But ignoring the peril did not dispel it."

An offsetting advantage was the Stirling's manoeuvrability - it had to be experienced to be believed. In the early career of the Stirlings, in 1941 and 1942, they had

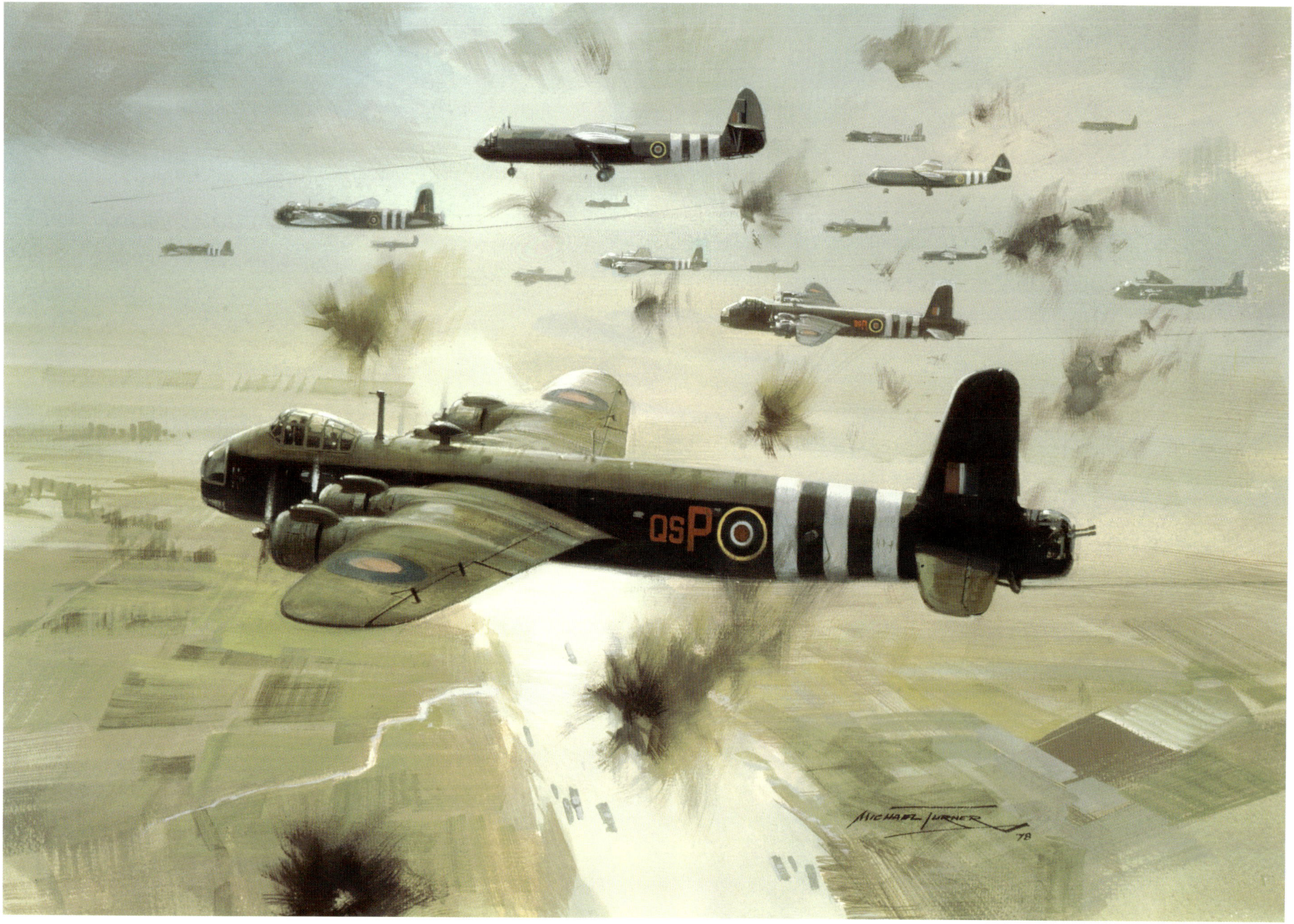
QSP
MICHAEL TURNER
'78

Short Stirling *Short Stirling IV glider-tugs of No 620 Squadron cross the Rhine on 24 March 1945, moments before releasing the Sixth Airborne Division in their attendant Horsa gliders. This Mark had four 1,650hp Bristol Hercules XVI engines.*

been employed on a considerable number of daylight operations against targets in Germany and elsewhere, during which they naturally came under fierce attack from German fighters. The Stirlings had acquitted themselves well. Not only did their agility make them difficult targets; but even with their standard .303 armament they shot down a number of their attackers.

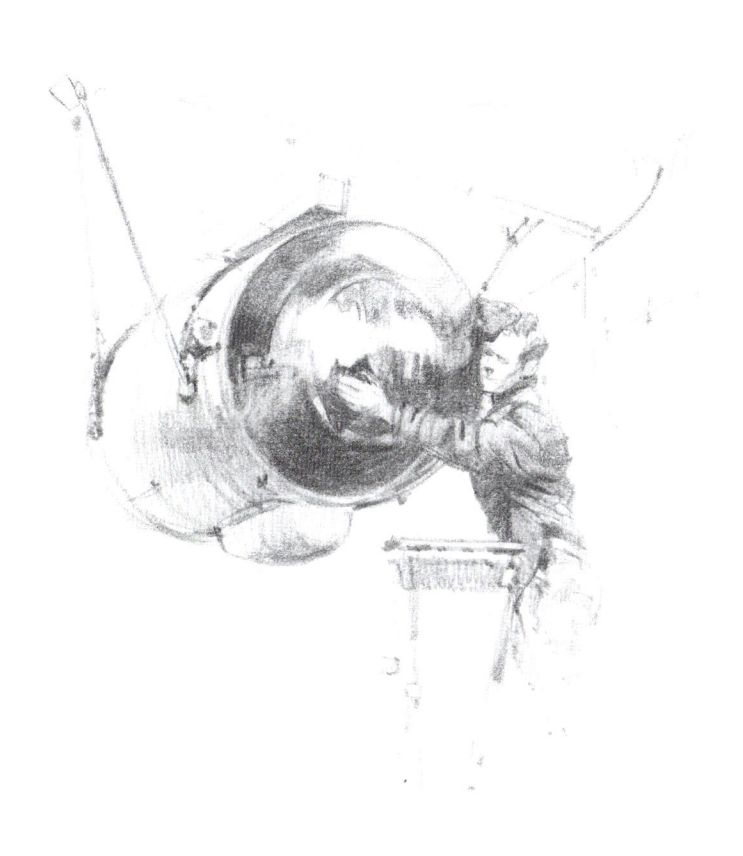

Consolidated Liberator

The B-24 Liberator, which first flew on 29 December 1939, is universally recognised for its huge contribution to the USAAF's daylight bombing assault on Germany during 1942-45. What is not usually recognised is the additional war record of the type in RAF and other Allied air forces during the same period. Slightly more than 2,000 Liberators saw service with the RAF alone, and many of these went to Coastal Command as VLR (Very Long Range) submarine-hunters over the Atlantic battle-area. Indeed, these maritime Liberators accounted for 100 U-boats sunk or seriously damaged - slightly less than a third of all U-boats accounted for by RAF aircraft. Other RAF 'Libs' saw plentiful action in the Middle East and over Burma and India, while some modified examples flew with Transport Command in the latter stages of the war.

Allied crews' reactions to the Liberator varied. One pilot, after his first flight in the type, called it ...a big, cumbersome, gormless pig . Nevertheless, with more experience he, like most pilots, came to regard the Liberator more kindly. Another pilot recorded: *"It was a great aircraft to fly and had almost no vices. Easy to handle and reliable. It was stable, had good range, a good turn of speed if required, excellent visibility for spotting submarines, and was an excellent instruments-flying aircraft. A third called it: The most comfortable aircraft for the pilot I've ever flown. The console was beautifully laid out insofar as control access was concerned, and the seat wonderfully adaptable with about four different adjustments... No one ever regarded the Liberator as a graceful aeroplane."*

Captain Eric 'Winkle' Brown, RN tested the Liberator against the Halifax and Lancaster at Farnborough in 1944. He reported on its general handling characteristics: *"Although the Liberator appeared on the scene some four years after the B-17 Flying Fortress, it had only a very small*

Consolidated Liberator *Liberators of No 356 Squadron head for their home base at Salbani, India after a bombing mission in Burma. The Liberator had a wingspan of 110ft, a length of 67ft 2in and a height of 18ft.*

advantage in speed over it, was more complicated to fly and handled less well. However, it had more development potential, and 19,203 were built, more than any other single type of American aircraft. It unquestionably proved a boon to RAF Coastal Command and, although I have never heard any pilot wax lyrical about its flying qualities, it proved to be a good solid performer, or as an ex-Liberator pilot put it, a grand old warrior. That makes a fitting epitaph for the B-24."

The last Liberator in RAF service was a GRVII with No 203 Squadron at RAF St Eval in June 1947.

Martin Baltimore

A direct development of the Martin Maryland, the Baltimore was produced specifically for the RAF, and first production examples began reaching Britain in October 1941. Their subsequent war service was confined to the Mediterranean area, where Baltimores entered operations with Nos 55 and 223 Squadrons in early 1942. For the following three years Baltimores were prominent in every Allied campaign in the Middle East, and in addition to nine RAF units were flown by two Royal Australian Air Force (RAAF) and three South African Air Force (SAAF) squadrons. In all, some 1,500 Baltimores were produced for the RAF.

Some of the earliest Wright Cyclone-engined Baltimores issued to No 60 Squadron SAAF for photo-reconnaissance were ill-received. To quote one unit pilot: *"They were not a patch on the*

Marylands being heavy and clumsy, though more powerful. Their Wright engines gave much trouble and couldn't stand up to desert conditions like the Pratt & Whitneys of the Maryland."

Later marks, fitted with the much more reliable Pratt & Whitney powerplants, were popular with their bomber crews, however, despite the cramped accommodation in the deep, narrow fuselages. The sheer strength of construction in a Baltimore paid dividends, especially during the latter war years when daylight formations of 'Balts' ran gauntlets of fierce, accurate anti-aircraft fire in target areas, such as Northern Italy.

Martin Baltimore *Baltimore IVs from No 223 Squadron approach their target in Northern Italy in 1944. It served around the Mediterranean until the end of hostilities.*

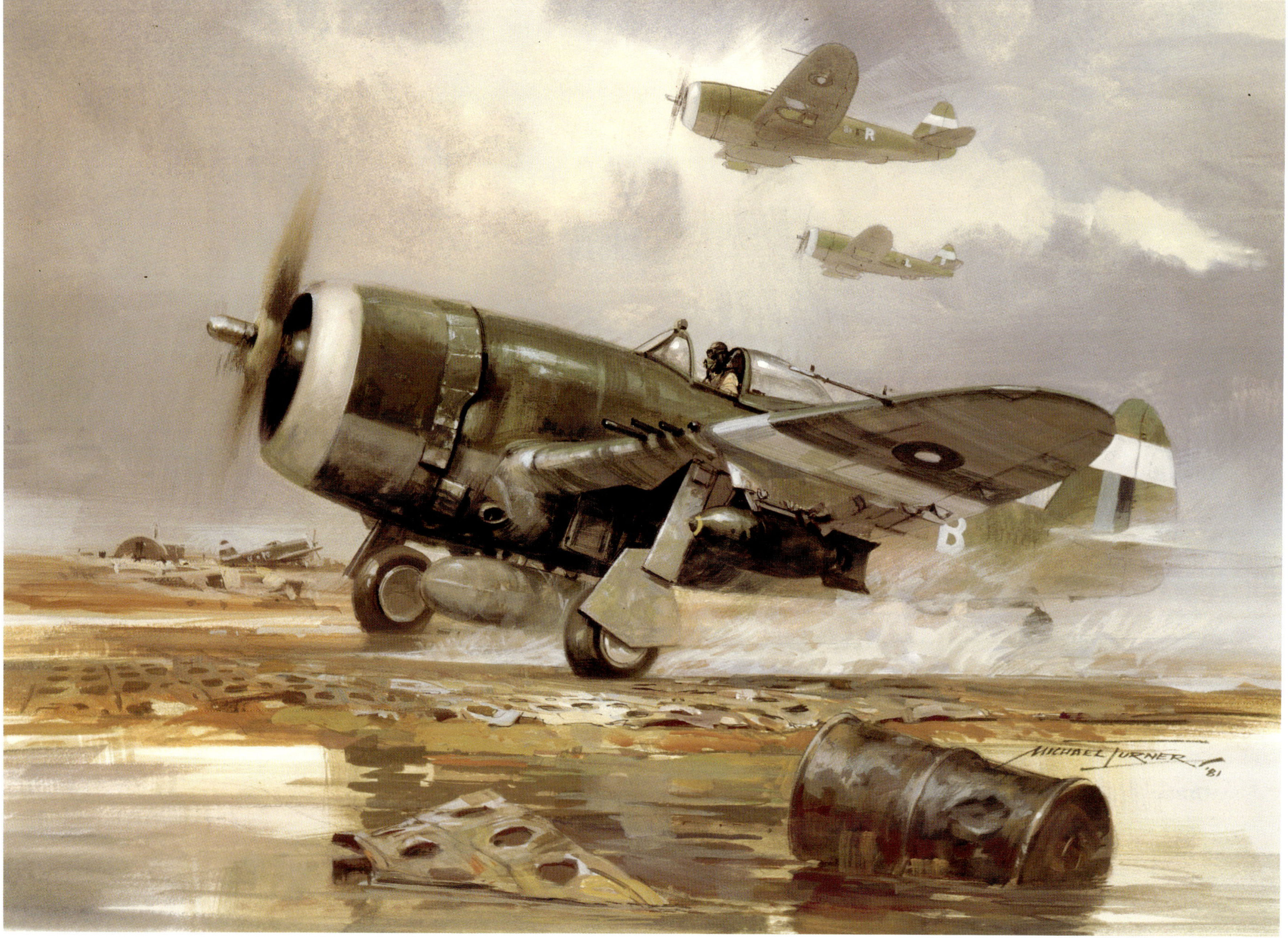
MICHAEL TURNER '81

Republic Thunderbolt

The Republic P-47 Thunderbolt - more usually termed 'T-Bolt' or 'Jug' (after Juggernaut) - was built in greater quantity than any other American fighter of World War Two; was the heaviest single-engine fighter in general operational use - it weighed twice as much as a Spitfire; and achieved its greatest fame as a long-range bomber-escort and low-level ground-strafer with the USAAF in Europe from 1943 to 1945.

A total of 830 Thunderbolts was ultimately transferred to the RAF, the first to reach squadron use being the initial examples received in May 1944 by No 135 Squadron in India. Subsequently a total of 16 RAF squadrons flew the 'Jug' - all in the Far East between 1944 and 1946. The climatic conditions over the Burmese jungles tended to exaggerate both the good and less favourable qualities of this ultra-heavyweight among fighters. On balance, however, the aircraft's poor rate of climb and turn over Burma were more than compensated for by its diving stability, high altitude manoeuvrability, and mainly trouble-free engine. A particular bonus was the design's ruggedness and sheer brute strength, which was blessed by every pilot who had to force-land or even crash-land.

The Thunderbolt's cockpit was ever a thing of wonder to British pilots more used to the tiny near-claustrophobic cabins of Spitfires and Hurricanes. As one RAF P-47 pilot quipped: *"In the Jug boredom on patrol was never a problem - one could always pass the time counting instruments and levers, or simply get out of the seat and have an invigorating run around the joystick...!"*

Republic Thunderbolt* A Thunderbolt II of No 134 Squadron taxies out on to a flooded airstrip in Burma late in a 1944 monsoon. This was the heaviest single-engine fighter at that time; as can be seen, it needed a very deep fuselage to accommodate the supercharger and ducting.*

Douglas Boston

Despite its outmoded defensive armament - the dorsal gunner had merely twin hand-operated machine guns - the Boston was in many other ways greatly superior to the Blenheim IV which it replaced in squadron service with No 2 Group, commencing in the autumn of 1941. The Boston was also the RAF's first tricycle undercarriage bomber to see general operational employment.

Mike Henry, DFC, an air gunner, has recorded his first impressions of the Boston: *"What a magnificent aeroplane it was. It was immediately apparent how much more powerful and manoeuvrable it was when compared to the Blenheim. A strange innovation was the duplicated flying controls in the gunner's cockpit, a stick and rudder bar, but no instruments nor could the gunner see where he was steering if he had to take control …Boston IIIAs had twice the power, carried twice the bomb load, but had only half the duration of the Blenheim."*

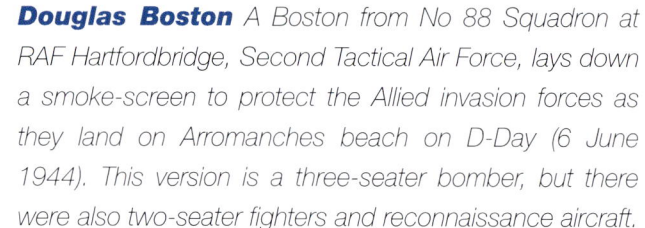

Douglas Boston A Boston from No 88 Squadron at RAF Hartfordbridge, Second Tactical Air Force, lays down a smoke-screen to protect the Allied invasion forces as they land on Arromanches beach on D-Day (6 June 1944). This version is a three-seater bomber, but there were also two-seater fighters and reconnaissance aircraft.

Boston crews flew many memorable daylight attacks over France and the Low Countries from 1941-44, even being used as smoke-screen operators during the June 1944 invasion of Europe. Further afield, Bostons of the RAF and SAAF played a significant part in the 1942-43 operations in the Middle East.

The Boston III proved an excellent bomber on daylight low-level operations over occupied north-west Europe. Flight Lieutenant R.A.Yates-Earle of No 88 Squadron wrote: *"A typical large-scale action at low level was an attack on the large Philips radio works at Eindhoven in Holland. We went in between Dunkirk and Ostend, hit the target and came out over the Hague. The type of formation we used for jobs like that was waves of eight aircraft flying in loose echelon."*

Supermarine Spitfire VIII

The Spitfire VIII, an unpressurised VII, appeared in three major versions, low (with clipped wings), medium and high altitude (with extended tips), varying in engines and wing spans according to its operational role. As a counter to the latest Focke Wulf Fw 190s and Messerschmitt Bf 109Gs in Europe and the Middle East, the Mark VIII proved to be superior in all-round performance, while in the India/Burma theatre it out-classed the Japanese Zero.

The Mk VIII was arguably the most advanced of the Merlin-engined fighters. Powered by a Merlin

Supermarine Spitfire VIII *Supermarine Spitfire Mk. VIIIs from No 607 Squadron pass low over the ruins of Naga village during the battle for Imphal, Burma.*

61 with two-stage supercharging this was built in F, HF and LF variants, later models of which had a raised pointed fin. Entering service in August 1943, it was also used in Italy, briefly in Russia and in the Far East, where they replaced the RAAF Spitfire Vs. Vokes Microvee air filters were standard fitments, to prevent ingestion of dust in desert and jungle warfare - an ancillary service never properly recognised.

With a top speed in excess of 400mph and fitted with extra fuel tanks, the Mark VIII could undertake long-range escorts and strafing sorties in the Japanese occupied areas. First to operate in Burma with Mark VIIIs was No 155 Squadron in November 1943, and by March 1944 eight squadrons were equipped. In total 34 Squadrons flew Mark VIIIs, and a total of 1,658 was ultimately built.

Supermarine Spitfire Mk XVI

The Spitfire XVI was the last major variant to be powered by the Merlin engine (1705hp Packard-built Merlin 266). It was normally operated with clipped wings as a fighter bomber for low-level ground attack against such targets as V-2 rocket sites. Later production Mk XVIs had a cut-down rear fuselage and bubble cockpit canopy. The first of 1054 aircraft entered service with No 602 Squadron at RAF Coltishall in November 1944. Post war they equipped Royal Auxiliary Air Force Squadrons and flew with Anti-Aircraft co-operation Squadrons until 1951.

Supermarine Spitfire XVI *In foreground is the machine flown by Flt Lt Raymond Baxter - picture depicts No 602 Squadron making a low-level precision attack on Baatsher-Mex building in The Hague, HQ of German V1/V2 research, on March 18th 1945.*

North American Mustang

Designed and developed from the outset for use by the RAF, the Mustang was the first-ever fighter produced by its parent company, North American Aviation. Initially fitted with an American Allison engine, the first Mustangs to be tested by the RAF proved disappointing for high altitude combat and were thus allotted to army co-operational roles, or tactical reconnaissance (Tac-R) as these duties came to be known. In this form a number of squadrons continued flying Mustangs in the Tac-R role until early 1945. The general opinion of the Mustang with the Allison engine was that it was an excellent aeroplane, docile in control, with several outstanding features, but that it lacked sufficient surge in engine power.   In late 1942, therefore, trials were flown of a Mustang fitted with a Packard-built Rolls-Royce Merlin engine. These showed that the Merlin-Mustang was more difficult to control, but was unquestionably superior in all combat facets. Within a year Merlin-engined Mustangs were operational with the USAAF based in Britain, fitted with extra fuel tankage, and acting as 'Little Brother' escorts for the American daylight bombers ranging over Germany. With more modifications and constantly increasing range potential, the Merlin-Mustangs became the undisputed finest operational fighter of its period. Mustangs next operated in the Mediterranean and Far East, while several years later the design was again operational with the USAF and RAAF in the opening phases of the Korean war.

Squadron Leader F E Dymond RAF (Retd) recalls the Mustang: *"In the latter half of 1944 I was stationed at RAF North Weald as a member of No 234 Squadron, one of the few operational units still flying the Spitfire Vb. In the September we were re-equipped, not as anticipated with the Spitfire Mark IX but with the Mustang III. It was a very pleasant aircraft to handle and although American-built we felt at home in it immediately, perhaps because of its Merlin engine.*

In December we moved to RAF Bentwaters where by early 1945 there were six squadrons of Mustangs. Our primary role was to provide long range escort to Bomber Command on daylight raids over Germany.

The recommended climbing speed for a fully loaded Mustang carrying drop tanks was 180mph, however when we climbed as a Wing of 36 aircraft it was easier to maintain formation by flying at 200 mph and climbing at 500 feet per minute. This slow climb was acceptable as our rendezvous point with the bomber force was not until we crossed the Dutch coast.

The aircraft was not designed as an interceptor but as a long range fighter and time to altitude was not a vital factor. With its large fuel-carrying capacity the Mustang gave us a range of action that we had never enjoyed with the Spitfire. In the latter one always had an eye on the fuel gauge but in the Mustang there were no such worries Not surprising really, with a maximum tankage of 349 gallons and a consumption rate of around 40 gallons per hour when cruising on weak mixture. Although I never flew there, Berlin was well within its reach with a margin for combat if necessary. It was a fighter with a terrific radius of action and practically viceless. Visibility from the cockpit was excellent thanks to the Malcolm canopy which was a British innovation and far superior to the original type fitted to the Mark III (P-51B and C). Another refinement was aileron trim control, hitherto unheard-of in single engined fighters but a welcomed feature on long sorties. As already stated it handled well and was a very stable weapons platform for its four 0.5in guns, and the other armament stores it could carry.

The Mustang was originally designed to meet British requirements and when it was eventually married to the Rolls-Royce Merlin engine I would not argue with those who claim it to have been the best Allied all-round fighter aircraft of the war, although some of our British fighters excelled in certain respects."

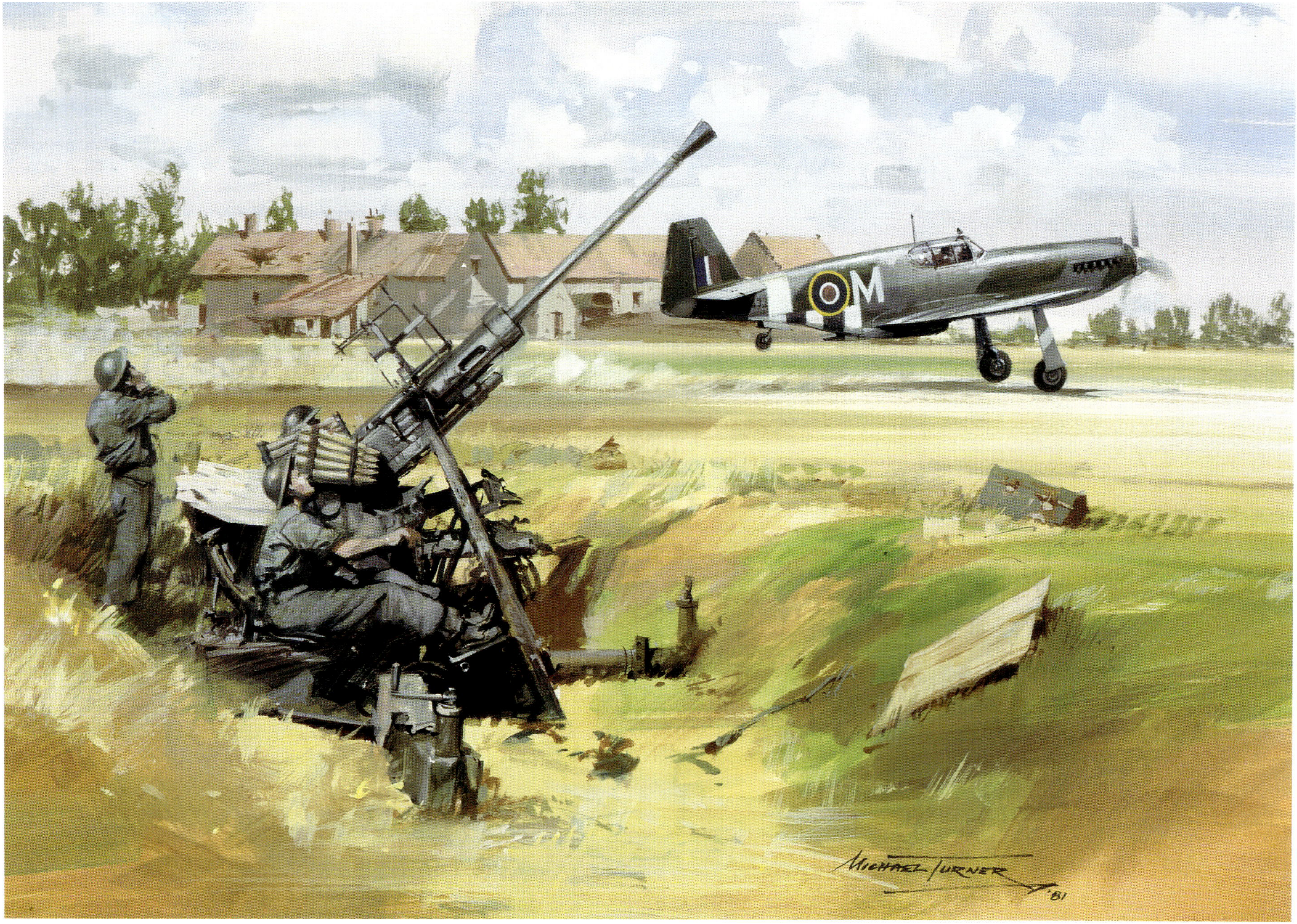
MICHAEL TURNER
'81

North American Mustang *A Mustang I from No 168 Squadron takes off on a reconnaissance mission from an advance airstrip in Normandy in summer 1944. This variant was fitted with the American Allison engine, the long-range fighter-escorts had the more powerful Rolls-Royce Merlin engine.*

Douglas Dakota

Any record of transport aircraft of the world over the past 60 years cannot fail to pay tribute to the Dakota, the doyen of such aeroplanes. A military descendant of the DC-3 airliner, the 'Dak' came into RAF use from April 1941 - the first 12 Daks going to No 31 Squadron in India whose prodigious supply record throughout the Far East campaigns has few if any peers. Dakotas, of every type, continued in RAF front-line service, though in diminishing numbers, until the ultimate RAF Dakota (KN645) was officially 'retired' on 1 April 1970. Almost 11,000 Dakotas were eventually built, of which some 2,000 were used by the RAF as the premier workhorse for supply and transportation in literally every battle zone of World War Two.

Every pilot who ever flew Dakotas developed a lasting affection for them, remembering their docility yet enduring toughness and stoic patience. Their feelings may possibly be summed by one ex-Dak skipper who once wrote: *"Having notched up over 8,000 hours on the 'Dak' I have nothing but affection and admiration for the old kite, and I can think of no other aircraft that could have taken the punishment that 'Daks' received weatherwise in SEAC (South-East Asia Command). For instance, I've had landing lamp glasses smashed by hailstones, wing rivets pulled, and the webbing straps that held the stretchers in position broken in turbulence - and still the old lady flew on."* Or as one anonymous scribe once put it: *"They patched her up with masking tape, with paper clips and strings - and still she flies, she never dies, Methuselah with wings."*

Robert Pearson, one-time Warrant Officer RAF, on Nos 437, 271 and 215 Dakota Squadrons: *"In wartime everything is a lottery. With flying training in South Africa completed. A toss of a coin decided whether I or somebody else should go to a squadron in the Middle East, carrying out shipping strikes in the Med. For me it was back to the UK, to life on a 'Dak' squadron - first as a second pilot, then as an aircraft captain - and a love affair with what must surely be one of the most remarkable aeroplanes of all time.*

So what, apart from its technical excellence, so endeared the 'Dak' to its crews and to everyone in uniform in war zones around the world? To pilots it was a thoroughbred, combining tenacity with impeccable manners - a delight to fly, forgiving and indomitable. One soon got used to what, in those days, seemed its large size - the cockpit some 20ft off the ground with the aircraft at rest, the 95ft wing span and those two marvellously reliable 1,200 hp Pratt & Whitney Twin Wasp engines. For the soldier wounded in battle it was the lifeline to salvation, however remote the location. For anybody else with the need or the wit to win a seat, it was an aerial bus to and

from all kinds of exotic and improbably destinations.

Even now, when occasionally a 'Dak' passes overhead, those sweet-sounding engines open the floodgates of memory. The comradeship, the endless toing and froing. The daily flights, in the winter of 1944-45, from our Gloucestershire base to forward airstrips in Holland with anything urgently needed which would pass through the wide double doors. The often atrocious weather of that winter; the low cloud, the mist, rain and snow and the need, come what may, to keep to the air corridors in sensitive areas. The pain of walking through a plane loaded with grievously wounded soldiers, their stretchers secured in tiers for the trip back to a British hospital. The one bemused soldier I so well recall who, within the space of a few hours, had been in action, wounded, capture by the Germans, liberated by our forces and put on the plane. But above all one remembers the humour and repartee of service life, and the joy of flying a delightful, responsive aeroplane.

On 24 March 1945, most memorable of days, the airborne crossing of the Rhine at Wesel by the British 6th and American 17th Divisions - a 200-mile stream of tugs and gliders (1,305) and transports with paratroopers (1,795). With a glider in tow the final stages were like a slow approach to Dante's Inferno. Dust, gun flashes, columns of oily smoke, burning aircraft and paratroopers and glider troops going down into battle while we turned for home."

Douglas Dakota *Douglas C-47 Dakotas drop supplies under heavy fire to the beleaguered airborne forces at Arnhem in September 1944.*

Hawker Typhoon

Entering service from July 1941, the Typhoon, or 'Tiffy' quickly acquired a reputation among the squadrons as a jinx aircraft. It had yet to resolve its teething troubles with its unproven Napier Sabre engine, while other minor aspects of actual performance gave few pilots confidence in going to war in this 'seven-ton brute'. Due in no small measure to the persistent faith in the design by Roland Beamont, who had helped in test development, however, the Typhoon slowly came to be recognised as a magnificent low-level attacker, packing a lethal punch of four 20mm cannons, with a turn of speed which completely outpaced any German fighter.

Above all, perhaps, was the extreme toughness of the design, both in construction and in appearance. Though initially intended as a high altitude interceptor in the defensive role, the Typhoon's true *métier* was as a low-level offensive fighter-bomber, where its near-400mph speed and solid stability in control augured well for its future. By 1944, Typhoons were being fitted with underwing rails for rocket projectiles and carriers for bombs - veritable flying arsenals, which were used to deadly effect in the first months of the Allies' invasion of Europe that year.

As one ex-No 609 Squadron member described the 'Tiffy': *"It was used initially to tackle low-flying Fw 190 hit-and-run raiders pecking around the south-east coast. Our Typhoons overtook these 190s like bats out of hell and then blew them out of the sky with the four 20mm cannons. The snag was that our lousy Sabre engines could be very temperamental - and engine failure at nearly 380mph at less than 200ft altitude was hardly a laughing matter. It was an ever-present nagging worry to the pilots, but we just pressed on and trusted our ground crews."*

Squadron Leader (later Air Marshal) Denis Crowley Milling formed the first Typhoon fighter-bomber squadron, No 181 (known as 'Bomphoons'). He recalled: *"As you dived down, you could look behind and see the heavy flak bursting to the rear. We developed a pretty good accuracy; on one occasion one of my bombs actually burst under an enemy aircraft as it was touching down. The whole essence was to hit and then get out fast; it did not pay to hang around."*

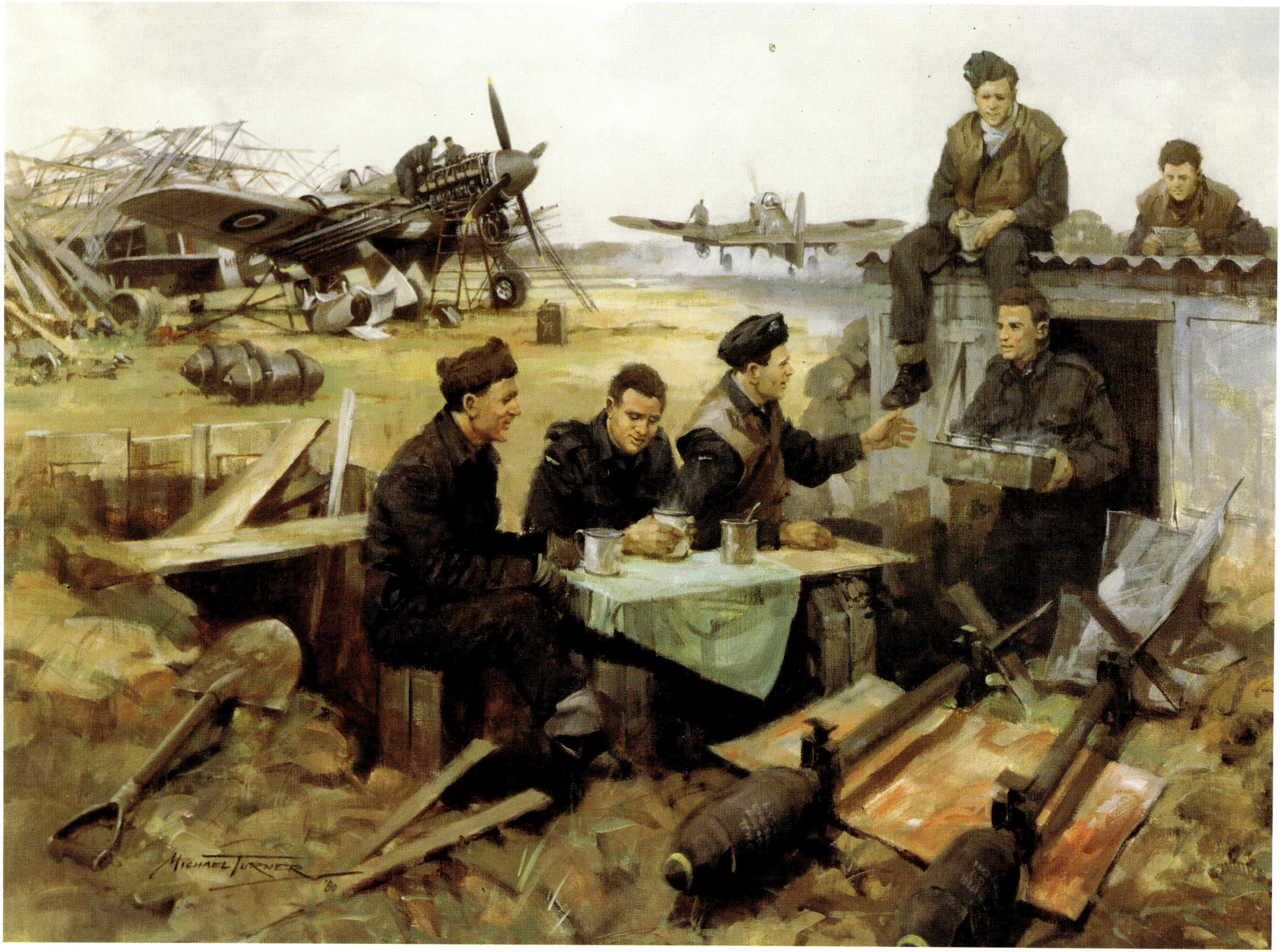
MICHAEL TURNER
'80

Hawker Typhoon *A ground crew takes a respite while in the distance a Typhoon undergoes maintenance. This was an overwhelmingly effective ground-attack fighter that destroyed numerous German tanks (particularly in the Falaise Gap) in Northern France during the summer of 1944.*

Hawker Tempest

The Tempest was basically a refined Typhoon - a 'Tiffy with the bugs ironed out' - and, indeed, was tentatively labelled Typhoon II in its original conception in 1940-41. A much thinner semi-elliptical shaped wing, plus more pleasing outlines to the fin and rudder marked the obvious external differences, and an uprated Sabre engine all helped the Tempest V under factory test to achieve a top speed in level flight of 472mph - faster than the contemporary official world speed record.

Roland Beamont, 'champion' of the parent Typhoon, also flew Tempests and his first impressions were highly enthusiastic: *"In the Tempest we had a direct successor to the Typhoon with most of the criticised aspects of the latter either eliminated, or much improved. Each flight brought greater enjoyment of and confidence in the crisp ailerons, firm though responsive elevator, good directional stability and damping giving high promise of superior gun-aiming capability, exhilarating performance and, with all this, magnificent combat vision, with windscreen forward frame members thinned down to a bare minimum, and superb unobstructed vision aft*

Hawker Tempest *A Hawker Tempest V from No 3 Squadron, flown by Flight Lieutenant Pierre Clostermann, engages in a dog-fight with Focke-Wulf Ta 152s (later edition of the 190) in April 1945.*

of the windscreen arch through a fully transparent sliding canopy."

The first Tempest Wing formed in April 1944 and they first saw action two days after D-Day. That same month, June 1944, brought the UK-based Tempests into combat with the German V1 'doodle-bug' flying bombs as these began their robot assault on southern England, and Tempests eventually destroyed 632 of them. The final months of the European war brought the Tempests into daily support tasks: ground-strafing enemy airfield locations, railways, roads, or other opportunity targets. Air opposition was sporadic but fierce, and included many clashes with Messerschmitt Me 262 jet fighters. Tempests remained in RAF squadron service until 1951.

Flight Lieutenant Pierre Clostermann, DSO, DFC, described a dogfight in the Tempest: *"I spotted a lone plane skimming over the tree tops in the direction of Bremen, whose tall chimney stacks looked positively medieval outlined against the dying sky.*

We were now over Bremen, and he was still about a thousand yards ahead. This business might take me rather far; I closed the radiator again and opened the throttle flat out. My Grand Charles responded at once. We were now over the first docks on the Weser.

Suddenly a salvo of flak shells blossomed between the Focke-Wulf and me - brief white flashes, mingled with brown balls which passed by on either side of me. More kept appearing miraculously out of the void. The automatic flak now chimed in and the orange glow of the tracer was reflected in the black oily water, from which overturned hulks emerged, like enormous stranded whales.

I concentrated on not losing sight of my Focke-Wulf - luckily he was silhouetted against the dying glow in the sky.

For a moment the flak redoubled in intensity then suddenly the tracers were snuffed out and disappeared. A bit suspicious! A glare behind me explained this curious phenomenon: on my tail were six 190s in perfect close echelon formation - exhausts white hot - pursuing me at full throttle.

With one movement I broke the metal thread to enable me to go to 'emergency', and shoved the throttle lever right forward. It was the first time I had occasion to use it on a Tempest. The effect was extraordinary and immediate. The aircraft literally bounded forward with a roar like a furnace under pressure. Within a few seconds I was doing 490 mph by the air speed indicator and I simultaneously caught up my quarry and left me pursuers standing.

I had soon reduced the distance to less than 200 yards. Although in this darkness my gun might rather dazzle me, I had him plumb in the middle and I fired two long, deliberate bursts. The Focke-Wulf oscillated and crashed on its belly in a marshy field, throwing up a shower of mud. He miraculously did not overturn. Without losing any time I climbed vertically towards the clouds and righted myself to face the others. They had vanished in the shadows. They must have turned about and left their comrade to his fate."

Gloster Meteor *A Gloster Meteor F3 of No 616 Squadron intercepts a V1 flying bomb over the Home Counties in 1944.*

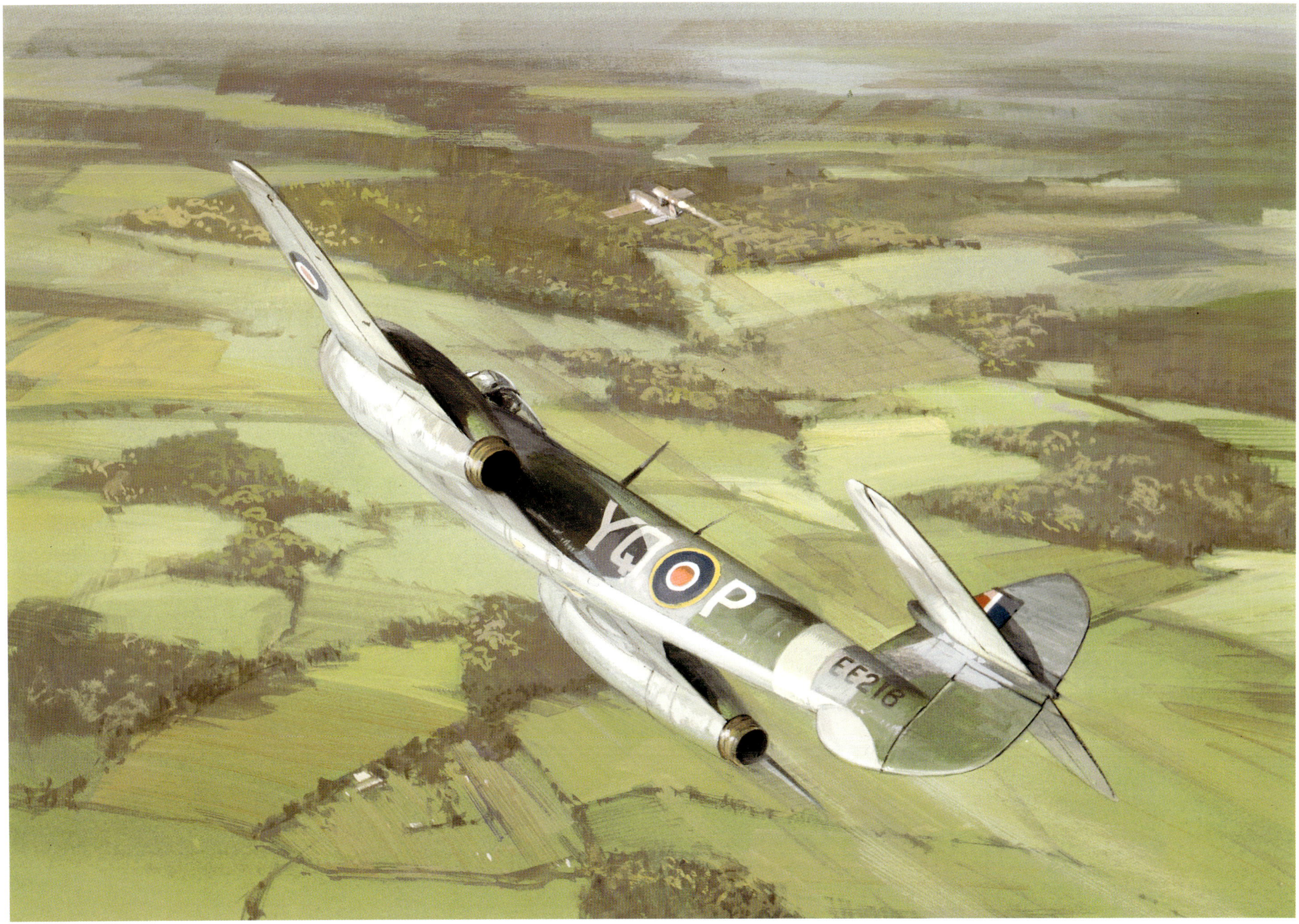
YQ
P
EE216

Gloster Meteor

The Meteor, or 'Meatbox', was the RAF's first jet fighter, and indeed the only Allied jet aircraft to see operational service during World War Two. It was the first jet-engined aircraft to enter full-production operational service with any air force in the world. Its planning was undertaken in 1940 (before the revolutionary Gloster E.28/39 single-engined jet had been built) but the first Meteor to actually fly (DG202) made its initial flight tests in March 1943. In July 1944, the first two that were operationally fit arrived at RAF Culmhead to begin re-equipment of No 616 Squadron - Britain's first jet fighter unit. Moving to Manston, No 616 Squadron commenced Meteor operations in July 1944, acting as interceptors against the V1 flying bombs, and eventually claimed 13 of these. During the last weeks of the war a handful of Meteors were stationed in Europe, but these saw no aerial combat. In successively improved versions, the Meteor was destined to remain the premier first-line aerial defender of Britain for some 12 years, while certain squadrons saw long service in Germany and in the Middle East.

It was built in thirty-four sub-types, with seventeen different types of power units. Many hundreds of Meteors were bought by foreign air forces in the post-1945 years, though none was ever required to fire its cannons in anger, except those used by No 77 Squadron of the RAAF which saw combat during the Korean War. During its long life the Meteor was subjected to a myriad of trials and experiments: in-flight refuelling, long-distance flights, high speed reconnaissance techniques, ejection seat trials, prone position pilot cockpits, radar tests. In particular, however, there were high speed record attempts. Meteor F4s were selected in 1945 for the RAF High Speed Flight, and Group Captain H. J. Wilson, DFC achieved 606mph. The following year saw more attempts to raise Wilson's record speed, and this was accomplished by Group Captain E. M. Donaldson with a recorded 616mph.

Former Hawker Siddeley test pilot Duncan Simpson remembers his step up from training on the Harvard to the Meteor T7: *"From the students' and instructors' point of view the two-seat Meteor T7 was a superb vehicle. View from the front cockpit was good, particularly forward, and from the instructor's rear seat it was adequate, despite the amount of metalwork in the massive hood, which opened sideways. Both cockpits were spacious and reasonably well laid out... Compared to the Harvard, the Meteor environment was spectacularly different."*

Post War

As in 1918, the end of the war in 1945 saw the RAF again suffer from drastic reduction not only in numerical strength but in financial provision, resulting in several years' delay in converting its first-line equipment from piston-engined designs to jet-powered successors. For the first six years of the 'peace', Bomber Command's squadrons continued to fly piston-engined Avro Lincoln and American B-29 Washington bombers, but in 1951 came the first English Electric Canberra jet-bomber squadron in service; while Fighter Command added DH Vampires to its Meteor units in defence of the United Kingdom.

Overseas squadrons, traditionally last in priority for new aircraft, plodded on operationally with piston-engined types, such as the Bristol Brigand and DH Hornet, until the mid-1950s; while Coastal Command had to be content with variants of the four-engined Avro Shackleton - itself a development of the wartime Lancaster bomber.

From 1955, new muscle was added to the RAF when the first of a trio of jet-engined heavy bombers, the Vickers Valiant, joined Bomber Command, followed later by the Handley Page Victor and delta-wing Avro Vulcan - a combination of nuclear-age bombers which were to comprise Britain's nuclear deterrent force until 1969. In the fighter field came the superlative Hawker Hunter, followed in 1956 by the Gloster Javelin interceptor, but it was to be a further five years before the RAF received its first truly transonic fighter, the magnificent English Electric Lightning. As the latter entered service, RAF Transport Command commenced up-dating its potential with jet-powered DH Comets.

English Electric (BAC) Lightning

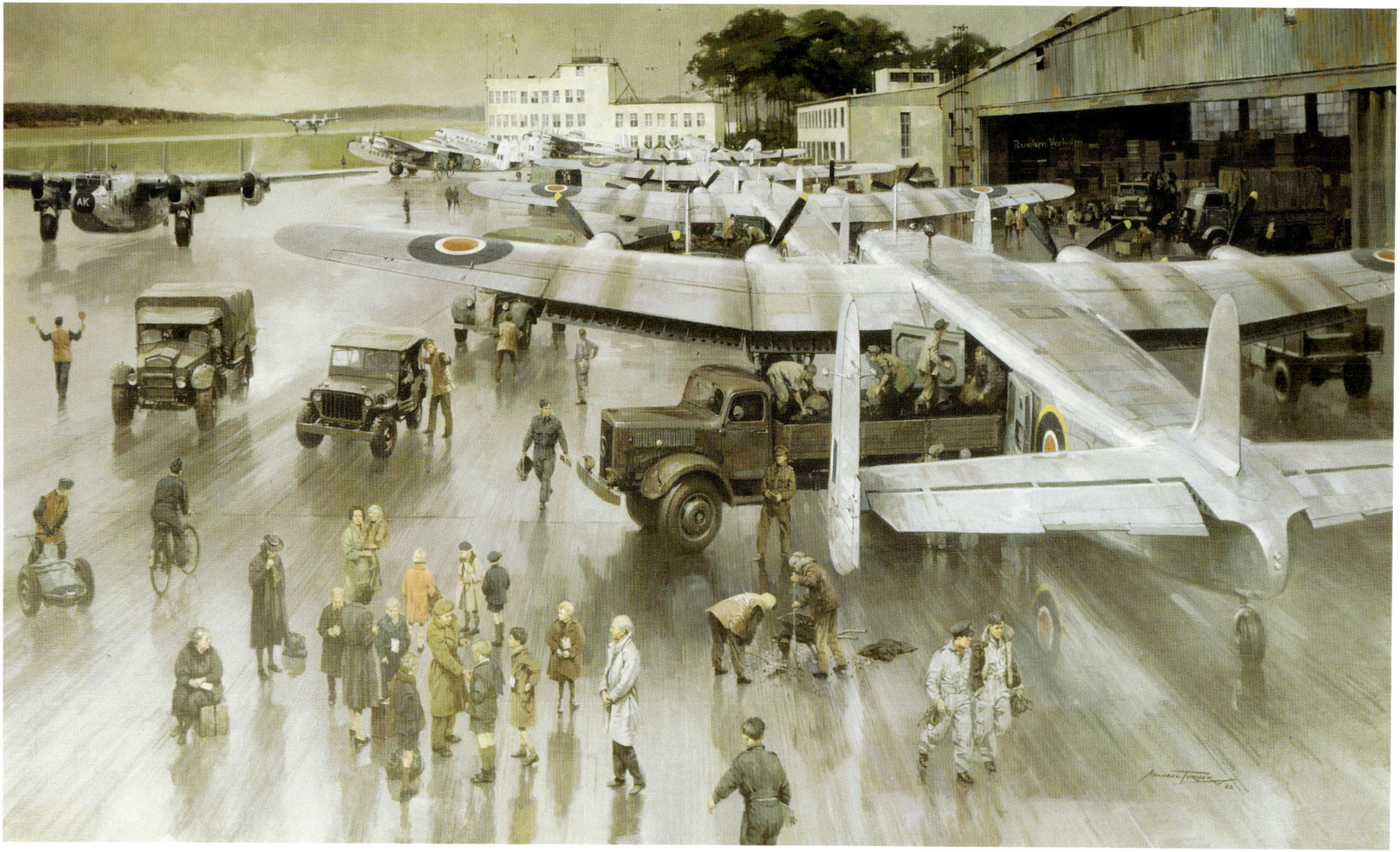
AK

Avro York

In many people's minds the lumbering Avro York is most associated with the immediate post-1945 era of RAF history, yet the aeroplane was conceived and first built in early 1942. It was a direct descendant of the mighty Lancaster from which it initially took its wings and tail unit. These were 'attached' to a much deeper, wider fuselage having roughly double the cubic capacity of its forebear, and the first York progressed from original drawings to the first prototype flight in a mere five months. Due to the contemporary Anglo-American agreement that all wartime transport aircraft were to be manufactured in the USA, the York was produced in small numbers at first, and several of the initial batches were immediately converted internally for VIP accommodation to ferry high-ranking politicians and Service chiefs, and on occasion royalty.

Thus it was not until 1945 that the first wholly-equipped York unit came into being when No 551 Squadron received its full complement of the type. The York's RAF heyday came in the late 1940s when it came into special prominence during the Berlin Airlift. In this Operation *Plainfare*, Yorks alone flew some 29,000 sorties and lifted nearly a quarter of a million tons of supplies, apart from being mainly responsible for the carriage of civilians - virtually half the RAF's total effort during this prolonged operation. Of a total of 257 Yorks eventually produced, 208 were delivered to the RAF, and the last of these in service (MW295) remained in RAF livery until 1957 when it was sold to a Middle East civilian airline. Though by no means as tractable to fly as its 'parent', the York was a patient packhorse which eventually accumulated a prodigious amount of vital, if mundane, flying miles.

Wing Commander Cyril Povey flew Avro Yorks for more than four years and took part in the Berlin Airlift: *"I went on to Yorks early in 1946 when I was transferred to No 246 Squadron at RAF Holmsley South near Christchurch. Our main task was to bring back from the Middle East and Far East people who were due for demob and take out replacements. I thought the York was a lovely aeroplane by the standards of those days. It was docile, pretty steady to fly and had no nasty vices. The engines were very reliable; in perhaps a couple of thousand hours of flying Yorks over a period of four years I had only one engine failure in the air, which is pretty good going.*

The York was not as beautiful an aeroplane to fly as, for example, the Mosquito and the Beaufighter. In fact, it was a lumbering heap as all transport aircraft were, but as 'transports' went it was a good aircraft. It was a much nicer aeroplane to fly than the Handley Page Hastings was, for example, although the Hastings was a more modern aircraft. I think all the York's virtues, especially its reliability, were shown to perfection in the Berlin Airlift.

When the Berlin Airlift began in 1948, No 246 Squadron went to Wünnsdorf near Hanover, which until then had been the base of some Vampire fighter squadrons. Then the whole place became a transportation set-up. The operation was very, very well organised from the start with improvements constantly being made.

Our Yorks mainly carried foodstuffs such as grain, tinned food, sacks of sugar, powdered milk, egg substitute and so on. All the seats had been taken out leaving the long fuselage completely empty and when we took off we were always crammed full of cargo. The few passengers we did carry were either very senior or were serious medical cases being flown out of Berlin for better treatment elsewhere. We would fly three return trips to Berlin a day, which took fourteen hours (the average flight time was about an hour) round the clock.

By the time the Airlift ended in May 1949, we had proved that it was possible to keep a large city supplied from the air, although there was an enormous amount of belt-tightening. I don't think the Communists ever imagined that we could do it but we did."

Avro York *One of No 51 Squadron's Avro Yorks, taking part in the Berlin Airlift in 1948, runs up its engines at Gatow airfield before returning to West Germany for more supplies.*

de Havilland Hornet

The aesthetically-appealing Hornet was not only the RAF's last piston-engined fighter to enter squadron service, but was also the fastest of its type and class. Patently derived from the huge success of the all-wood Mosquito, the Hornet was nevertheless an entirely new design. Its conception was as a long-range interceptor, capable of matching any Japanese fighter, for use in the final stages of the Pacific campaigns. Great attention was paid to reducing cross-sectional area in fuselage and engines in order to enhance speed, and basic armament comprised a four 20mm cannon battery in its slender belly.

Planned and built in 1942-43, the prototype Hornet first flew in July 1944 and immediately exceeded its expected performance figures, reaching a maximum speed of 485mph.

The first production Hornet reached the RAF in February 1945, but it was not until March 1946 that the first fully-equipped squadron was declared operational, this being No 64 Squadron based at RAF Horsham St Faith (now Norwich Airport). Only three other UK-based squadrons were Hornet-equipped thereafter, and these became Meteor jet fighter units by 1951.

That year saw the Hornet finally move to the Far East, when three other squadrons in Singapore and Malaya received Hornets, and flew these almost daily on operations against Chinese communist

de Havilland Hornet *A pair of Hornet F3s from No 41 Squadron at RAF Church Fenton soon after take-off. They are painted in the camouflage worn by long-range intruder aircraft of the period.*

'bandits' in the prolonged Operation Firedog until in turn being replaced by jets from 1955. In Malaya the Hornet's cannons were supplemented by underwing rockets and carriers for up to 2,000lb of bombs. A fully navalised version, the Sea Hornet, was also built in reasonable numbers, but equipped only two squadrons fully; while the final variant was the PR 22 - a high-speed photo-reconnaissance machine which saw limited use.

Avro Lincoln

Designated originally the Lancaster IV or V (according to type of engines fitted), the Lincoln was built to a 1943 specification and intended for use in the Pacific war against Japan. First flown in June 1944, Lincolns were first issued to Nos 44 and 57 Squadrons late in 1945, and eventually equipped 20 RAF squadrons. The design was historically significant as being the final piston-engined heavy bomber to see RAF squadron use, though some were complimented by Boeing B-29 Washingtons for a brief period.

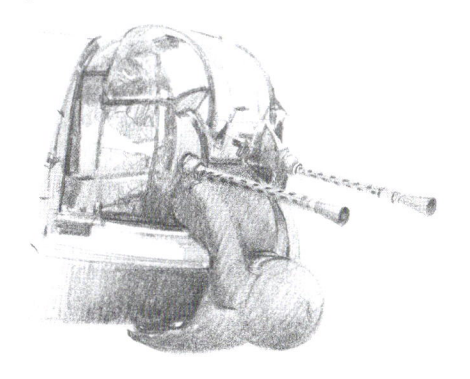

Avro Lincoln *Avro Lincolns of No 7 Squadron on a bombing mission against Malayan terrorists in 1954. The aircraft was a development of the Lancaster, but its improvements included a greater wing-span, improved engines with four-blade propellers and a longer fuselage.*

The aircraft's extended range and bomb load capacity - 14,000lb at maximum storage - led to a variety of active operations in the various post-1945 uprisings and rebellions in overseas zones; notably during the Malayan Emergency and the anti-Mau Mau campaign in Kenya. In these periods, UK-based Lincoln squadrons were detached for one or two months in rotation to appropriate RAF bases overseas. The Lincoln's high altitude performance also saw the type employed in a wide variety of purely aeronautical experiments. Batches of Lincolns were bought by Australia and Argentina for normal bomber roles, while individual examples undertook a number of very long distance flights in the interests of research.

Finally withdrawn from RAF first-line use by 1963, the bulky Lincoln - its wings spanned 120ft - was not a particularly easy bomber to like. It handled reasonably well and performed its duties doggedly, but as one Lincoln pilot put it: *"The sheer size of this black beast was frightening at first acquaintance, but the most vivid memory of several years in a Lincoln's driving seat was the noise inside the cabin. After four or more hours up front in a Lincoln, my hearing was semi-defective for hours afterwards."*

Bristol Sycamore One of No 194 Squadron's Bristol Sycamore helicopters landing on an improvised pad high in the Malaysian mountains in 1955.

Bristol Sycamore

The Sycamore prototype (Bristol Type 171 Mark 1) first flew in July 1947, and improved variants were first delivered to the RAF for operational use in April 1953 with No 275 Squadron at RAF Linton-on-Ouse.

As such the Sycamore was the first British-designed and produced helicopter to enter RAF service.

Fitted with a 550hp Alvis Leonides 73 piston engine it had a crew of two and could carry three passengers. Having a Westland hydraulic winch, over a sliding door, this was the first use of a helicopter for Search and Rescue (SAR).

Its initial role was for SAR in Fighter Command, but in later years the type was used to good effect in Malaya, Cyprus, Kenya and Aden on active operations. Eventually seven squadrons were equipped with Sycamores. From 1963 Sycamores operated in Borneo, but the helicopter was not really suitable for 'hot and high' conditions, and serviceability was a problem. They were withdrawn from front-line duties in October 1964. A small number of HC14s remained at RAF Northolt for passenger carrying duties until August 1972.

Bristol Brigand

The Brigand's main operational contribution, between 1950 and 1954, was as a light bomber or, more usually, a ground-attack strike aircraft. Its original conception in 1942, however, had been as a torpedo-bomber replacement for the Beaufighter which was temporarily fulfilling such a role with Coastal Command at that time. The prototype Brigand first flew in December 1944 and owed much to its stablemate the Buckingham bomber design, and although initial deliveries to the RAF were torpedo aircraft.

Bristol Brigand *Two Brigands from No 84 Squadron let loose a salvo of rockets at a terrorist position in Malaya in 1952. The Brigand had been developed from the Beaufighter, but was radically adapted into a three-seat ground-attack aircraft.*

These were soon converted for the pure bombing and strike role and then reallocated to units based in the Middle and Far East commands. Indeed, the Brigand, which was another development of the Beaufighter (page 104) served in a wide range of environments that were unsuitable for aeroplanes such as the wooden Mosquito.

In Malaya Brigands served briefly with No 45 Squadron before being replaced by de Havilland Hornets, while those allotted to No 84 Squadron at Tengah continued anti-'bandit' strike sorties until as late as 1953, when - resulting from a number of fatal crashes due to structural reasons - No 84 Squadron was 'disbanded' in situ and its Brigands reduced to scrap on site. Thereafter the only Brigands in service were flown as radar navigation trainers on UK-based OCUs until early 1958 when they were finally withdrawn from service.

An ex-signaller on No 84 Squadron remembers the Brigand as: *"...a noisy, sweaty aircraft in which to operate. The Perspex glasshouse for the crew was like a sauna bath when one climbed in for a strike sortie from Tengah. Operating at jungle-height was never comfortable, while the wings always appeared to be ready to part company with us every time we went into a rocket attack dive. My pilot usually referred to the kite as 'the black bastard'... I shared his opinion".*

Supermarine Spitfire F22 *Supermarine Spitfire F.22's sporting the colours of No 603 (City of Edinburgh) Squadron in 1951.*

Supermarine Spitfire F22

From the F21 Spitfire version came two more distinct variants, the F22 and the F24. Both had rear-view bubble canopies and more slender rear fuselages than the F21, but in most respects differed only in minor details. Production of F22s commenced in March 1945 but only 260 were eventually built. These equipped only one regular RAF unit, No 73 Squadron in Malta, but twelve Royal Auxiliary Air Force squadrons were re-equipped with the type, where it became the major aircraft type in service from 1946 to 1951. Though little used by the RAF, several batches of F22s were acquired by the Rhodesian and Syrian Air Forces and a handful flown by the Royal Egyptian Air Force. In RAuxAF service the F22 achieved one minor claim to fame, being one of the very few Spitfires of any type to wear colourful unit markings as per pre-1938 RAF markings on overall silver paint finishes.

de Havilland Vampire

A contemporary of the Gloster Meteor, the de Havilland Vampire jet fighter was designed in 1941 but did not reach RAF squadron service until 1946. For the following five years Vampires established a high reputation for their aerobatic qualities and formation flying displays in Europe and abroad. Though generally superseded in Fighter Command by the Meteor by 1951, the Vampire created many firsts in RAF history. Six aircraft of No 54 Squadron at RAF Odiham made the first RAF jet crossing of the Atlantic in July 1948; it was the first jet fighter to see service in both the Middle East and Far East areas; it was also the first jet aircraft to be issued to units of the Royal Auxiliary Air Force. In December 1945 a navalised Sea Vampire became the first pure jet ever to operate from an aircraft carrier.

Initially known as the Spidercrab, it featured a short central nacelle, built of wood with a pressurised cockpit forward of the engine, with wing-root inlets and short jet pipe. The tail was carried on twin booms above the jet efflux. It was the first Allied aircraft to exceed 500mph in level flight.

From 1950 to 1954 the only Vampires to fire their cannons in anger were those equipping two squadrons of the Far East Air Force (FEAF) based in Singapore and Hong Kong, which flew numerous sorties in the Malayan anti-'bandit' campaign.

Always popular with its pilots, the Vampire (along with the Meteor) was equally popular with its ground maintenance crews - a relatively rare attribute. Its compact design and easy access for servicing, re-arming and refuelling, enhanced its reputation among the ever-toiling 'erks' - one of whom has described the Vampire as: *"the neatest little jet fighter ever invented, even if it did suffer from ducks' disease!"*

Chris Ashworth, a Vampire T11 instructor, recalled that: *"It was very easy to start, taxi, take-off and land. The view from the cockpit was good and the controls well co-ordinated. The Vampire was an excellent trainer because it needed a light touch to be flown accurately, a useful cross-country machine because it was comparatively economical on fuel, and quite good for aerobatics, especially in the looping plane. During formation flying, much more anticipation was required than on propeller-driven aeroplanes, both to catch up and slow down. Circuit flying was straightforward unless it was raining. Then it could be difficult to see forward through the flat windscreen, especially at night. Perhaps one of the most off-putting features was the strange noise sometimes produced by the Goblin engine."*

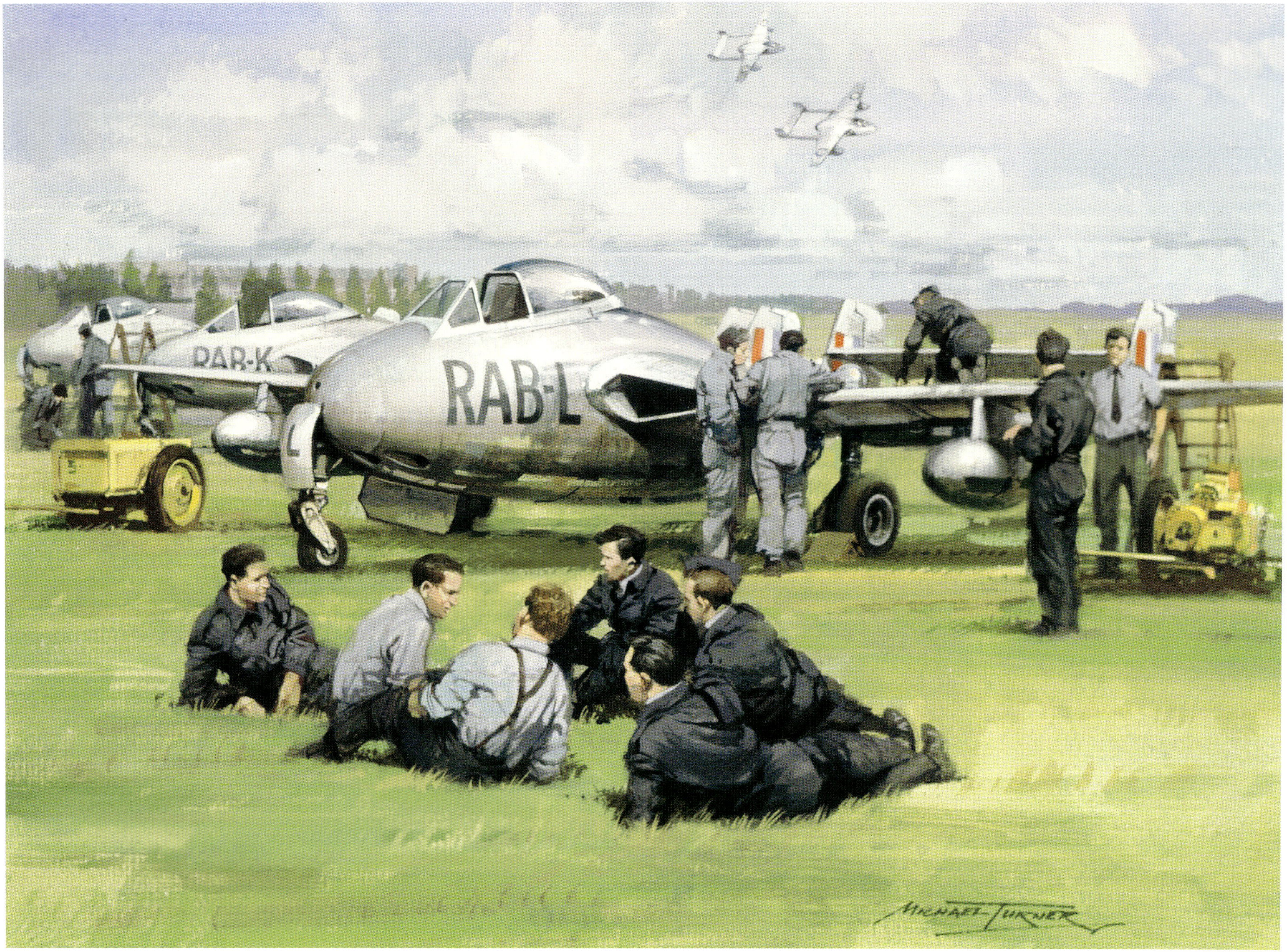
RAB-K
RAB-L
MICHAEL TURNER

de Havilland Vampire *Vampires of No 501 (County of Gloucester) Squadron, Royal Auxiliary Air Force between sorties during summer camp at RAF Odiham in 1949. This single-seater jet fighter was powered by a Goblin turbojet engine rated at 3,100lb of thrust and had a maximum speed of 540mph.*

Blackburn Beverley

Good looks, plus an ability to carry bulky and heavy loads in and out of short fields, seldom go hand in hand, and the Beverley was no exception. A military version of the intended civil transport GAL Universal Freighter of 1946 genesis, the Beverley came into RAF service from March 1956, when No 47 Squadron began the changeover from the unit's Hastings aircraft. A simple, unpressurised aircraft with fixed landing gear the lumbering Beverley was, at that time, the largest aircraft ever seen in RAF livery, and its design incorporated no few general innovations for its designated role as a freight and troop carrier. It attracted the nicknames of 'Barrack Block' and 'Pregnant Portia'.

The rear-loading doors - then unique in RAF experience - permitted easy access for a wide variety of loads; while the aircraft's remarkably short take-off and landing runs enabled the gentle giant to operate to and from bald desert airstrips at will. Only five squadrons were equipped with Beverleys and a mere total of 47 machines were actually produced for the RAF; yet these gave some 12 years' faithful, virtually

Blackburn Beverley *A Beverley on a desert airstrip in Aden while another circles overhead. This transport aircraft was the largest aeroplane to be seen in RAF service up to that time, yet it could take off and land in a surprisingly short distance.*

trouble-free operational service before finally being retired in 1968. During those years Beverleys saw active operations in several trouble-spots around the globe, particularly in Aden, Kenya and during the brief Kuwait 'oil crisis', while in early 1966 three of No 47 Squadron's amiable mammoths were 'detached' for 18 months to Da Nang Air Base in Vietnam to assist in lifting relief supplies to the interior of that war-ravaged country. Others flew over the Malaysian jungles from Singapore bases, and some participated in the Brunei uprising.

A Beverley pilot recalled his time with No 47 Squadron at RAF Abingdon: *"Greeted at first by RAF aircrews with some dismay as an ugly monster, the 'Bev' quickly earned our affection by its robust reliability when operating in challenging terrain, such as desert landing strips, and its endless adaptability to carry heavy loads of all descriptions. There was a short period when Beverleys were grounded following a spate of engine fires in the air, but this was rectified by introducing a later variant of the Bristol Centaurus engine which proved to be trouble-free, and they went on to earn great laurels."*

Gloster Meteor F8 Three Meteor F8s of No 601 (County of London) Squadron, RAuxAF based at RAF North Weald, practice aerobatics while on a summer camp in Malta before the RAuxAF disbanded in March 1957.

Gloster Meteor FR9 Meteor FR9s from No 79 Squadron, on exercises with the British Army in Northern Germany, flown by Ray Hanna.

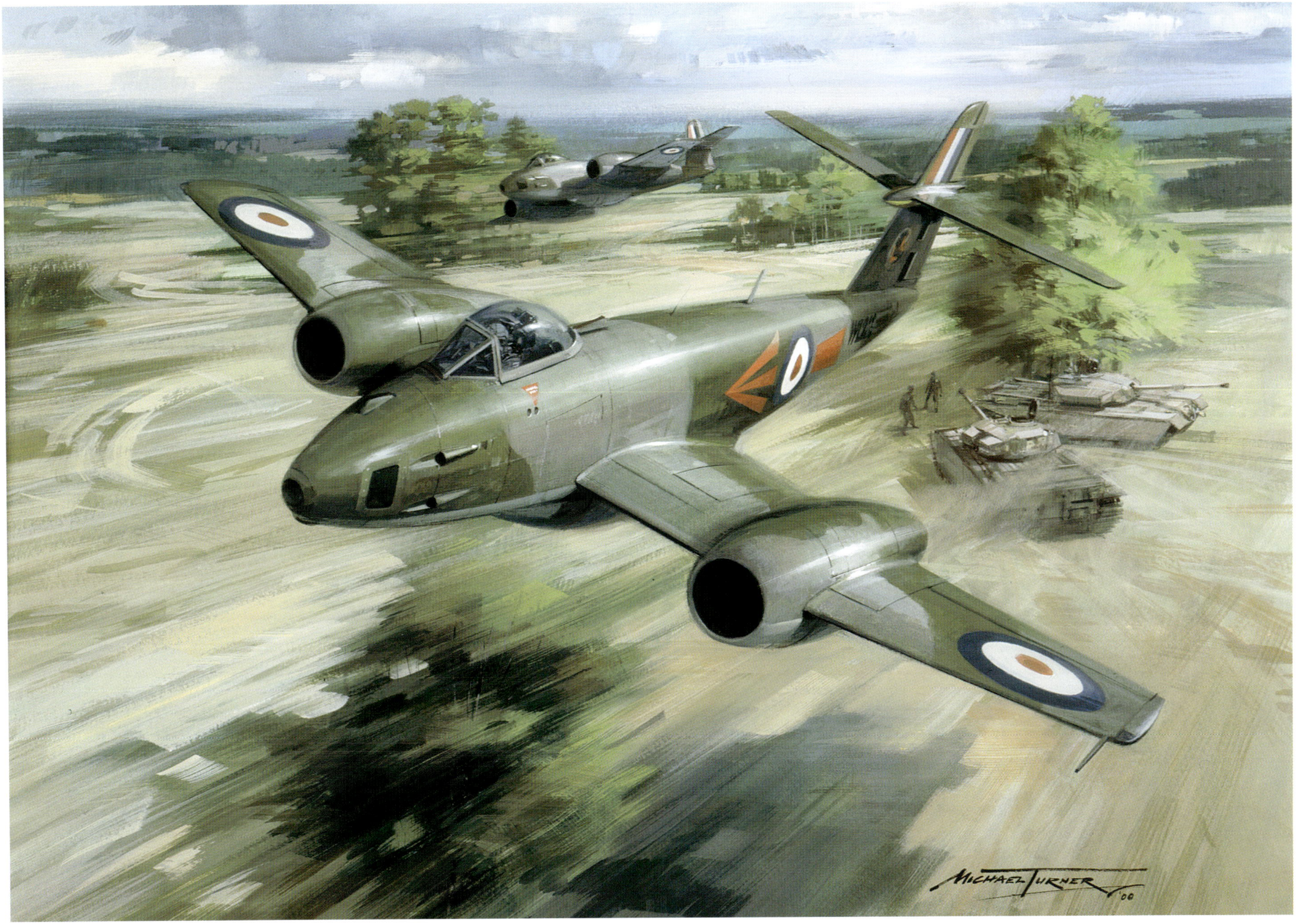
MICHAEL TURNER

Gloster Meteor F8

Though many different marks of Meteor served with the RAF at various periods, probably the best-known was the Mark 8, which from 1950 to 1956 was the main single-seat day fighter of the UK-based RAF. The F8 was in essence a much-improved F4, with longer fuselage, uprated engines, and a modified cockpit to accept a better-vision canopy and an ejector seat. Armament remained the same, but all-round performance was noticeably improved, giving the F8 a top speed nudging the 600mph mark. The Meteor F8 was gradually replaced on the first-line squadrons from 1956 onwards, but the type lingered for several more years as a target tug.

The F8 was the only 'peacetime' Meteor to see active service in the Korean War, when No 77 Squadron RAAF exchanged their Mustang fighters for Meteor F8s in early 1951. Actual war operations by the Australians began in late July and continued until the end of the war in July 1953.

Squadron Leader Bill Waterton, DFC, GM, Gloster's chief test pilot, flew many of the various marks of Meteor:

"The prototype Meteor 8 was smooth and pleasant to handle. It was faster than the Mark 4 despite its extra weight - 15,200lb against 14,700lb. During trials I reckoned it was doing 605mph at 5,000ft, and I put this down to the cleaning-up of airflow over the improved tail. While the Mark 4 pitched and bucked when approaching the speed of sound, the very first 8 simply showed slight trim changes and dropped a wing. It was lighter to manoeuvre and an easier spinner. Its ailerons were still heavy, however, and remained so until new spring-tabs were introduced. In production, however, Mark 8s did not repeat the prototype's pleasant characteristics...."

Supermarine Swift

Significant as the RAF's first-ever swept-wing fighter in operational squadron use, and also the first RAF aircraft with powered ailerons, nevertheless the Swift's only true claim to fame came in September 1953, when Lt Cdr Mike Lithgow RN established a new world speed record of 737mph in a specially-prepared Swift. The Swift was produced as a 'safeguard' high altitude interceptor in case the Hawker Hunter, then being built, proved to be disappointing in service. In the event it was the Swift which was considered a somewhat dismal failure for its intended role.

A host of modifications and trials failed to give the design the essential attributes of a first-line defender, and its later variants were accordingly converted to low-level high-speed tactical reconnaissance machines. The difficulties which were encountered were such that the Swift was eventually withdrawn from Fighter Command in May 1955, and the Mk 5 version was modified for service as a fighter-reconnaissance aircraft.

In squadron use the early marks were underarmed - just two 30mm cannons and assorted rocketry at best - while the aeroplane's undesirable longitudinal control characteristics and engine deficiencies condemned it for the particular needs of the UK-based Fighter Command. Based in Germany, just two squadrons were equipped with the later fighter-recce (FR) version of the Swift and these performed satisfactorily in their tasks. This FR version was the first RAF jet in squadron service to incorporate a re-heat engine capability, and remained in service from 1956 to 1961.

Supermarine Swift *A Supermarine Swift FR5, operated by No 79 Squadron in Germany from 1959 to 1961, on a low-level sortie.*

Handley Page Hastings

Superseding the Avro York as the RAF's standard long-haul transport aeroplane, the Hastings served with RAF squadrons from 1948 until the type's official retirement in 1968. Almost immediately after reaching its first squadron, the Hastings was in action - participating in the latter stages of the Berlin Airlift. During its 20 years service the Hastings served the RAF magnificently. Like all 'willing workhorses' in the RAF's history, it undertook an astonishingly wide variety of tasks: freighter, paratroop conveyor, meteorological surveyor, ambulance, VIP luxury transporter, radar bombing trainer, navigational instructor, heavy cargo lifter - these and other minor roles were all grist to the Hastings' mill. Nor were these roles always carried out in peaceful skies.

Apart from the emergency measures of Operation *Plainfare*, the capacious Hastings saw active service during the Malayan Emergency (Operation Firedog), the Korean War, and, in 1956, in the Suez Crisis (Operation *Musketeer*).

The demise of the Hastings was eventually due simply to fatigue - literal fatigue of its airframe components; but by the time of its withdrawal from RAF squadron use, the type had flown more than 150 million miles, and 'lifted' some one and a half million passengers and nearly 200,000 tons of freight over virtually every part of the globe.

Its splendid service history fittingly continued its parent firm's long tradition of providing dependable 'heavies' for the RAF which had begun in essence with the Handley Page O/100 biplane behemoth of 1914-15.

A Hastings pilot engaged in the Berlin Airlift recalled: *"The Hastings, which had only just entered service, had its teething problems and, with its conventional type of undercarriage, had difficulty with a crosswind* component when this was stronger than 20 knots. This compared unfavourably with the USAF C-54 Skymaster, which had a tricycle undercarriage and was able to operate in considerably more severe conditions. The first Hastings squadron had been deployed to Western Germany at short notice, well ahead of schedule, but this was justified by the high standards of flying under the exacting conditions of the Airlift."

Handley Page Hastings *Hastings from No 511 Squadron, Transport Command, drop the parachutists of the Third Battalion, Parachute Regiment over Port Said during the 1956 Suez Crisis. The Hastings was the RAF's standard transport plane for over a decade.*

de Havilland (Canada) Chipmunk

Designed and built by de Havilland's Canadian company, the tandem two-seat Chipmunk was a direct successor to the firm's Tiger Moth for 'ab initio' training in the RAF. After the war the RAF had an urgent need to replace its Tiger Moths, particularly with the post-war Reserve Flying Schools and University Air Squadrons. As elementary instruction aircraft, Chipmunks, which first flew in May 1946 at Toronto, were in RAF service from 1950 to 1973 in sporadic phases - depending on whatever contemporary fashion in flying instruction was in vogue with the RAF - and were considered to be delightfully easy aeroplanes to operate, with good handling characteristics and a high degree of aerobatic capability in the hands of an experienced pilot.

Able to operate comfortably from even small grass airfields, Chipmunks provided a first taste of flying for many thousands of RAFVR (Royal Air Force Volunteer Reserve) and National Service pilots, apart from regular RAF personnel, and was the type chosen for the initial flying instruction undertaken by HRH the Duke of Edinburgh in 1952, and subsequently by Prince Charles and Prince Andrew.

Because of the expansion of the RAF, due to the Korean War, additional Chipmunks equipped

de Havilland Chipmunk *A trainee pilot puts a de Havilland Chipmunk through its paces. This two-seater trainer was a direct successor to the Tiger Moth (page 69).*

Basic Flying Schools that were set up for the instruction of National Service Pilots.

The Chipmunk was used by AEF flights until the late 1990s.

Flight Lieutenant Peter Bouch who flew the Chipmunk with the Flying Selection Squadron at RAF Swinderby recalls: *"It was robust, simple to operate, yet because of a tailwheel configuration quite demanding in its handling - particularly on or near the ground. It was a very basic, simple little machine, with nicely balanced controls, fully automatic, spinnable and ideal for the full RAF primary flying syllabus. It could operate equally well from grass or concrete, but being light it made it vulnerable to strong and cross winds, so we had to be careful with it. Having said that, it was the best aircraft for the job. It is a much loved old aeroplane, excellent for the task and outlasted many of its successors."*

Vickers Valiant

The Valiant, as Britain's first operational four-jet bomber, exemplified RAF Bomber Command's true transition from the piston-engined force of the 1940s to the nuclear deterrent bomber strategy of the 1950s and onward. It also gave practical 'birth' to the RAF's V-bomber force created to implement that fresh strategic policy.

Entering squadron service in April 1955 - two years before its compatriots the Avro Vulcan and the Handley Page Victor - the Valiant was the first V-bomber to release bombs in anger when it flew operations in the Suez Crisis; while in 1956 and 1957 Valiants were responsible for dropping Britain's first atom bomb and hydrogen bomb respectively during nuclear trials in the Pacific. It remained in squadron service for almost ten years, during which period reconnaissance and in-flight refuelling tanker variants were also introduced. In the latter role the Valiant extended the RAF's flexibility in striking power globally, and a number of successful intercontinental long-range flights by various Valiant crews emphasised this versatility. Despite the seeming complexity of such a radically new concept of bomber, the Valiant was found to be relatively easy to service and maintain, while its handling qualities were considered generally good by its air crews.

Official disbandment of the Valiant V-force was announced in February 1965, due to a number of metal fatigue defects discovered in main wing spars, and the design swiftly faded from the RAF scene. Nevertheless, the Valiant had spearheaded the RAF's entry into the 'nuclear club' and its pioneering experience was the foundation for Britain's future strategic policies in bombing operations.

Chief Technician Fred Flower served as a crew chief on Nos 18 and 49 Squadron for several years:

"With the introduction of the V-bombers, of which the Valiant was the first, the RAF decided that it would need an aircraft servicing chief on American lines, and in consequence many senior NCO airframe and engine fitters had to do a pretty concentrated crew chief's course involving the maintenance of the airframe, engines, electrics, and a fair knowledge of the radar and wireless equipment fitted. The course was about nine months and was very concentrated - too concentrated, especially if you weren't from Bomber Command to start with. The Valiant introduced the complexities of electricity on a large scale, as most of the major operating procedures - flap operation, airbrakes, undercarriage retraction etc - called for electrical power where they would normally have been hydraulic.

As crew chief, you were in charge of the servicing, and in theory, wherever the aeroplane went, you went with it. This sometimes involved what were called 'lone rangers', overseas postings where you flew with the aeroplane, with no-one at all to help with the maintenance except the air crew you were

Vickers Valiant *A Valiant B1 of No 148 Squadron based at RAF Marham lands at RAF Luqa in Malta. This was the first time that the British V-bomber force had been in action, and XD814 was the first aircraft to bomb during the Anglo-French intervention in the Suez Crisis in Egypt during October 1956.*

with. The ideal thing was for a crew chief to be assigned to one aeroplane, and to stay with it; though obviously if someone went on leave or was sick, you ended up looking after more than one aeroplane.

It says a lot for the Valiant that we could cope with that requirement, but I have horrible memories of changing fuel tanks with the temperature way below zero; the fuel tanks were rubber cells and the cold did nothing to make the rubber flexible. Given a warm hangar, then even the job of changing fuel tanks was considerably eased, but a lot of the servicing had to be done outside and it was nothing unusual to see engine changes going on outside."

Gloster Javelin

The largest fighter ever adopted by the RAF up to that time, and the world's first delta-winged operational aircraft, the Javelin owed its basic shape, in part, to the results of studies undertaken by a few German scientists for the Luftwaffe and subsequently analysed by RAE Farnborough shortly after the close of World War Two. Its initial trial and test programmes resulted in the deaths of two test pilots and illustrated several serious handling and flying defects, but steady modification and improvement in the light of experience allowed the Javelin to be introduced to RAF squadrons from February 1956, two years after the Hunter's operational début. Compared to the Hunter, the Javelin's all-round performance was inferior, but its accommodation for extra radar and other black box equipment made it highly suitable for night interception roles.

At least nine distinct Marks of Javelin were built, but the initial Mark Is issued to the RAF were considered by many pilots to have been the best version for squadron use. It was generally thought of as a pilot's aeroplane, with all-vital equipment and controls close to hand, easy to operate, and simple to check. Cockpits were thought to be well-designed, comfortable to use, while handling was considered excellent. Its greatest fault - common to most marks of Javelin - was its poor stall recovery characteristics; normal recovery in a Mark I being almost impossible and, in part, responsible for several aircraft and crew losses in operational use.

Bill Waterton, who flew in many of the Javelin prototypes' test trials and was awarded a George Medal for bringing back a Javelin which had shed its elevators due to excessive flutter, said of the aircraft: *"The Javelin was easy to fly, had an excellent performance and showed great promise. It had some dangerous tendencies too, such as reversing her longitudinal control (the stick had to be pushed instead of pulled) near the stall, tightening into the turn, and pitching strongly nose-up when the flaps were extended."*

Gloster Javelin *A Javelin FAW7 from No 23 Squadron takes off from a rain-soaked runway at RAF Coltishall, Norfolk in 1959. This was the RAF's first delta-wing fighter and was also the first designed to fly in any weather and at night.*

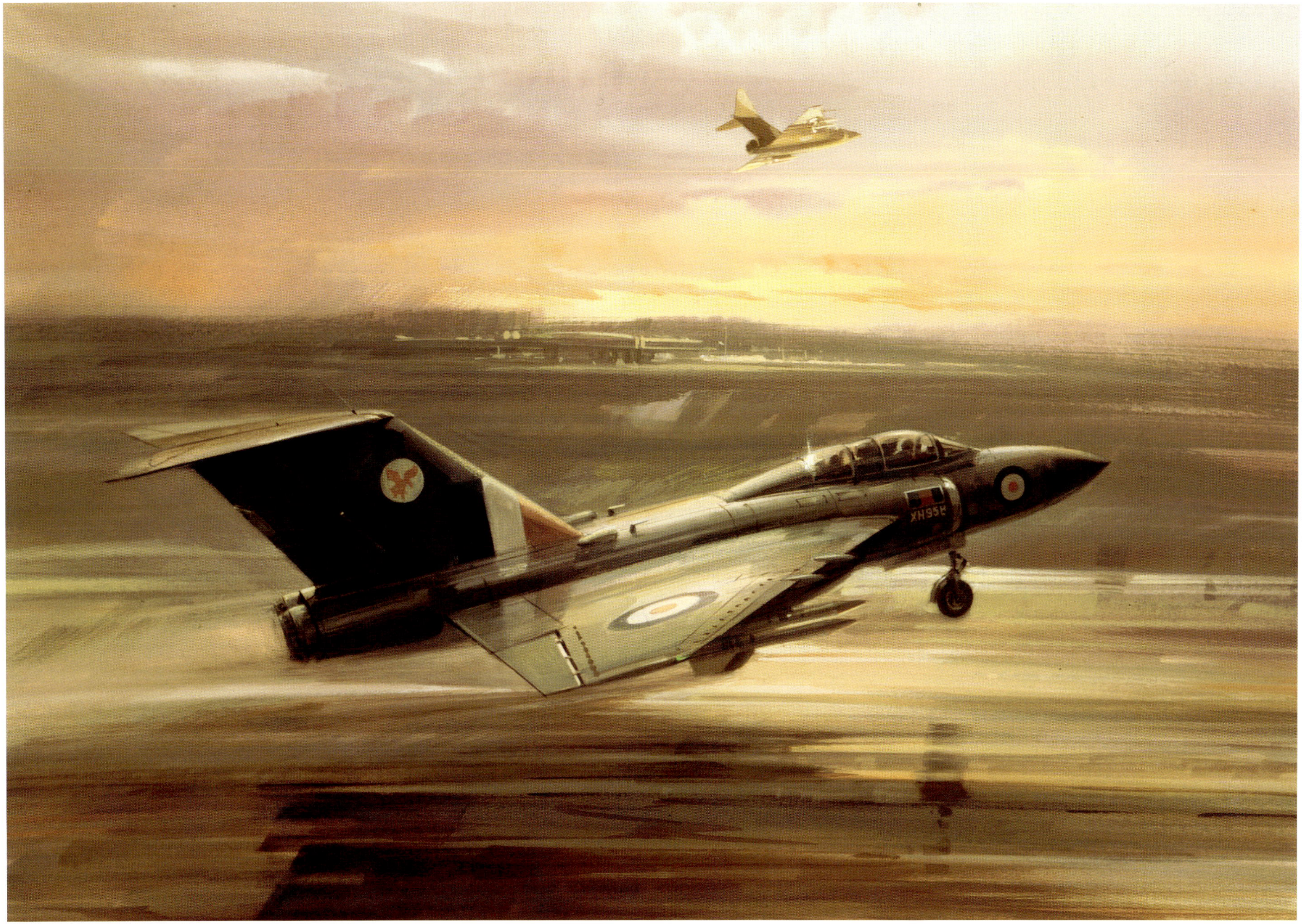

Westland Belvedere

Helicopters, now very much part of the everyday aviation scene, were not used operationally by the RAF until 1945, and even then merely by introducing British-built American designs. The efficacy of the 'chopper' for frontline tactical use became well evident in the Malayan Emergency operations, apart from its widespread use by the USAF in the Korean War; hence British interest was stimulated in several aircraft firms. Bristol's (subsequently taken over by Westland) twin-engined, twin-rotor Belvedere - the first of its class in RAF service - entered squadron usage in late 1961, and was designed to fill several support roles, including trooping, freight supply, and casualty evacuation for ground forces. Capable of lifting some 6,000lb - internally or externally - Belvederes saw widespread action during their eight years' RAF service, operating in Europe, Aden, Africa and in the Far East during the 1962-66 Brunei campaign. Though designed for one-engine reliability if required, the Belvedere's all-round performance was never outstanding, and its squadron crews were never entirely enthusiastic about the type; indeed, several crashes at Aden in 1965 brought the design into dubious repute for a time.

Wing Commander J. R. Dowling, MRE, DFC, AFC had wide experience of the Belvedere. He not only formed the initial Belvedere Trials Unit but also later commanded a helicopter Wing in Borneo

Westland Belvedere *A Belvedere of No 26 Squadron, based in Aden, lifts a 105mm howitzer into position for J Battery, Royal Horse Artillery, during the Radfan operations in South Arabia in 1964. This was both the first twin-rotor helicopter and the first turbine-engined helicopter to enter service in the RAF.*

which included the Belvederes of No 66 Squadron:

"The Belvedere had a number of firsts to its credit. It was the first helicopter specifically ordered to provide tactical support for the Army; it was the first twin rotor helicopter and the first turbine-engine helicopter to come into RAF service.

Basically, the Belvedere was two Sycamore helicopters joined together, back to back. Its twin rotor design meant that it did not have the centre-of-gravity problems that are bound to affect a single rotor helicopter, since such a configuration ensures that there is no residual torque to be corrected and produces a further advantage in that the aircraft is not sensitive to wind direction when it is hovering. In other words, the Belvedere could hover as efficiently cross-wind as into the wind, unlike a tail-rotor helicopter.

Production models of the Belvedere appeared in late 1961, at which point development stopped for financial and other reasons. In fact, the Belvederes which were put into service were described by the designer as mere operational models. Certain mistakes were made, the most tiresome of which concerned the starting system whose unreliability was a major problem. There were also other technical problems, most seriously with those operating in Aden, but in general the aircraft was eminently satisfactory from a flying point of view.

Unfortunately, the Belvedere had a comparatively short lifetime. There was no hard and fast strategic case for having helicopters of that size in long-range support to the Army and short-range support could be adequately dealt with by first the Whirlwind and then the Wessex. Now the RAF has Chinook helicopters, which the Belvedere resembled in many ways. I think the Belvedere came too soon; it was too early for its own good."

Hawker Hunter

The elegant Hunter endeared itself to all who were privileged to fly it. In the words of the distinguished fighter pilot Peter Wykeham: *"The slim fuselage, thin swept-back wings, tailplane and fin, and the delicate balance and proportion of the whole aircraft were the very poetry of motion."* Anyone fortunate enough to have witnessed the breathtaking formation aerobatics of No 111 Squadron's *Black Arrows* in the 1950s, or No 92 Squadron's *Blue Diamonds* in the early 1960s could only agree with that description.

As the RAF's first supersonic operational fighter, the Hunter initially equipped No 43 Squadron in 1954, and became Fighter Command's standard single-seat fighter until being gradually replaced by the English Electric Lightning from 1960 in Britain. Later marks of Hunter continued in front-line service overseas until 1971, playing a major active role in operations in the Middle East and Far East.

Squadron Leader Neville Duke, the wartime fighter pilot who had much to do with the development flying of the original Hunters, has put on record his thoughts: *"For me there is no greater satisfaction than sitting in the cockpit of the Hunter, beautiful in design and construction, representing the thought and skill of so many people, and feeling it respond to the slightest movement of your fingers. It lives and is obedient to your slightest wish."*

From a Service viewpoint, an ex-No 8 Squadron Hunter pilot once remarked: *"When I arrived on the squadron I had some years of fighter experience behind me, but after only one sortie in a Hunter I felt I'd never really flown a fighter before. Its touch was perfect, control a real enjoyment, and manoeuvrability a wonder. I've flown more modern fighters since, but none compare with the superb Hunter."*

Rod Dean, who had 20 years and nearly 3,000 hours of association with the Hunter in the RAF recalls: *"I was sitting on the runway at RAF Chivenor, home of RAF fighter pilots, in Hunter F6 XG131 on 25 November 1964, for my first solo. The Hunter groundschool, four hours in the Hunter 'box' and four hours dual in the T7 had*

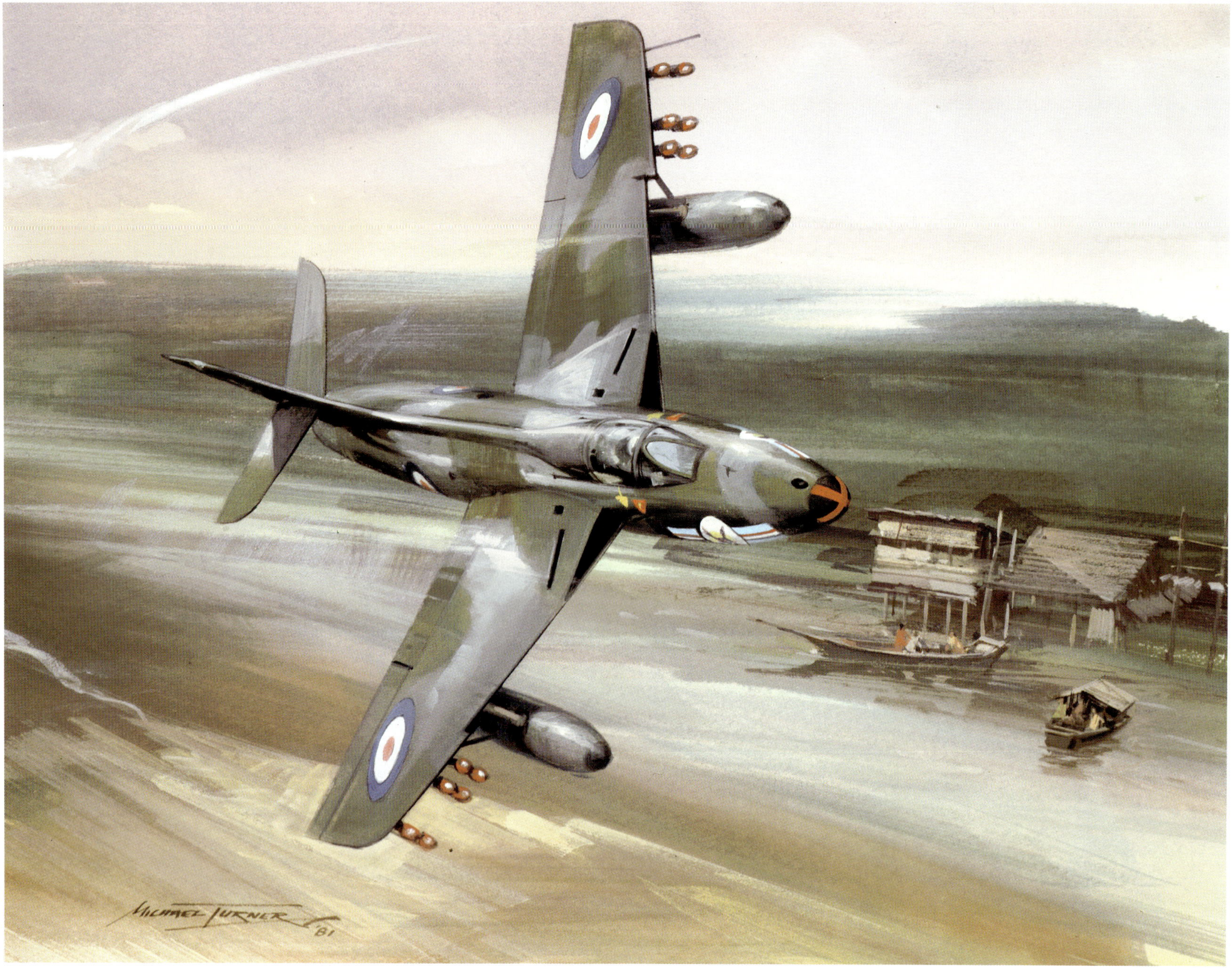
Michael Turner '81

Hawker Hunter *A Hawker Hunter FGA9 from No 20 Squadron, the Far East Air Force, flies past a native settlement in Borneo during the mid-1960s. The Hunter was a superbly versatile combat machine that could be a fighter, bomber or reconnaissance aircraft.*

prepared me for this moment - my first ever flight in a single-seat Hunter. There was no preparation for the noise of 10,000lb of thrust, the view (the T7 was fairly claustrophobic) and the sheer exhilaration of being airborne in one of the best British fighters ever. The low-speed handling was impeccable, with plenty of warning before anything unusual happened."

Westland Whirlwind

The patent success and versatility of the American Sikorsky S-55 helicopter led to its adaptation by the RAF from 1953, retitled as the Westland-built Whirlwind. It also entered service with the Royal Navy, and was progressively modified and improved. Its duties were widely varied: jungle rescue and evacuation, air-sea rescue, communications, troop transport, VIP transport, emergency medical transportation, and a dozen other roles.

The early versions were fitted with piston engines, but replacement of these with turbine powerplants lengthened the useful life of the aeroplane, and added reliability and greater range to its performance. Whirlwinds saw operational service with the RAF during the Borneo confrontation of the 1960s, adding the supply role to its ubiquitous tally of duties; and, in several cases, being converted for use as a gun or missile carrier for low-level strafing sorties.

Apart from its purely military or naval roles, it was a familiar sight to the civil population around Britain's coastline, and in its rescue role has saved the lives of several thousands of holiday-makers and maritime crews in distress.

Flight Lieutenant D. P. Holmyard was a navigator who flew in the Whirlwind on numerous Search and Rescue missions, including those with No 21 Squadron at RAF Manston:

"The Whirlwind had a crew of three: pilot navigator/winch-operator and winch-man. Its radius of action was 90 miles, which allowed it to undertake inshore and coastal missions while the Sea King helicopters performed the longer missions.

The outstanding feature of the helicopter was its precision and manoeuvrability in calm conditions. It could be steered to hover within merely a few inches of movement; that was everything you could want from

Westland Whirlwind *A Whirlwind HAR10 from 'D' Flight, No 22 Squadron based at RAF Manston, Kent on Search and Rescue Duties, picks up a survivor from a stricken yacht. The winchman is lowered by the navigator, who also calls out guidance to the pilot.*

a machine that needed to do precision winching such as is necessary when picking up an injured person from a ship with a lot of rigging lines, or from a cliff with a large overhang. In such a situation the navigator/winch-operator acted as the pilot's eyes, directing him upwards and downwards, backwards and forwards, to the left and right.

The winch-man was lowered, and came off the winch-hook to look after the injured person while the Whirlwind held off, then reconnected himself and the injured person was pulled up and taken back to shore.

The Whirlwind was eventually phased out of Search and Rescue Operations. In time, instead, would be seen flights of Sea King helicopters dotted around the UK in overlapping circles."

Hawker Siddeley Gnat

The Folland-designed Gnat fighter was never adopted by the RAF in its intended role, but its conversion to a two-seat advanced jet trainer was accepted by the service, and the latter version began its service with the Central Flying School (CFS) in early 1962.

The series of small, light, high-performance jet aircraft by Folland began with the Midge fighter which first flew in August 1954, and continued with the Gnat private venture single-seat fighter which made its maiden flight on 18 June 1955.

Capable of becoming supersonic in a shallow dive, the nimble Gnat offered all the necessary handling and flying characteristics of the modern jet interceptor to its pupil crews, and was fully aerobatic at low or high altitudes. This latter quality was never better exemplified than its many public performances with the CFS's formation team, the *Red Arrows* of the 1970s.

Flown in superlative style by instructors from the CFS, the *Arrows* brought the art of formation aerobatics to the peak of perfection, thrilling millions of spectators all over Europe until 1979, when it was superseded by the Hawk.

It was introduced to replace the Vampire T11 as the RAF's standard advanced fighter in Flying Training Command. In 1964 No 4 FTS formed its own aerobatic team with Gnats painted all-yellow and known as *Yellowjacks*.

Considering its power - an ability to reach Mach 0.97 in level flight - yet astonishing manoeuvrability and instant, positive control, it is seldom realised just how relatively small the plane was. Its wings spanned a mere 24ft, while overall length extended to just 31ft and 9in. It stood a mere 10ft 6in off the ground at its maximum height, making it a very compact aeroplane indeed.

When one considers the multi-million pounds' cost of producing a present-day single-seat military jet aircraft, the sheer economy in costs, materials and labour-hours needed to produce a true lightweight, operational interceptor or strike aeroplane - the Gnat's original conception - is still perhaps worthy of attention. Its arrival on the military scene was, perhaps, ill-starred, coming into being at a period of governmental retrenchment in military expenditure.

Sqn Ldr Ray Hanna, member of the original team and founder leader of the *Red Arrows* recalled his early days on the jet trainer: *"The Gnat was the second, maybe third generation jet, with powered controls, swept wings and with all sorts of modern avionics very similar to the*

Hawker Siddeley Gnat *Gnats of the RAF Red Arrows aerobatic team, led by Squadron Leader Ray Hanna, perform at the 1968 Royal Review at RAF Abingdon. This highly manoeuvrable aircraft entered service in 1954 and for more than two decades it was the RAF's standard advanced jet trainer.*

Lightning. My first impressions of the Gnat were just that it was totally delightful, and very, very sensitive after the Meteor. In a sense it was much nicer to fly than, say, the Hunter, and of course the two were always being directly compared. It suffered from lack of thrust over 25,000ft, but low down it had all that was necessary. The low wing loading made it a very manoeuvrable aeroplane, particularly at low altitude, but it did bump around in turbulence. It was a totally delightful aeroplane, and during the five years at the Red Arrows, it never suffered any major failure or major accident."

Avro Shackleton

The value of the four-engined landplane in the long-range maritime role was proved during World War 2 by the use of the American B-17 Flying Fortress and B-24 Liberator with RAF Coastal Command. When these Lend-Lease aircraft were returned to the US the RAF sought a development of the Avro Lincoln. This emerged as the Avro Shackleton, a maritime reconnaissance version of the bomber. This retained the Lincoln's wings and undercarriage, but had a re-designed fuselage and was fitted with four Rolls-Royce Griffon piston engines driving six-bladed contra-rotating propellers.

Early MR1s had a short nose with chin radome, but the MR2 introduced a long streamlined nose and a new type of semi-retractable 'dustbin' radome aft of the wings. After five years in service, the MR3 was introduced which had a nosewheel undercarriage and featured wingtip tanks. To assist take-offs with heavier loads later models were fitted with two Bristol Viper auxiliary turbojets in the outer engine nacelles.

Sergeant Signaller 'Dinty' More AFC remembers that the Shackleton with its large crew requirement engendered 'a great spirit'. He recalls: *"I look back on the Shackleton with great affection. It did not quite have the 'aura' of a Lancaster, but it was more comfortable than a Lincoln. It was noisy, it vibrated, it was draughty, it threw exhaust stubs, its heaters did not work properly, but in its day it was the best anti-submarine aircraft in the world. It had a rest bed, a galley, new radar sonics and you could actually walk around in it."*

With the arrival of the Nimrod MR1 in 1979, Shackletons were withdrawn from service with the maritime reconnaissance squadrons. But this was not the end of its RAF service. Following the demise of the Royal Navy's big aircraft carriers, and with them the Fairey Gannet AEW3s, the RAF assumed the role of providing airborne early warning aircraft to counter low-level intruders probing the UK air defence region. Twelve Shackleton MR2s were converted to AEW2 configuration, with a large radome under the nose. No 8 Squadron was re-formed in 1972 to operate the AEW2s until their replacement with the proposed Nimrod AEW3. The service of this 'stop-gap' aircraft was much longer than planned, after the cancellation of the AEW Nimrod programme. No 8 Squadron's Shackletons remained operational until the Boeing E-3D Sentry AEW1s service début in July 1991.

Avro Shackleton AEW2 *Avro Shackleton AEW2 WL747 'Florence' of No 8 Squadron passes over the Rock of Gibraltar, on detachment from RAF Kinloss, during 1971.*

de Havilland Comet

Internationally famed as the world's first jet-engined commercial airliner, the prototype DH106 Comet first flew on 27 July 1949. The obvious potential for RAF long haul transportation led to modified Comet Series 2 aircraft being introduced to RAF service in July 1956, and No 216 Squadron at RAF Lyneham became the first military jet transport unit in the world the same year.

The Comet 2, modified for service with the RAF, pioneered the use of the pure jet for military transport duties. Transport Command took delivery of 15 Comet C2s from 1956. The first operational flight was made on 23 June 1956 when a Comet flew the Air Minister to Moscow for the Soviet Air Forces day.

In February 1962 the RAF began receiving Mark 4 variants, again via No 216 Squadron, which increased passenger accommodation from 44 to 94, or could be converted to carry 12 stretchers, 47 'sitting patients' and six medical attendants with full medical facilities in a casualty evacuation role. The 4C was the final production version, continuing the stretched fuselage of the 4B with the wings of the 4.

Comets flew emergency services to Malta and Cyprus during the Suez crisis and regular sorties to Australia and Christmas Island in the Pacific. These jets brought the most distant parts of the Commonwealth to within less than two days travelling time from the UK, and the Far East inside 24 hours.

Comet 2s were withdrawn from RAF service in May 1967, and Mark 4s were eventually withdrawn from squadron use on 30 June 1975 with the disbandment of No 216 Squadron. Two units, Nos 51 and 192 Squadrons, flew Comets R1s on signal duties.

BAC Jet Provost

The Hunting Percival Provost of the 1950s was the RAF's ultimate piston-engined standard basic trainer, and from it was developed the BAC Jet Provost in accordance with a contemporary training policy for 'all-through' jet aircraft instruction for embryo RAF pilots. The neat Jet Provost entered service in 1955 and its easy-to-handle characteristics quickly proved popular with instructors and pupils.

Gradually improved and modified, later versions of the Jet Provost formed the equipment of several RAF aerobatic formation teams for public exhibitions and displays in the late 1950s and early 1960s. In late 1969 the final variant, the T5, entered RAF service, having a pressurised cockpit and many of the most modern avionics incorporated. With its maximum speed well in excess of 400mph, and an ability to operate above 35,000ft, the T5 Jet Provost could thus accustom its crews to the demands of modern jet operations. HRH Prince Charles received his advanced flying instruction in a Jet Provost at RAF Cranwell, going solo after just eight hours' dual control.

de Havilland Comet *A de Havilland Comet C4 of No 216 Squadron, on a trooping flight to the Far East from its base at RAF Lyneham.*

Group Captain John Lacock spent several years flying the Jet Provost, and training pilots on it: *"Many of our trainee pilots came from the University Air Squadrons where they had been flying piston-engined Bulldogs, but the Jet Provost was used for basic pilot training since the early sixties and 'ab initio' pilots went straight on to them. The basic course was 150 hours, which took about ten months to complete, before you went on to the advanced trainer Hawk.*

In some ways the jet is an easier plane for young people to come on to than a piston-engined aircraft. When you apply take-off power to a piston engine plane, for instance, it tends to turn sideways and go off the runway, which can be quite difficult for a student to cope with initially. The jet pointing right down the centre line with the thrust light pointing straight forward goes straight down the runway rather than turning. Another problem with earlier trainers was the fuel-induced piston engines. These meant that there was an unpleasant smell that pervaded the cockpit, and the environment for the new student could be very upsetting. Many young people feel a certain amount of travel sickness when they get airborne for the first time and that was accentuated by the smell of gasoline fumes. There are none in the jet, and the Mark 5 had a pressurised cabin, very similar to sitting in a sports car.

It is, like all good training planes, one that handled conventionally and did not spring surprises on the inexperienced pilot.

When we got back to flying after a spell in a desk job, the first thing we did was a refresher course

BAC Jet Provost *The instructors of No 1 Flying Training School, RAF Linton-on-Ouse, Yorkshire indulging in mirror formation practice in 1969.*

in a Jet Provost, and it's something that we all thoroughly enjoyed. Under the old system we used to keep all pilots in current flying practice by closing the office on certain days each month when we would go up; but that was a difficult system to work and made people thoroughly dangerous. Nowadays you are assigned to a squadron for six months at least, and the basic training was then done on a Jet Provost to get your flying skills back to decent speeds before you go on to other planes. So as a result it was plane we all felt a good deal of affection towards."

English Electric (BAC) Lightning

On the introduction of the superb Lightning in 1960, RAF Fighter Command entered a new era, for the Lightning was its first true supersonic fighter. Capable of achieving a speed of Mach 2 in level flight (more than twice the speed of a Hunter), the Lightning was also the real beginning of defensive aircraft that had been designed from the outset as a complete weapons system; this was a radical change from the hitherto design philosophy of producing a fast fighter and then 'adding' its offensive armament.

Designed initially by W. E. W. Petter of the English Electric Company, the Lightning was a bold step into the future; in effect the company had undertaken the design and production of a transonic, operational fighter in a single stage, and the result was a superlative aircraft by any criterion. It was received with acclaim by its RAF pilots: handling was excellent - a pilot's aeroplane - and it packed the necessary punch and urge to tackle any other aircraft in existence then.

In June 1960 the first Lightning squadron, No 74 'Tigers' at RAF Coltishall, received its first examples of the new fighter, and was declared fully operational by early 1961. Thereafter the Lightning became the RAF's standard defensive fighter until well into the 1980s. For the greater part of its long service the Lightning, in most of its many forms, lived up to the succinct opinion of Squadron Leader J. F. G. 'Swazi' Howe who, as commander of No 74 Squadron in 1960-61, flew the first operational example: *"We know that we can catch any current bomber, and...we know that we can outfight any fighter. This knowledge that we have the finest interceptor in the world gives the pilots tremendous confidence."*

One Lightning display pilot recalled his sequence: *"I started the acceleration for the display, but left the reheat until the airfield boundary. Easing down to 250ft, trimming load free at 550kts and lined up with the display axis. Reheat in and wait for the light-up - both lit - good! Reef into a 90 degree bank turn, away from the crowd, to let them hear the roar of the burners and then cancel - airbrakes out to kill the speed and tighten the turn. Hold six degrees until 420kts, then airbrakes in, play the g against speed to arrive pointing at the crowd centre at 380kts. Pull up to the vertical - reheat lit and quarter roll onto the display axis - keep pulling to complete the loop....I looked over my shoulder to see the airfield and reflect on how lucky I am to be paid to do the job!"*

English Electric (BAC) Lightning Lightning interceptors of No 11 Squadron from RAF Binbrook tail chase through storm clouds over Lincolnshire in 1974.

McDonnell Douglas F-4 Phantom

McDonnell Douglas F-4 Phantom *A Phantom FG1 of No 43 Squadron, based a RAF Leuchars, Fife gains height to shepherd a Soviet Tu-20 Bear (top) high above the North Sea.*

The RAF's enforced budget cuts of 1965 and 1968 cancelled orders for the British TSR2 and American F-111 strike aircraft intended to ultimately replace the ageing Javelins and NF Meteors in squadron use, and left the Lightning as the RAF's sole standard interceptor. Accordingly, a previous order for F-4 Phantoms for the Royal Navy was supplemented by orders for more F-4s for the RAF as interim replacements until the Jaguar became available.

The first Phantom arrived in Britain in mid-1968 and by the end of 1969 a total of 168 Phantoms had been delivered for the RAF. Supersonic in speed and capable of lifting up to eight tons of modern offensive armament, the Phantom had already been in use by American air services since 1960, and its employment as a pure fighter in the Vietnam conflict proved relatively successful, with USAF F-4 crews claiming a total of 108 MiG enemy jets shot down.

In RAF service the F-4 was used in two main forms: as a defence interceptor, and as a low-level attack and reconnaissance aircraft.

With the demands on the interceptor fighter after the Falklands conflict, there was a shortage of F-4s with the home-based units. No 74 Squadron was reformed at RAF Wattisham in 1984 and 15 secondhand US Navy F-4Js were purchased, becoming known as F-4J(UK) and retained their General Electric J79 engines. These aircraft remained on strength until 1991.

Following the service entry of the Tornado F3 from 1987, the Phantom was progressively phased out. RAF Germany's last Phantoms, those of Nos 19 and 92 Squadrons at RAF Wildenrath, were finally stood down in January 1992, and the last squadron in the UK, No 74 at Wattisham, retired its Phantom FGR2s the following October.

One pilot wrote: *"When you watch the Phantom take-off, you see its arched nose and down-swept stabilator separated by a bulky midriff that looks as awkward as a goose with drooping tail feathers and a middle-aged spread."* Another was more outspoken: *"When I first saw a Phantom I thought it so ugly I wondered if it had been delivered upside-down."* They all changed their views after it entered service.

Squadron Leader Graham Cullington on the Phantom:
"The Phantom was a relatively easy aeroplane to fly, and indeed I believe that in the United States it was even flown by National Guard pilots, who only flew it at weekends. It was a typically American plane in many respects; for instance, its cockpit was larger than you usually found in a British-designed aeroplane and this undoubtedly helped the pilot's efficiency. Although the Phantom was a heavy aeroplane, and consequently less manoeuvrable than many others, what made it a great air defence aeroplane was its excellent weapons capability. The Phantom's weapon load and radar performance undoubtedly made it one of the world's finest all-round combat aircraft."

Air Chief Marshal Sir John Allison on the handling abilities of the Phantom: *"Before the Tornado was so named its official designation was MRCA, which stood for "Multi-Role Combat Aircraft". Sadly, this laudable design aim was never realised and two very different versions had to be built.*

The irony is that a genuine multi-role fighter was already in Royal Air Force service in considerable numbers. That aircraft, the versatile McDonnell Douglas Phantom, was capable of every role ever conceived for a tactical fighter - classic all weather air defence, air superiority, escort, nuclear strike, conventional bombing, defence suppression and fighter reconnaissance.

The Phantom was not without its drawbacks, of course. Like the Tornado, it was a high wing loader and lacked the agility of present generation fighters. It was also quite challenging to fly.

Its curious shape arose through its genesis from the F101 Voodoo. That aircraft suffered from uncontrollable pitch up if the angle of attack (alpha) limits were exceeded, because of aerodynamic blanking of the tail surfaces. So the designers of the Phantom bent the stabilator (as the Americans call it) dramatically downwards to keep the tips flying in clean air during manoeuvre. That destabilised the machine laterally, for which the fix was the 12 degrees upwards slant of the outboard wing sections. That in turn obliged the designers to use inboard ailerons and spoilers for lateral control. Because the spoilers were largely blanked from the airflow at high alpha, the aircraft suffered more than most from adverse yaw. The Phantom also exhibited a mild degree of dynamic instability in pitch and, to make things worse, gave the pilot very few stick force of positional cues during manoeuvre. These factors in combination, together with oceans of induced drag at high alpha, meant that departure from controlled flight was never very far away in the kind of operational flying demanded, for example, in air combat. The golden rule when needing to roll while pulling was "if it buffets, use your boots". In other words, to retain control, the pilot had to use the secondary effect of rudder and keep the stick centralised.

But for those who mastered her, the Phantom was an immensely capable and enjoyable aircraft to fly. Certainly, no other aeroplane gave me such satisfaction. The Phantom was, in my opinion, the best all round warplane flying anywhere in the world in the 1960s and 1970s and, although eventually superseded by more agile machines, it has held a deserved place in the front line of many reckonable air forces through subsequent decades."

Handley Page Victor

The last of the RAF's trio of V-bombers to fly, the graceful, crescent-winged Victor was incidentally the last Handley Page bomber to be ordered for the RAF. Deriving from the 1946-47 decision by the British government to develop the atomic bomb and a four-jet engined bomber force capable of delivering nuclear weapons, the first prototype Victor made its initial flight in December 1952.

Prolonged trials and testing - including several crashes and crew deaths - resulted in the first operational squadron, No 10 at RAF Cottesmore, only receiving its first Victors from April 1958.

As other units gradually began receiving Victors for the nuclear bomber role, development continued to produce Victors for other tasks; these were chiefly the strategic reconnaissance, or flying camera-ship, role and, by 1965, as in-flight refuelling tankers. From 1964 modified Victors began to be flown in a very low-level bomber role, while adaptability trials were carried out to marry the Victor to the Blue Steel missile. By the close of 1968, however, bomber versions of the aircraft were phased out of squadron service. This left only the high-speed tanker version to continue its vital contribution to the RAF's global flexibility and mobility in a role initially pioneered by Valiants of No 214 Squadron, commanded then by Wing Commander M. J. Beetham (later ACM Sir Michael, Chief of Air Staff), but which from 1965 was taken over by Victors.

Squadron Leader A. Kearney flew Victor tankers for several years. Here he discusses the process of refuelling both from the tanker's and the receiver's viewpoint: *"The role of the Victor tanker changed over the years. Its primary role in the 1960s was that of strategic deployment: we would take people out to Singapore three or four times a year and we also did some work with the Navy. In recent years, though, the emphasis has completely changed. Deployments then became a secondary feature, instead the primary role of the tanker in a tactical sense became to refuel the aeroplanes of UK air defence or maritime air defence.*

Handley Page Victor *A Victor K2 Tanker from No 57 Squadron extends its fuel hoses to refuel a Lightning of No 5 Squadron. Lightnings normally refuelled at altitudes above 30,000ft, which is significantly higher than more modern aircraft.*

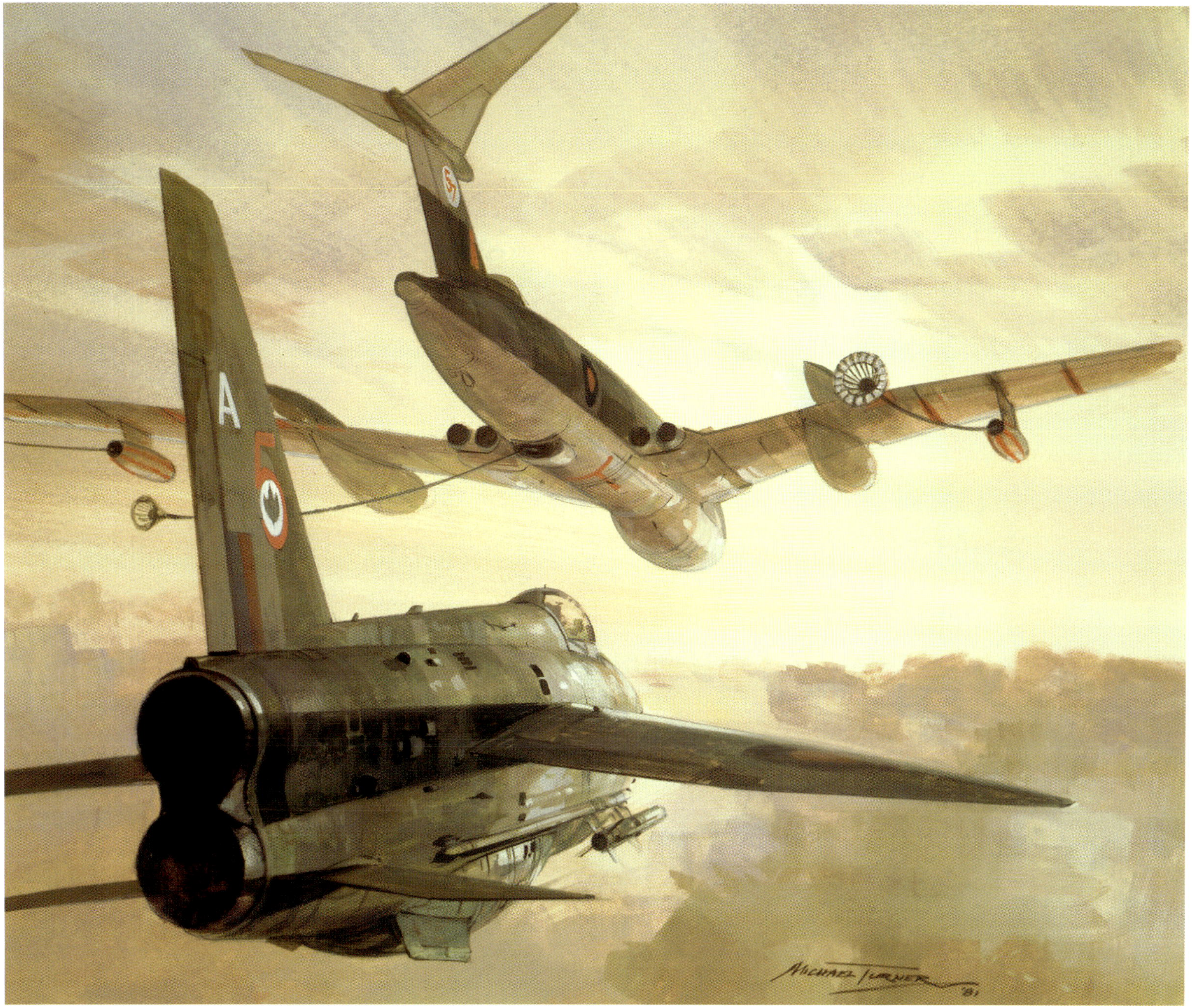
A
MICHAEL TURNER
'81

The aim of the tanker pilot is to make a rendezvous, get on a tow line and give as much fuel as possible to the receiver. Most refuelling takes place at altitudes in the mid-twenties (such as at 25,000ft) although some of the newer aircraft prefer to be lower at about 20,000ft. The Lightning performed best in the mid-30s, but that was exceptional; that altitude was good in terms of ordinary deployment but would be a little more vulnerable during hostilities. In close formation where one Victor was refuelling fighters, then the fighters had to manoeuvre while the Victor maintained position. However, we regularly had three or four Victors in formation perhaps joining up with a flight of Phantoms, and for that situation the Victor pilots were quite skilled in formation flying.

Refuelling is fairly simple for a tanker. It's a crew effort in terms of getting to the rendezvous and bringing the aircraft together, but once this has occurred it becomes a very passive manoeuvre from the tanker's point of view. Hoses are trailed and the receiver comes in to make contact. The tankers do day and night refuelling, and the latter is probably the most demanding task for any pilot in the tanker force.

To refuel, the receiver has to fly in very close formation, which is quite difficult in a large aeroplane, get in very close into a stabilised position 8-20ft behind the centre hose and make that final contact. In daytime there are visual cues; the markings that run across the wings are a help initially and the pilot can see the hose and orientate himself to the aeroplane and to the horizon.

At night most of the visual cues are gone. All that remain are the centre-line lighting where the hose leaves the aircraft and the hose itself. The procedure is carried out purely by sight and, because there is no visible horizon, there can be a mild sense of disorientation. In practical terms, if you are in current receiver practice, by day you should make contact within four attempts - I would say that at night this number is probably doubled."

During the Falklands conflict, Victor K2s made an outstanding contribution to the success of the campaign - tanking the 'Black Buck' Vulcans and other aircraft in the South Atlantic. Their final call came in the Gulf campaign of 1991, prior to being retired at the end of 1993.

English Electric Canberra

English Electric Canberra *A Canberra B2, serving with No 231 OCU up from Wyton in 1989, enjoys clear sky above a cloud covered East Anglia.*

The sleek and deceptively slim contours of the Canberra tended to hide the fact that besides being Britain's and the RAF's first jet bomber, it proved to be one of the most versatile and adaptable aircraft designs in the annals of aeronautical history. Designed to a 1945 Air Ministry specification, the prototype first flew in May 1949, and began to re-equip RAF squadrons from May 1951. With an internally-stowed bomb capacity for up to 6,000lb, and speeds well in excess of 500mph, the Canberra inaugurated a new era in British bombers. Since that time the development potential of the basic design has been exemplified by a proliferation of variants: a ground attack, photo-reconnaissance, nightfighter, radar and ECM dual trainer, target tug, crewless 'drone', night interdiction - these were merely the major roles undertaken by Canberras over the years. Canberra crews became the first to operate jet bombers in the Far East, flying anti-terrorist bombing sorties in Malaya; while the Suez Crisis in 1956 saw Canberras used as strike bombers against Egyptian airfields and installations.

Long-range overseas flights were undertaken without problems by various Canberra formations during the early 1950s, and individual machines set up fresh speed records for such items as trans-Atlantic double flights.

Bomber Canberras were finally phased out

of first-line use by the end of 1961, but PR versions are still in service in 2003. In all, some 40 RAF squadrons flew Canberras at some period of the design's outstanding life during which a grand total of 27 Marks of this long-lived and versatile aircraft were built.

Wing Commander Colin Adams has described the photo-reconnaissance work of the Canberra:

"The Canberra PR7, and subsequently the PR9, was the backbone of the photo-reconnaissance force, with squadrons in the UK, Germany, Malta, Cyprus and the Far East. But the plane really came into its own during the Borneo confrontation. The plane was originally designed for high-level reconnaissance with a set of six cameras for vertical work, but it could also do oblique and low-level work. Normally in the Canberra the navigator takes the pictures lying in the nose, where there is a sight for him. He has to be very accurate, particularly for mapping work where you have to get the photos overlapping to complete the picture. Some of the early versions had an extra navigator taking pictures out of the back of the plane, as the pilot cannot see behind him.

The surveying work was used for all sorts of purposes. Some squadrons were for reconnaissance on the battlefield, photographing troop movements and military installations. But I have done many other jobs too. In England I have done tasks for the Ministry of Housing and local government, surveying potential sites for new towns in West Sussex - which rather horrified me as I come from around there - and photographing the approach roads into London to

English Electric Canberra *An English Electric Canberra B(1)8, on detachment with No 59 Squadron in Cyprus, flies low over the moonlit castle at Kyrenia.*

work out traffic patterns and establish where to put new roads. Often we would do a job for the local government when we've finished our military task. In Trinidad we were doing a survey of the island, and the government also asked us for some pictures of the harbour to help build a new harbour wall; and while I was doing a complete mapping survey of the New Hebrides there was a boat lost and I sent the Canberra out to find it. I've used the Canberra to photograph aircraft accidents and train crashes. Photo-reconnaissance is one of the most fascinating roles in the RAF, as a result; you can visit a lot of interesting places and you can actually see what you have achieved.

The Canberra is now an old plane. Photo-reconnaissance has never had such an important role as it had in the Second World War; the Canberra was going to be replaced by the TSR2 before that was scrapped. Many of the surveying jobs can now be carried out rather better by satellite, which can give higher resolution pictures. But many countries can't afford to pay for a satellite survey, and if there is a Canberra there, they still got us to do the surveys for them."

The photo-reconnaissance versions have been particularly long-serving, becoming the last variant to remain in front-line use with the RAF. In the last decade they have been used operationally over the Gulf, Bosnia and other parts of the Balkans, Afghanistan and - in 2003, Iraq - on UN intelligence-gathering sorties.

Hawker Siddeley Buccaneer

The rapid development of radar for detection of enemy aircraft - the prime ingredient of the RAF's struggle in 1940 and in subsequent night operations over Britain and Germany - led logically to urgent considerations in the post-1945 RAF to aircraft capable of penetrating enemy territory under the existing radar defence systems.

The Buccaneer, originally designed and developed by Blackburn, was the first RAF aeroplane specifically designed for such a task - ultra low-level sorties deep into hostile countries to avoid any radar 'umbrella'. It was originally conceived for naval carrier operations and equipment of RN units commenced in 1961.

In 1968, with the cancellation of contracts for re-equipping RAF squadrons with the swing-wing F-111, however, orders were placed for Buccaneers to fill the gap in the RAF's front-line units, and these began reaching RAF squadrons from late in 1969. At speeds approaching Mach 0.85, Buccaneers in their prime role usually flew at less than 200ft altitude, literally hugging the terrain in any attack approach. Actual flying, navigation and eventual target acquisition relied almost entirely on highly sophisticated black box instrumentation, radar, television guidance and predicted flying patterns for operations.

The aircraft's structure was specially strengthened to withstand the inevitable buffeting, stresses and fatigue of 'grass-cutting' altitude flying; while low altitude manoeuvrability was reported as excellent.

Stan Hodgkins of No 208 Squadron (1977-1980): " 'Measured with a micrometer, drawn with chalk and hewn with an axe'. This was the nature of the beast as it was explained to us when we were introduced to the Buccaneer on day one at 237 OCU.

Eight of us, the whole course, were at the time standing on the roundel near the port wingtip looking with awe at the rest of the mighty 'banana jet'. The surface beneath our feet did indeed feel as if it was carved from solid steel. The other striking feature as we looked across was that there was not a single straight line on the fuselage - it was all voluptuous curves and bulges. It occurred to me that if Rubens had lived in our times he would have had to have painted the Bucc!

'To be empowered' is often heard these days but unless you have been on board a Buccaneer fast and low, about its normal business, you can't really know the

Hawker Siddeley Buccaneer *A Buccaneer S2B from 237 OCU, RAF Honington builds up a condensation barrier on a fast low-level run off the East Coast. The Buccaneer functioned as both a low-level strike and reconnaissance aircraft.*

meaning of the expression. One just felt unstoppable and part of a hugely capable weapon. With its combination of long range, superb handling at low level and with a heavy weapons load (mostly internal and therefore drag-free), it could deliver a big punch deep into enemy territory.

Of course it had shortcomings - no defensive armament for one, but if we kept our nerve and stayed 'in the weeds' at maximum speed, no fighter or missile could get a bead on us in those days and the bad guy ran out of gas and we could slow down to our 'normal' cruise speed of 420 knots.

The Buccaneer's other great lack was a modern navigation system and here I must pay the greatest respect to those top men - the back-seaters - they were the reason why the Bucc was so effective. I am sure all the best navigators and observers were sent to Buccaneers. From the pilot's point of view I can only marvel at the precision of navigation and co-ordination they achieved as they sat in that 'ergonomic slum' of a back seat, equipped only with a map and stopwatch - all this normally in a radio-silent environment. Also, unlike the all singing Jaguar our nav-kit didn't 'dump' just when it was needed!"

An RAF Buccaneer pilot from the 'Desert Pirates' said: "Of all the RAF elements in Desert Storm in 1991 the Buccaneer force proved the most vital and the fastest to respond. Without the help of a 33-year old bomber - more at home skimming the cold waters between the UK and Iceland than at medium altitude over Iraq's arid wastes - Tornados would have spent the war scattering 454kg (1,000lb) *bombs only slightly more accurate than did Lancasters in World War II. Buccaneers allowed the Tornado force to regain the accuracy of attack lost when missions were transferred to above 20,000ft to evade SAMs and AAA surrounding targets. Like many aircraft in the war, the aged Buccaneer was fighting its last campaign."*

The last Buccaneer was retired from RAF service in April 1994.

Lockheed Hercules

With the drastic reduction in Britain's overseas territories and commitments overseas following World War Two, the crucial need for mobility of the much-reduced RAF's potential striking force and of the army provided a much greater requirement for large, long-range aircraft capable of transporting troops and supplies over vast distances at very short notice. Interim designs such as the Hastings and Beverley filled the medium range role in this context, followed by the Argosy in the 1950s and 1960s.

To supplement these air carriers, the RAF purchased a fleet of 66 of the giant American Lockheed Hercules tactical transport - known to its USAF crews as the 'Herk' or 'Herky-Bird'- but in the RAF as 'Fat Albert'. Able to lift almost 100 passengers and kit over ranges up to 4,700 miles, the Hercules first joined No 36 Squadron at RAF Lyneham in August 1967 (11 years after its original acceptance by the USAF). Within a year, four more RAF squadrons were declared operational on the Hercules, including No 48 Squadron based at Singapore.

Powered by four Allison turbo-prop engines, a loaded Hercules can accomplish a cruising speed of nearly 370mph. Despite its size - its wings spanned nearly 133ft, and fuselage length was almost 100ft - the Hercules was relatively simple to operate and handle.

The new generation C-130J Hercules has now entered service with the RAF and has a new 'glass' cockpit, head-up displays, much improved avionics and Allison AE2100 turboprops driving scythe-shaped, six-bladed propellers.

Wing Commander Tony Webb AFC, who took part in Operation *Agila* recounted some of his experiences of flying the Hercules in the former Rhodesia: *"The operation lasted for over three months and Operation* Agila *provided an outstanding example of the adaptability of the Hercules. The confidence in the aircraft and the remarkable resilience it gave to crews is a tribute to Lockheed's excellent aeroplane. Other aspects of reliability were underlined by the astonishingly high success of the daily programme."*

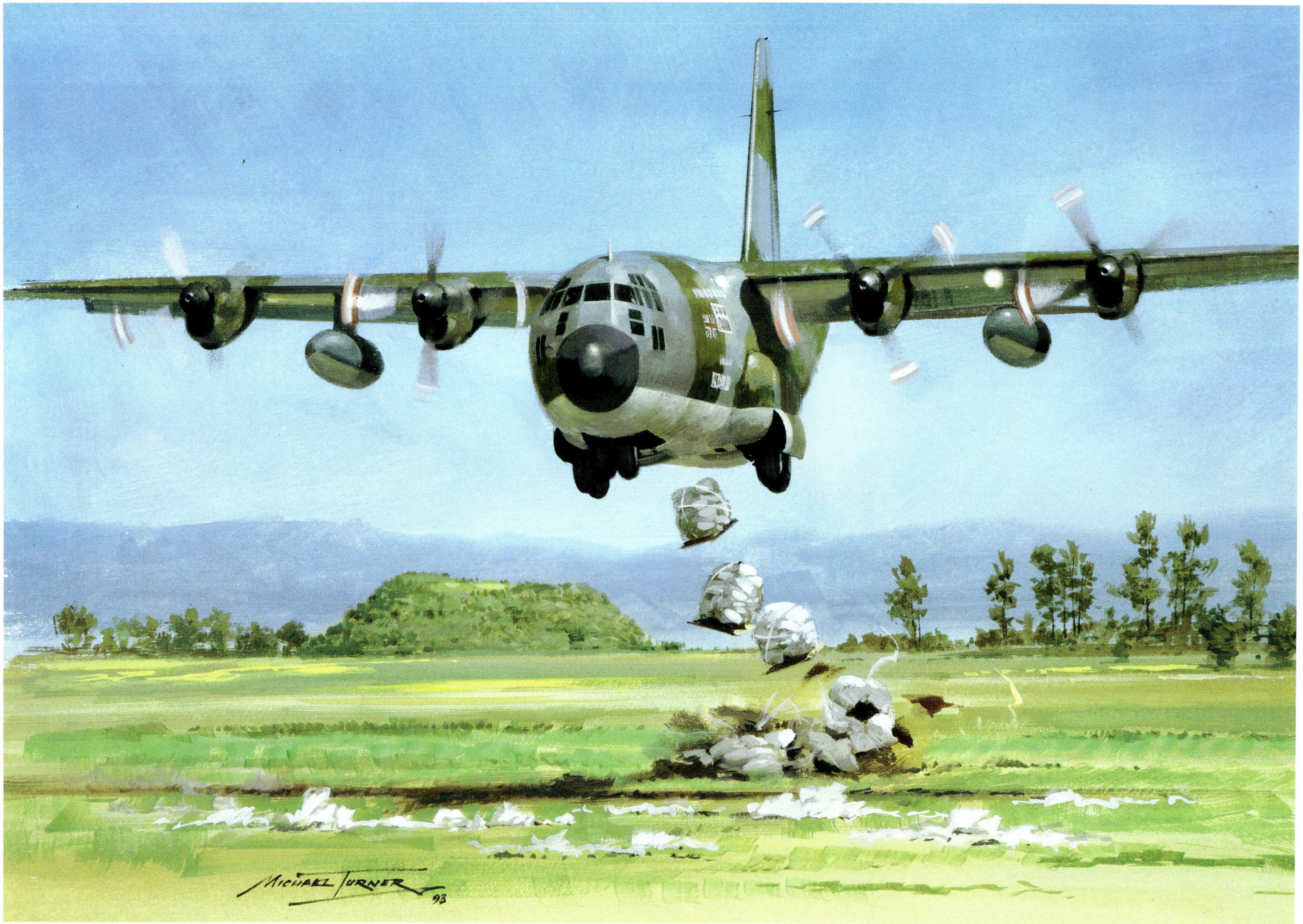
MICHAEL TURNER
93

Hawker Siddeley Nimrod

One of the longest serving front-line RAF types, the Nimrod long-range maritime reconnaissance aircraft has been operational since July 1970. It was the first land-based four-jet maritime reconnaissance aircraft to enter service in any of the world's air forces, and reflected the very latest concepts in anti-submarine warfare. Developed from the de Havilland Comet airliner, the Nimrod was designed to replace the Avro Shackleton. A weapons pannier was added beneath the cabin, giving a distinctive 'double bubble' cross section which necessitated an increase in fin area. A magnetic anomaly detector (MAD) 'stinger' was added to the tailcone, a search radar to the nose and a fin-top radar to house ESM equipment.

Originally the Nimrod MR1 equipped five squadrons in the UK and one based in Malta. The British withdrawal from Malta rendered these eight surplus, and some were used for the abortive AEW3 programme in the 1980s.

In the mid-1970s the initial MR1 versions began to be upgraded to MR2 standard, with much enhanced electronics and the addition of in-flight refuelling probes. The Falklands War resulted in underwing hardpoints being used by front-line Nimrods for the first time, carrying AIM-9 Sidewinders. Wingtip Loral ESM pods were also added.

Nimrods played an important part in the

Hawker Siddeley Nimrod *A Nimrod MR2 from RAF Kinloss overflies a Russian nuclear submarine on the surface in the North Atlantic, during its vital surveillance of the Iceland/United Kingdom Gap in the late 1980s.*

Lockheed Hercules *A Lockheed C-130K Hercules from No 74 Squadron making a supply drop in 1985 during the Ethiopian famine relief operations.*

Falklands conflict and in Gulf operations from 1990 onwards.

Squadron Leader Tony Cowan described a long-range sortie from Ascension Island during the Falklands conflict: *"On 15 May 1982, we took off in Nimrod MR2 XV232 and No 201 Squadron crew 7 at 0857hrs for a flight which lasted 19 hours and five minutes, extensive cloud having prevented the use of satellite-derived information. We flew south to a point 150 miles north of Port Stanley and then west until approximately 60 miles off the Argentine coast. XV232 then tracked north-east at between 7,000ft and 12,000ft, parallel with the coast and its Searchwater radar was used to survey a strip 400 miles wide and 1,000 miles long, confirming that all Argentine warships were still successfully blockaded in port by the threat of British nuclear-powered submarines. It was a fine day and the aircraft was vulnerable during some segments of that flight, but the Nimrod was successfully recovered to Wideawake without incident after a total of three air-to-air refuellings and having travelled 8,300 miles. This was the longest sortie by any aircraft during Operation Corporate and one of the longest RAF missions of all time."*

Currently three squadrons of Nimrod MR2s are based at RAF Kinloss in Scotland. A number of Nimrods are being converted by BAE Systems into the MR4 version with new wings and engines.

Hawker Siddeley (BAe) Harrier GR1 and GR3

The conception of vertical flight ability is hardly new, but its application to the aeroplane in the military context was only truly exemplified successfully over 40 years ago, when the Hawker P1127 first demonstrated vertical take-off and hover, or V/STOL as it was termed. Final development of the P1127 resulted in the Kestrel fighter - the first jet V/STOL aircraft put into RAF service. A supersonic development of the Kestrel was planned, then cancelled by governmental order, and instead a subsonic variant was progressed as a ground-attack fighter for the RAF, in the Harrier. Similar in appearance to the Kestrel, nevertheless the Harrier was virtually a completely new project with only some 5% of components common to both designs.

First to convert to the operational Harrier were the pilots of No 1 Squadron RAF in mid-1969, and initial reaction to this highly unorthodox fighter may be summed in the description given by one of those No 1 Squadron pilots: *"The Harrier seemed at first sight to be almost deformed. Her squat bulbous fuselage crouched over a set of wheels like a broody hen on the nest... the whole aeroplane seen from afar when approaching to land strongly resembled some sort of flying ant... yet she breathed that indefinable sense of power. Her hunch-backed shape seemed to exude a threat to pounce on anyone foolish enough to walk by and ignore her. The cockpit was snug, and festooned in admirable logic with a multitude of miniature gauges, switches, lights and levers."*

Apart from its upward take-off and hover capability, the Harrier handled well in the conventional performance envelope at up to near-Mach 1 speeds; while in its later forms it carries formidable armament, and adds a new dimension to tactical air warfare over land or at sea.

According to Air Vice-Marshal Hine, who commanded the RAF Harrier

Corps in Germany in 1974-75: *"The Harrier is virtually unique, as the only plane to combine the characteristics of the high-performance ground-attack jet with the capabilities of the helicopter. The particular advantage of this is that instead of being confined to a vulnerable main airfield, we have been able to develop the concept of the 'dispersed site operations', with only six or eight aircraft at each site, hidden in a wood. The plane can take off and land on fields of hard grass, or on two or three hundred metres of straight road. As well as the safety advantage, this can mean that the Harrier can be used well forward in support of ground forces, maybe only ten minutes away from where operations are taking place, whereas the nearest airfield may be 25 minutes away. The result is you can do many more sorties in the course of a day than with a conventional aircraft; so that even if the Harrier does not carry as large a payload as a conventional plane, the number of weapons on target in a day can be higher.*

There are a number of reasons why no other country has yet successfully developed a V/STOL aircraft. The first is that many people think that the dispersed site operations are too complex logistically. That is not really true, especially if the site is within 20 miles or so of a main base; the equipment required to maintain a Harrier force in Germany for instance was considerably less than the Army required for an armoured regiment. Another criticism is the Harrier's relatively short range and small weapon capacity. But that is not a criticism of the V/STOL concept itself, and the Harrier is very much a first-generation V/STOL plane. I'm sure that future designs will overcome these limitations, especially as the vertical take-off capacity is of much less importance than the vertical landing, which is essential to get the plane hidden quickly. And perhaps another reason is the not-invented-here syndrome.

The bulk of the Harrier's flying is done at very low levels. You can get a pretty rough ride of course but it is a very safe plane. This is borne out by the

Hawker Siddeley (BAe) Harrier *A Harrier GR1 takes off from a dispersed site in winter. This was the first vertical take-off plane to enter RAF service, which it did in 1969, and was certainly the forerunner of numerous similar aircraft.*

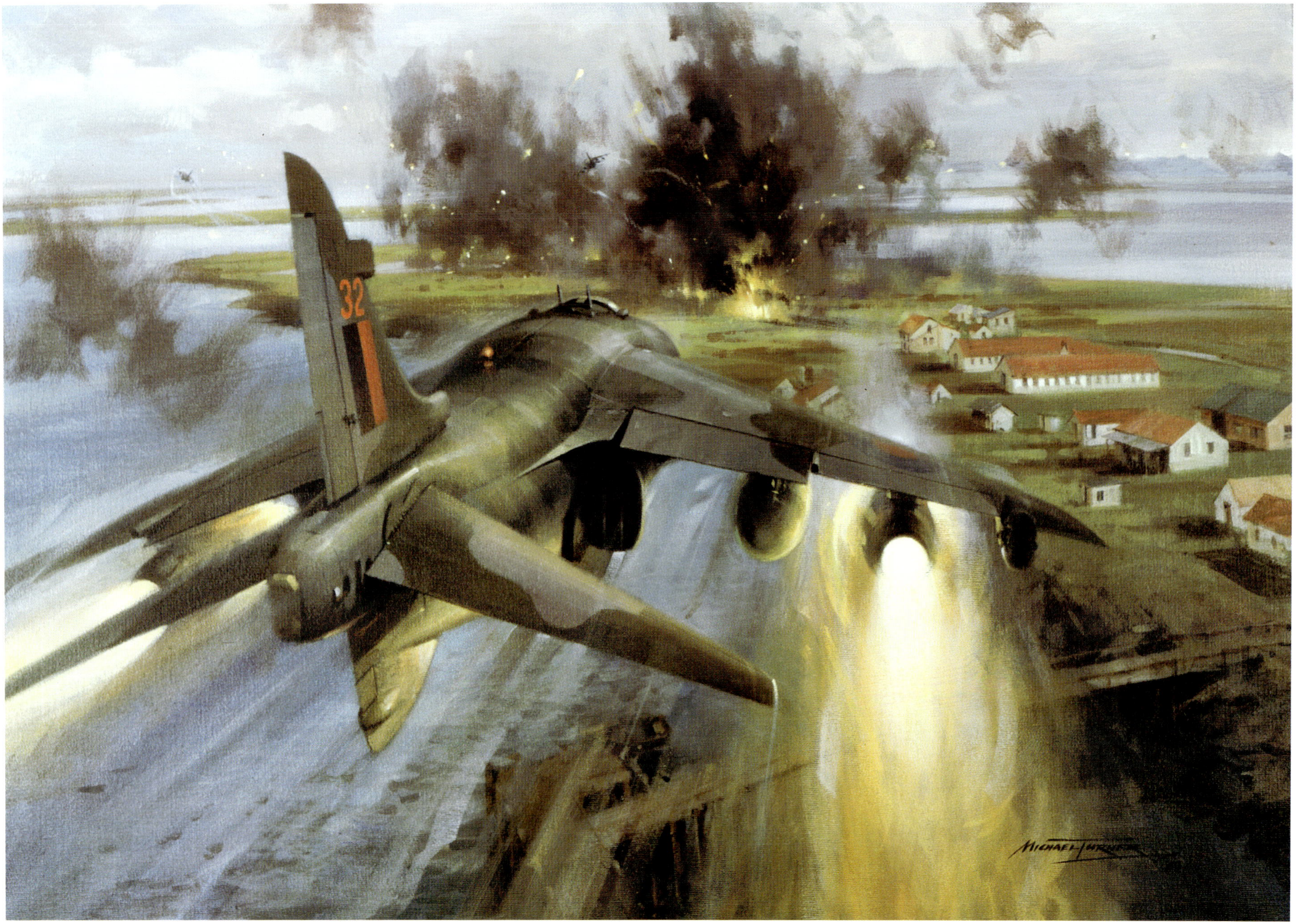
32
MICHAEL TURNER

Hawker Siddeley (BAe) Harrier *Harrier GR3s of No 1 Squadron making a low level strike at Goose Green during the Falklands campaign.*

fact that we teach people to fly a Harrier in all its modes in 21 sorties only, a total of 13 hours. It's extremely exhilarating to be flying at 250ft at 550kts one moment, and then, literally in the space of ten miles to slow down to the hover and land on a 50- or 70-foot square metal pad in the corner of a field and 30 seconds later to be inside the wood in a hide being turned round. The V/STOL capability gives the Harrier another unique feature, in its turning performance.

Though in normal flight it is very similar to other conventional aircraft, you can vector the nozzles to increase your rate of turn, and alter the angle of attack in the aircraft in combat. You can literally make the Harrier turn a corner using thrust vector acting in a centripetal sense. This feature enables the Harrier to survive in combat against the aircraft of an inherently much better performance. The real payoff comes at lower speeds when the conventional planes begin to run out of lift and the rate of turn falls off markedly, while you can move the Harrier about on its axis. And so you can bring guns to bear, even at very low speeds, which would be impossible for conventional aircraft."

Avro Vulcan

The doyen of the RAF's trio of V-bombers, the delta-wing Vulcan was ordered into quantity production before the first prototype had even flown. First to equip with the type was No 83 Squadron in July 1957, followed by No 101 Squadron in October of the same year. Third to receive Vulcans was the much-publicised No 617 Squadron, in May 1958. The early B1 versions could carry a bomb load of 21,000lb with ease, and general handling and maintenance was found to be surprisingly conventional considering the design's unconventional appearance.

Designed by Roy Chadwick, the Vulcan was the world's first delta-wing heavy bomber. The Vulcan nicknamed 'Aluminium Overcast', was a bold design, which in service ably met the RAF's changing operational requirements for nearly 30 years. Forming a key part of Britain's nuclear deterrent throughout much of the Cold War, four Vulcans were kept at immediate readiness to be airborne in two minutes from the start of the engines,

Avro Vulcan *A Vulcan B2 of No 617 Squadron from RAF Scampton passes over Fylingdales Early-Warning Radar Station in 1975.*

at each operational base.

After some three years extensive RAF use on global flights and weapon-testing, the B1 was gradually superseded by the larger, better-powered B2 versions commencing in 1960. The B2 offered superior high-altitude performance and extended range (some 4,600 miles without refuelling) and became the main vehicle for the 'stand-off' bomb/missile technique then being used by RAF Bomber Command, particularly with the Blue Steel missile. From 1966 Vulcan B2s were further modified to undertake ground hugging penetration roles, and three years later the Blue Steel partner was withdrawn, leaving the aircraft with conventional war loads. From the early 1970s Vulcans replaced Victors in the strategic reconnaissance (SR) role.

With replacement by the Tornado GR1 imminent, the Vulcan force was due to disband in 1982 - however, as is now legendary, the Falklands War halted these plans. The extraordinary Black Buck operations on ultra long-range strikes on the Falklands, refuelled by Victor tankers from Ascension Island, gave the bomber its first actual taste of combat.

During the Falklands conflict six Vulcans were converted as air refuelling tankers and were flown by No 50 Squadron - the last RAF unit to operate the Vulcan when these K2s were withdrawn in March 1984.

Group Captain John Lacock on the Vulcan: *"I first became involved with Vulcan operations in 1968 when stationed at Goose Bay in Labrador, and a year later joined No 44 Squadron at RAF*

Waddington, which also operated Vulcans. The aircraft had the dual capability of carrying both conventional and nuclear weapons, and it also performed strategic, or maritime, reconnaissance duties on No 27 Squadron. The wonderful thing about the aeroplane was that it was designed to operate as a high-altitude weapons system, but because of the improvements in surface-to-air systems in its lifetime it was forced into use in the low-level role, which was a much more demanding physical regime for an aircraft, and adapted to this role extremely successfully.

The mark of a 'thoroughbred' aeroplane, such as the Vulcan, is flexibility in the basic design that allowed improvements to the performance of the various parts of the aircraft over the years, especially the engines and electronic systems. In the 1960s, the Vulcan was re-equipped with uprated engines to allow the aeroplane to carry the weight of the forthcoming Skybolt missile, the successor to Blue Steel. The missile was cancelled, but the Vulcan crews have had the benefit for well over a decade of engines capable of producing much more power than the aircraft normally needed to carry out its basic role on the squadrons, which is an appreciable safety factor.

The Vulcan was definitely a 'pilot's aeroplane' - I have never yet encountered an RAF pilot who disliked flying it. It was possibly the most spectacular airframe as a display vehicle for the RAF that we have ever had, and is certainly the only large delta wing aircraft that stood the test of time as a display vehicle"

Scottish Aviation (BAe) Bulldog *The Duke of Kent takes a flight with Flight Lieutenant Ian Lawrence while on a visit to the University of Oxford Air Squadron, at RAF Abingdon on 27 June 1979.*

Scottish Aviation (BAe) Bulldog

Originally designed and built by the now-defunct Beagle Aircraft company, whose first example made its initial flight in May 1969, the diminutive piston-engined two-seat Bulldog was taken over by Scottish Aviation for export production but was ordered for the RAF in 1972. Entering RAF service from April 1973, the Bulldog replaced the Chipmunk as the standard 'ab initio' trainer for embryo pilots prior to jet instructional machines. Fully aerobatic, with ample modern instrumentation, the aircraft provided a near-ideal introduction to Service flying. By the close of 1975 Bulldogs were the full equipment of all the University Air Squadrons, thereby enabling would-be Service graduates to prepare for their future career.

Squadron Leader H. Harvey, MA discusses the Bulldog:

"The Scottish Aviation Bulldog was widely used in the Services as a basic trainer, both by the Royal Navy and, more widely, by the Royal Air Force with the 16 University Air Squadrons. At RAF Abingdon there were two University Air Squadrons, that of London which had nine aircraft with eight instructors and about 80 students, and Oxford with four aircraft, four instructors and 33 students.

We found the Bulldog ideal for training novice pilots. They were reasonably sturdy and resilient with a good record of serviceability although they did have a few teething troubles initially. With a fuel capacity of 32 gallons the Bulldog had a range of over 300 nautical miles at its cruising speed of 120 knots which afforded a wide scope for student cross country flights. In fact I never knew a situation where anyone was embarrassed for fuel, whereas on the Chipmunk, which the Bulldog replaced, this did sometimes occur.

One feature we lacked on the aircraft was navigation aids. This did present a challenge to the instructors when flying above total cloud cover.

The students, most of whom had never flown an aircraft before coming to us, attended for flying training once a week during term time. With occasional extra sessions they could reach 35 hours in a year by which time they were ready for their Basic Handling Test. Apart from normal aircraft handling they were proficient enough to perform stalling, spinning and the basic aerobatics. One feature of the Bulldog was that it requires positive spin recovery action which, in a training aircraft was, in my view, a very worthwhile facet. It was also cleared for the full spectrum of aerobatics but, because our aircraft engines were not fitted with the inverted oil system, we were not cleared for sustained inverted flight for more than eight seconds.

By the end of their second year our students were competent at instrument flying and cross country navigation, and the few who completed a third year learned formation flying and had a basic grounding on low level navigation. We found that at this stage there was little left in the Bulldog to stretch the student pilot who was then ready for the greater demands of the Jet Provost at RAFC Cranwell."

The Bulldog was replaced by the Grob Tutor in the late 1990s.

Hawker Siddeley (BAe) Hawk

The most successful modern, two-seat, advanced jet trainer produced in western Europe, the Hawk has gone on, in its second generation, to become an equally successful weapons platform. The original ideas included the importance of a baseline for the aircraft's development. Subsequent perseverance by engineers and marketeers, demonstrations by test pilots and RAF pilots, has resulted in 16 world air arms operating the Hawk today.

In a bid to rationalise all pre-operational training within the RAF, the tandem, two-seat, multi-purpose jet trainer Hawk was designed to replace the Gnat, Hunter and Jet Provost in most aspects. With a maximum speed approaching 600mph, and built-in provision for fitting bombs, guns and missiles, the Hawk offers a package deal for all stages of jet instruction to future squadron crews. The design first entered RAF service in mid-1977 at No 4 FTS, RAF Valley and at CFS. Its high-placed rear seat for an instructor permits an excellent field of vision, while the all-round performance of the Hawk gives the student pilot unsurpassed grounding in his future trade.

Hawks have also formed the equipment of the RAF's premier aerobatic and exhibition formation team, the *Red Arrows*, since 1979 exemplifying not only the supreme skill and precision of the team's crews but demonstrating the agility and exacting control responses inherent in the Hawk. The red-

Hawker Siddeley (BAe) Hawk *A Hawk T1A from No 234 Squadron lets loose a salvo of SNEB rockets on the Pembrey Range off the coast of Dyfed.*

painted aircraft, with their eye-catching smoke, have entertained airshow audiences in Britain and across Europe, North America and the Middle East on countless occasions. The team has consistently demonstrated the high qualities of the Hawk wherever they have displayed. This highly visual promotion of the aircraft has undoubtably assisted the manufacturer in securing overseas interest and sales.

In its service career, the Hawk has fulfilled - and in many cases exceeded - the objectives of the design team. The aircraft has proved to be a safe, rugged, reliable and highly adaptable and to date has over 750,000 flying hours with the RAF. As for adaptability and mission flexibility the Hawk's service record speaks for itself. Having begun life as an advanced flying and weapons training aircraft, it was soon adapted for display flying with the *Red Arrows.*

In addition to its tactical weapons training role, the TWU Hawks were given a front-line role and allocated to 'shadow squadrons' that would, in times of crisis, be capable of carrying out limited combat missions. Originally, the aircraft operated restricted ground attack missions but the decision was taken in 1980 to extend this role to include a limited air defence capability. Between 1983 and 1986, 88 Hawks T1s, including the aircraft flown by the *Red Arrows,* were modified by BAE SYSTEMS to carry AIM-9 Sidewinders air-to-air missiles, for close air defence of vital assets such as airfields and radar installations.

Squadron Leader Brian Hoskins, once the leader of the *Red Arrows,* has a high opinion of the Hawk:

"I converted to the Hawk in the summer of 1979, when the Red Arrows *were still flying the Gnat, so that I was able to collect the first Hawk from British Aerospace on 15 September 1979. The team started flying the aircraft extensively from October, and it said a lot for the aeroplane that over just one winter period we were able to prepare for our normal* Red Arrow *displays in it. We began doing our displays again as usual the following April.*

The Hawk is undoubtedly a more advanced plane than was the Gnat, and it's a very comfortable one to fly. Its major advantages are that it is extremely reliable, and both carries more fuel and has a far more efficient engine than the Gnat. As a result, we can get a much greater flexibility in diversion: we can finish one display and go on much further than we could before. Last year, we did more than 120 displays, and the aircraft performed very well indeed. I cannot visualise any limit on the time we shall use the Hawk. I would think it will be in RAF service for very many years, and will be flown by the Red Arrows *for a long time to come.*

The displays we do with the Hawk are essentially the same as we did with the Gnat. But we do need rather more anticipation than we needed with the Gnat; the Hawk has forced us to change our technique a bit, especially with the throttle. In particular you need to use the air-brakes against power much more than in the Gnat.

Another feature of the Hawk is that it is an excellent trainer. It is supersonic, you can fly it on long sorties, you can spin the aeroplane, and, of course, it is very easy to handle in aerobatic formation. A real advantage is that, as well as serving as an advanced trainer, you can use it for weapon training. It's a marvellous training aeroplane; its wing is very strong and produces plenty of lift; and when you get into the Hawk the good thing is that it feels as if the entire plane really has been designed to help you do your job. Everything is exactly as it should be to make it easy for you to fly. In fact, I would think that the Hawk's only fault as a trainer is that it may be just a little too easy to fly."

Hawker Siddeley (BAe) Hawk *The RAF* Red Arrows *synchro pair in their scarlet Hawks perform a cross-over during the team's display at the 1991 Fighter Meet at North Weald.*

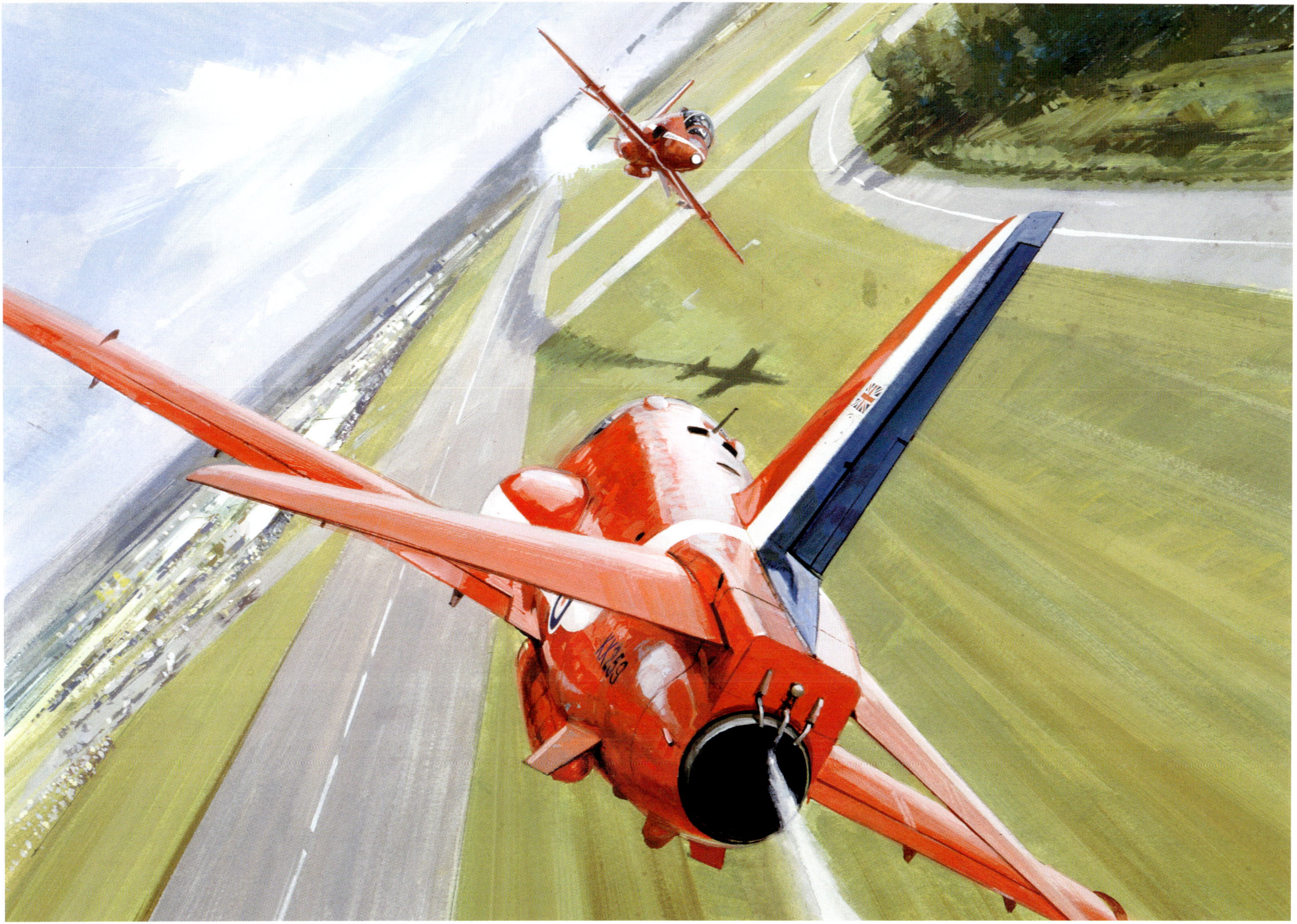

SEPECAT Jaguar

The Jaguar ground-attack fighter represented the first of a new breed of European aircraft. Its design conception gave priority to the low-level assault role, with traditional fighter air-to-air combat capability of a high order yet secondary in consideration. An Anglo-French project from the outset, the Jaguar first achieved operational status on joining the Escadron 1/7 'Provence' of the French Armée de l'Air in June 1973, while the first Jaguar-equipped RAF unit was No 54 Squadron at RAF Coltishall, Norfolk in September 1973.

The RAF acquired a total of 203 Jaguars fitted with a very accurate attack system to operate at low level. At its peak in the mid-seventies it equipped eight front-line RAF squadrons from 1974 replacing Phantoms as a major element in RAF Germany's tactical air capability, until the arrival of the Tornado in 1985.

In the context of the RAF's equipment Jaguars thereby superseded F-4 Phantoms in the ground attack role, leaving the latter for solely interception duties. Packed into its deceptively slight fuselage are a host of computerised technological advantages, including a weapon-delivery system flexible enough to tackle virtually any form of target in any sort of circumstance, but especially at low level and at high speed. Such is the precision of the technical ironmongery that the traditional duties of a navigator and a bomb aimer are automatically carried out for the pilot by his black boxes.

The first RAF attack aircraft to be sent to the Gulf following Iraq's invasion of Kuwait in 1990, the Jaguar GR1A served throughout *Desert Storm* without an aircraft being lost through enemy action. Although the Jaguar then had 18 years of service behind them they still proved to be one of the most cost-effective weapons in the RAF strike armoury. At Incirlik, in Turkey, Jaguars operated until 1993 as part of Operation *Warden* to defend the Turks in Northern Iraq. The aircraft then continued their support of UN duties, within the NATO deployment at Gioia del Celle, supporting Operation *Grapple* over Bosnia and later over Kosovo. Some subsequently participated, alongside Harrier GR7s, on Operation *Deliberate Force*.

As Paul Millett, then BAC Military Division's chief test pilot has recorded: *"Pilots of the last generation of jet ground attack aircraft find that the task of flying a high-speed, low-level mission has been revolutionised. The Jaguar has been designed and developed with the*

SEPECAT Jaguar *A Jaguar GR1, operated in the photo-reconnaissance role by No II (AC) Squadron, makes a low pass over NATO vehicles in Western Germany during a sortie from RAF Laarbruch in 1980.*

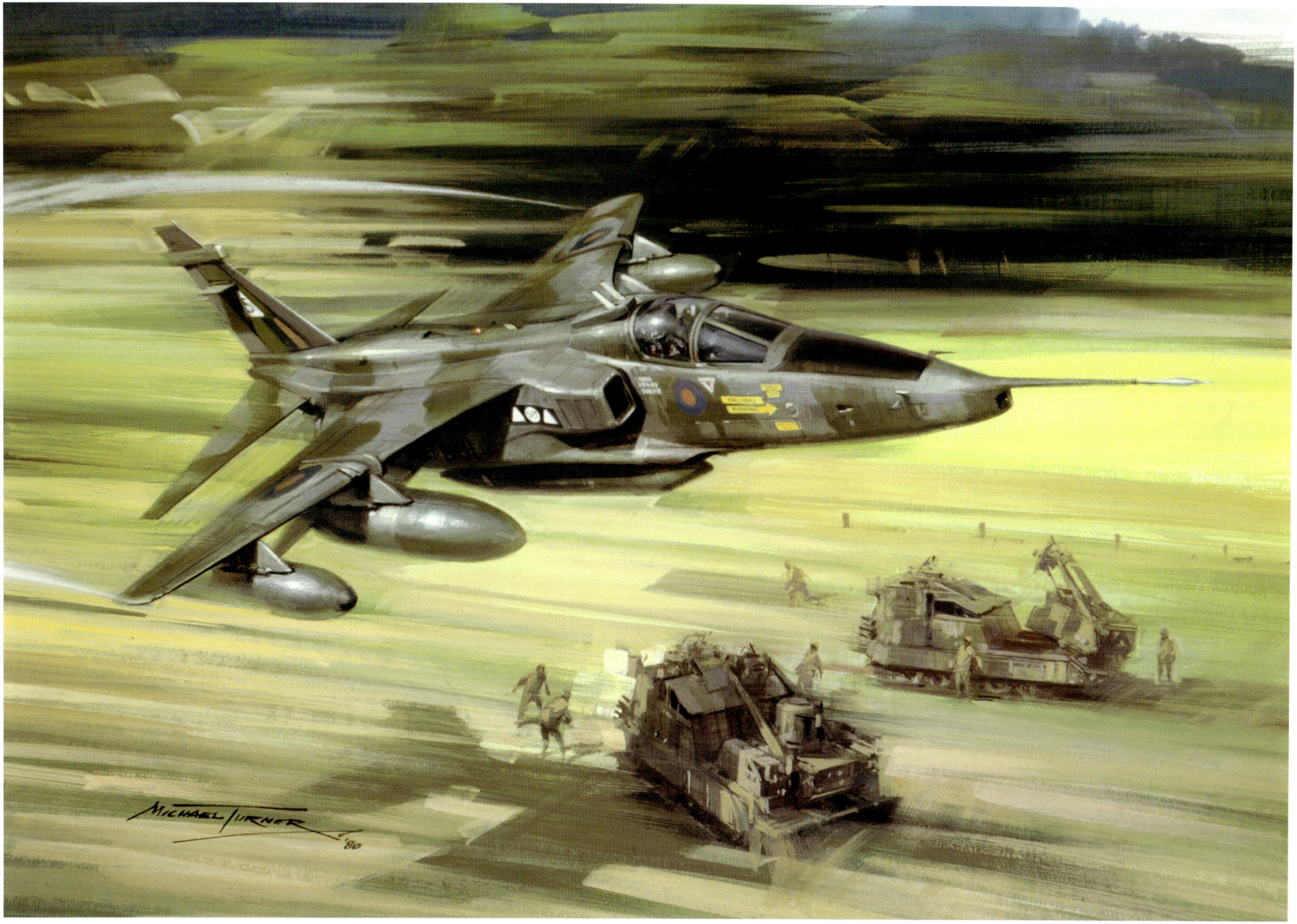
MICHAEL TURNER

aim of lifting a large and varied weapons load from a small airfield, taking these weapons through defended territory to a pinpoint target, attacking that target with maximum accuracy and returning safely to base. All pilots who have flown the Jaguar to date have been delighted with its handling characteristics."

Wing Commander John Walker, Officer Commanding the Jaguar Operational Conversion Unit in the early 1970s, described the aircraft as: *"A very high performance little ship. It certainly gets out and gets up very fast indeed - to the point that it surprises Lightning pilots. For the first time we have got an aircraft where you can virtually guarantee, on interdiction-type targets, making the very fast, low-level, straight pass attack. The aim of weapons delivery is to put the bomb on the target, and that's what the Jaguar does better than anything else we have."*

Westland/ Aerospatiale Puma

A development of the French SA300, the Puma resulted from a 1968 Anglo-French manufacturing agreement and the first British-produced Puma HC1 made its initial flight in November 1970.

It was designed for a wide range of duties, including casualty evacuation, troop transport and as a helicopter gunship. The type's twin-doors and

Westland/Aerospatiale Puma *A Westland Puma, on detachment to Belize with No 230 Squadron, during a counter-insurgency exercise with a Harrier.*

spacious cabin make the type popular with its Army users, who also appreciate its versatility.

The first Service example was delivered to the RAF in January 1971, and No 33 Squadron became the first Puma squadron from September 1971. Nineteen HC1s took part in the 1991 Gulf War, supporting ground forces by airlifting troops, freight and, often, ammunition. It has seen operational service in Northern Ireland for many years and during the last decade has been involved in the Gulf, the Balkans and Afghanistan. It has also served with the Army in Germany, Cyprus, Zimbabwe, Mozambique and on NATO exercises in Norway. Forty HC1s were built, serving with Nos 33 and 230 Squadrons and No 1563 Flight.

A recent upgrade has dramatically reduced the aircraft's vulnerability to hostile ground fire. Improvements include updated missile approach warning detection, IR detection and flare dispensers as well as better avionics.

An RAF Puma pilot reported on the Puma deployment to the Gulf in 1991: *"A composite RAF Puma squadron was assembled from No 33 Squadron at RAF Odiham and No 230 Squadron from Gutersloh, Germany. We air-freighted from RAF Brize Norton in USAF C-5 Galaxies and initially operated from Ras al Ghar. Our prime duty involved carriage of up to 16 troops or 2.5 tonnes of underslung loads, such as ammunition. We remained close to the troops, leaving Jubail for King Khalid Military City (KKMC) on 20 January and then proceeded as General Schwarzkopf's 'left-hook' thrust into Iraq was prepared. Night-vision goggles were regularly used and the uprated navigation equipment proved a godsend in the featureless terrain. The Coalition advance in the land war beginning on 24 February was so swift that ground-refuelling and re-arming parties had difficulty in keeping up with the helicopters as they accompanied the leading elements of UK forces deep into Iraq."*

Panavia Tornado GR1 and GR4

The RAF version of the Tornado IDS was the GR1 with 229 examples delivered, primarily for operation in the strike/attack role. It was the first swing-wing aircraft to enter RAF service and has been an outstanding success both as an international collaborative venture and as a military weapon. The Tornado performed well in the Gulf War, in Bosnia and the Balkans and more recently in Gulf War II carrying out the low-level interdiction role, for which it was designed. The GR1 was first flown on 14 August 1974 and entered RAF service in July 1980. At its peak it equipped eleven front-line squadrons, both in Germany and the UK. The basic strike/attack GR1 spawned two sub-variants - the GR1A reconnaissance variant and the GR1B maritime attack version. The GR1 featured seven weapons pylons, three under the flat-bottomed fuselage and two on each of the moving part of the wing and the pylons move as the wing is moved. The pylons and aircraft systems can accept all NATO weapons, plus AIM-9L Sidewinder missiles for self defence. All GR1s have now been upgraded to the GR4 with the aid of a major MLU (Mid-Life Update) programme.

Squadron Leader Dick Garwood, piloting GR1 ZA400 describes the first hunt sortie for Iraqi 'Scud' missiles on 18th January 1991: *"Our first mission was against the elusive mobile launchers from which the Scuds were being launched against Saudi Arabia and Israel. This threatened to bring Israel into the conflict. It was a very, very black night; probably one of the darkest I have ever flown on. Once you get out over the desert, especially over Iraq, there are no lights on the ground. We saw the odd Bedouin encampment flash by on the left-hand side of the wing. Flying at 200ft with 'hard ride' selected on the terrain-following radar, and at speeds between 540 and 580kts, the sortie lasted two hours, involving nearly 60 minutes over Iraq. We brought back images of a Scud launcher in firing position, and secured media headlines for the Tornado GR1A on the first night of the operations. On landing back at Dhahran, the Tornado was found to have a single flak hole in the top of the rudder."*

Air Vice-Marshal Glenn Torpy, air officer commanding 1 Group, and RAF and UK component commander in the Gulf in the Spring of 2003 said of the upgraded GR4: *"Initial RAF assessments of the upgraded Tornado GR4 indicate the recently improved strike fighter and its new weapons provide a solid foundation for the UK's future strike capability.*

The upgraded aircraft's greatest testament was its performance in the Gulf, particularly during the first three months of 2003."

Group Captain Greg Bagwell, group captain offensive strike RAF 1 Group, said the GR4's expended: *"27 Storm Shadows, 360 Enhanced Paveways, 255 Paveway II/III LGBs and 160 weapons, including the MBDA Alarm 2 anti-radiation missile during the 2003 Iraqi war."*

Panavia Tornado GR1 One of the RAF Tornado GR1's makes a night strike on an Iraqi airfield during the Gulf War, jettisoning its JP233 dispensers as the runway cratering bomblets explode behind it.

Panavia Tornado GR4 Operating out of Ali al Salem in Kuwait, fully-armed Tornado GR4 ZA614/AJL of No 617 Squadron on a bombing mission over Iraq during Operation Telic in March 2003. A total of 18 GR4s from Nos 2, 9, 31 and 617 Squadrons, on deployment, were involved in the operations over Iraq.

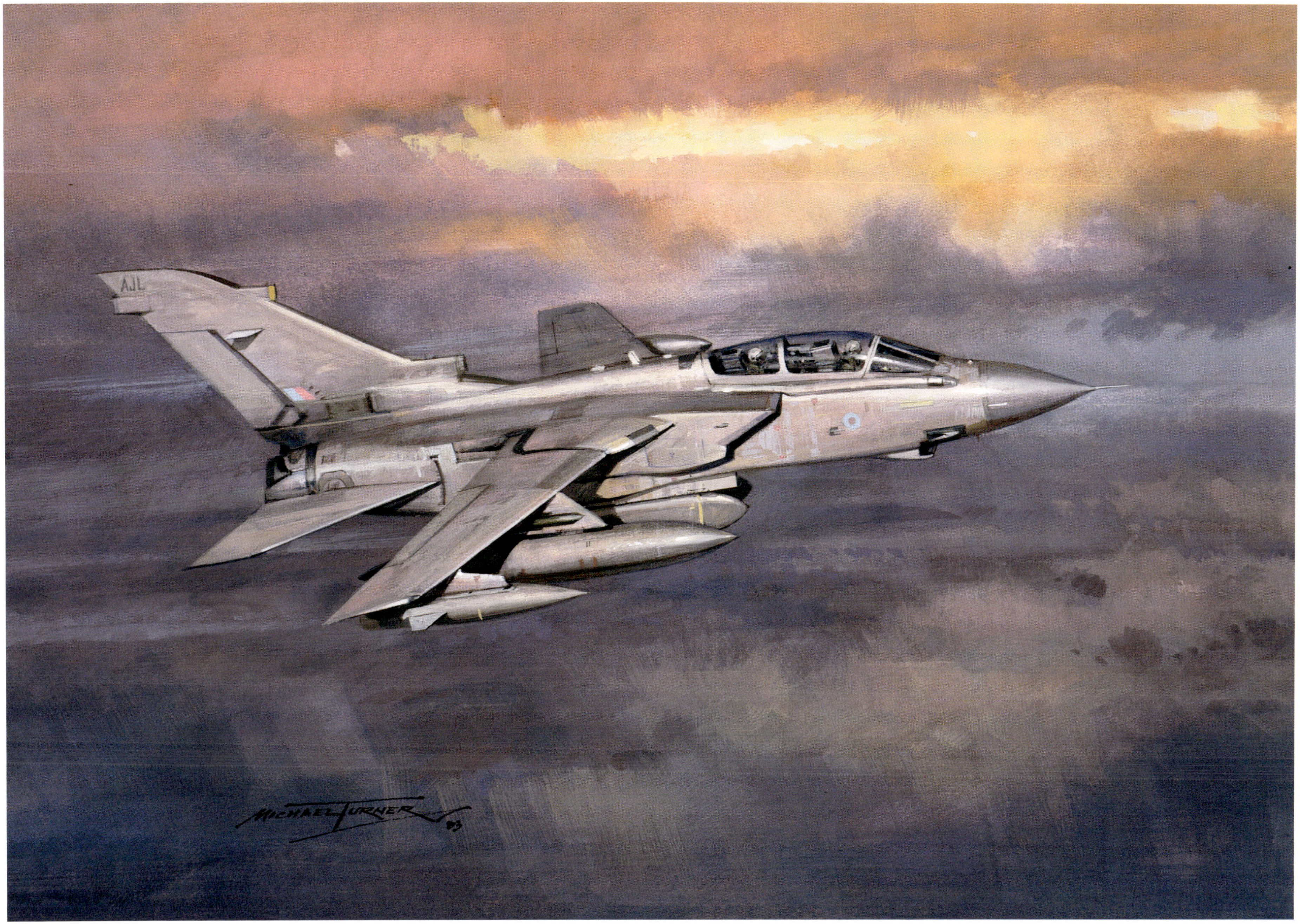
AJL
MICHAEL TURNER

Panavia Tornado F3

When the Multi-Role Combat Aircraft (MRCA) was under review by various NATO member countries, the interceptor role was considered for the aircraft in addition to the IDS version, but was rejected by all except the UK. The RAF requirement was for the air defence of the UK, which needed an aircraft with long-range, all-weather capability and the ability to intercept and destroy at considerable distances from the coast. Hence the Air Defence Variant (ADV) was born, and 165 of the total planned build of 385 Tornados for the RAF were the ADV version. The main change was a 1.36m (4ft 5.5in) fuselage plug, providing an extra bay forward of the wing box for a fuel tank and a longer radome. The extra length also allowed the carriage of four Skyflash missiles under the fuselage. Despite the changes, the ADV retained an 80% commonality with the IDS version. The first F3 flew in November 1985 and entered service on 28 July 1986, and at its peak the RAF had five Tornado F3 squadrons.

The only export order for the F3 came from Saudi Arabia, who received 24 from 1989. The RAF has subsequently leased 24 F3s to the Italian Air Force pending the arrival of the Eurofighter Typhoon. RAF examples have recently undergone the Capability Sustainment Programme (CSP) which equips the fighter for AMRAAM and ASRAAM missiles, JTIDS and Successor IFF.

Panavia Tornado F3 A Panavia Tornado F3 of No 23 Squadron from RAF Leeming in 1991.

Wing Commander Robin Birtwistle, Commanding Officer of the F3 OEU stated: *"the ADV upgrade has not only given the F3 the capability to employ the new AIM-120 AMRAAM missile, but in 2002 the RAF declared the Advanced Short-Range Air-to-Air Missile (ASRAAM) ready for operational use on the F3, as a replacement for the AIM-9L Sidewinder.*

ASRAAM has an acquisition and track performance significantly better than that of the AIM-9 Sidewinder and has a robust counter-measures capability. The weapon will provide a first shot in most scenarios, and as standard equipment with the F3 is an enhancement to the aircraft's capabilities. It will give our crews an edge in obtaining air superiority.

With its new capabilities, the RAF Tornado F3 is a popular and potent platform. The arrival of the Eurofighter Typhoon in front-line service over the next few years will open the way for the F3 to be equipped for new missions and new capabilities. The final chapter for this workhorse is still some way off."

Boeing-Vertol Chinook

A development of the 1956 basic Boeing-Vertol CH-47, the Chinook was first ordered for the RAF in 1978, and the first examples delivered in November 1980 to No 240 OCU. The first operational Chinook unit was No 18 Squadron at RAF Odiham followed by No 7 Squadron. Of four Chinooks sent to the Falklands campaign three were lost at sea on the *Atlantic Conveyor* leaving just one, ZA718, to continue the workload of all

Boeing-Vertol Chinook *A No 18 Squadron Chinook helping with the clearing up of the airfield at Port Stanley, after the Falklands conflict.*

four. In total the RAF took 41 Chinook HC1s, equivalent to the American CH-47C.

All remaining HC1s were subsequently upgraded to HC1Bs with new engines and glass-fibre rotor blades in the late 1980s. During 1991-1995 further upgrading to HC1Bs was incorporated in 33 aircraft and later to HC2 standard. Chinooks operated with Nos 7, 18 and 78 Squadrons, the latter based in the Falklands. Each Chinook could carry a 28,000lb load on a triple cargo hook, or up to 55 men, 24 stretchers, or other internal loads. Fifteen HC1Bs flew during the Gulf War with the Coalition forces with duties including transporting prisoners of war. It has also seen recent service in Sierra Leone, the Balkans, Afghanistan and Iraq.

Squadron Leader Ian Rose, a Flight Commander with the Rotary Wing Operation Evaluation and Training Unit comments on the Chinook: *"It takes more than learning to fly a Chinook for RAF Support Helicopter (SH) crews, who have to be capable of operating effectively, and to survive, in today's multi-threat environment. New global strategic concepts and rapid deployment force structures, all now rely on helicopters to provide much of their mobility and tactical flexibility. Chinooks have to undertake a wide range of missions from peace-keeping to full regional conflict. It can carry M60D and M134 Miniguns, for gunnery sorties, the latter being purchased for Desert Storm. These had been manufactured and used by the US Army as a dedicated air-to-ground weapon. The Chinooks are now fully equipped with a comprehensive aids suite, weapons and electronic countermeasures."*

Shorts Tucano

Winner of the RAF's AST412 requirement for a Jet Provost replacement, the Shorts S312 Tucano was selected in March 1985 as the RAF's future basic trainer. It was built by Shorts of Belfast under licence from the Brazilian aircraft manufacturer Embraer, and a total of 130 aircraft was delivered.

Flying instruction using Tucano T1s began at No 7 FTS, RAF Church Fenton in late 1989. T1s differed from Brazilian Tucanos in having a higher-powered Garrett turboprop, a new cockpit layout with British equipment, and some airframe strengthening. The first Tucano T1 made its maiden flight on 30 December 1986. Exports were made to Kenya and Kuwait.

The Tucano was the first tandem-seat basic trainer to reach the RAF since the Chipmunk was issued back in 1950. All subsequent 'ab initio' and basic trainers such as the Prentice, Provost, Jet Provost and Bulldog featured side-by-side seating for the instructor and pupil. With advanced trainers the trend back to tandem seating began with the Gnat in the early 1960s and was firmly established with the Hawk from 1976 onwards.

Shorts Tucano *The Tucano turboprop trainer replaced the Jet Provost in 1989 in the basic flying training role. Tandem seating gives the Tucano a more slender fuselage, and because the cockpit wraps around the pilot he has everything to hand, as it is in all fast jets - and is much better for the student on solo sorties. Here ZF409 is being readied for a training flight with No 3 FTS at RAF Cranwell (for which the Tucano carries the rear fuselage blue band) in the mid-1990s.*

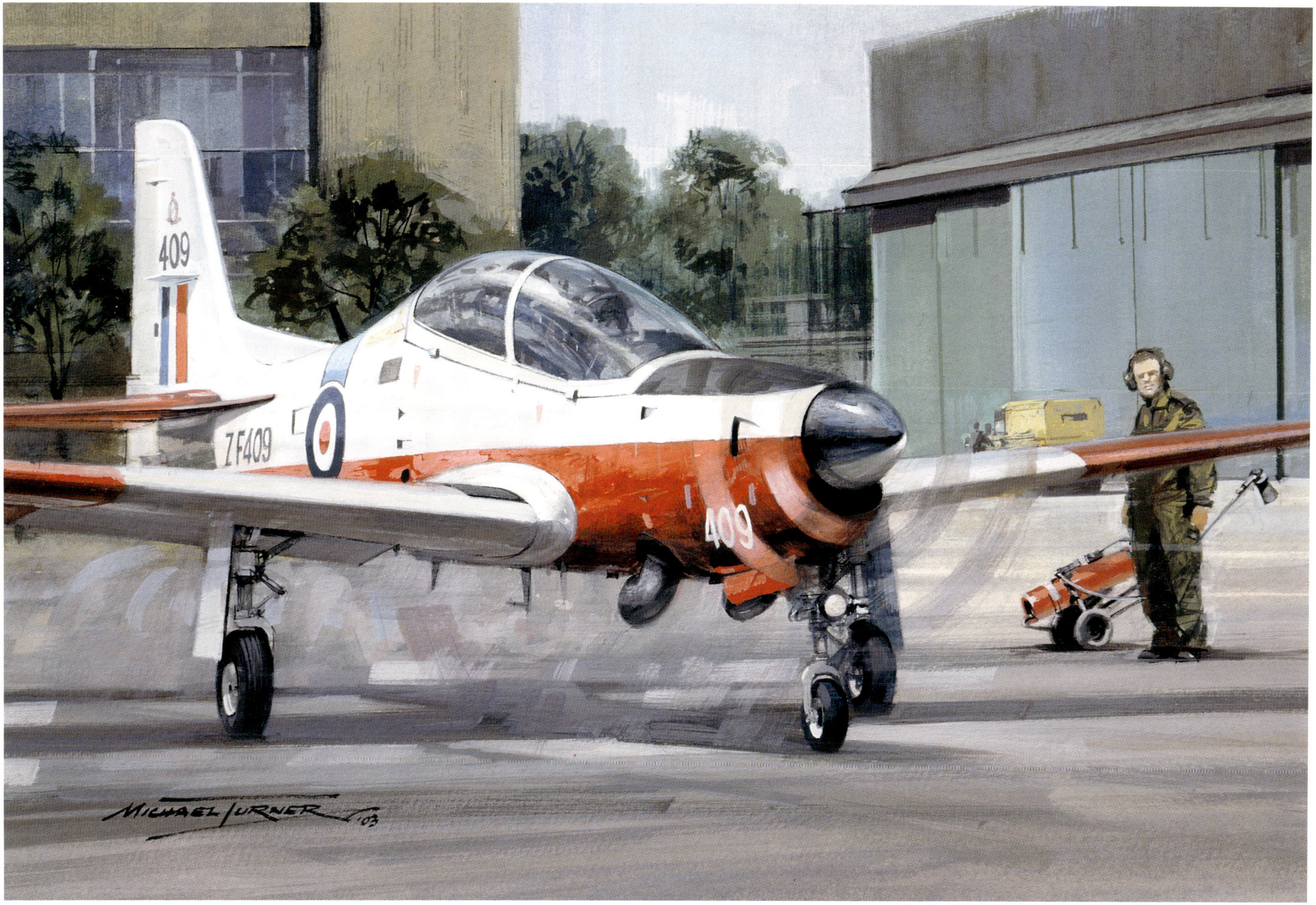
409
ZF409
409
MICHAEL TURNER '03

Westland Wessex

The RAF's Wessex stemmed from a Royal Navy requirement 50 years ago. Westland acquired a licence to build the Sikorsky S-58, using a Napier Gazelle turboshaft in place of the S-58s Wright R-1820-24 piston engine. A subsequent RAF requirement for a powerful troop-carrying, casualty and SAR helicopter led to the Wessex Mk 2, powered by two coupled 1,350shp (1,006kW) Rolls-Royce Gnome H.1200 free turbine engines.

The first HC2 was flown on 18 January 1962 and in the summer of 1962 a Wessex Trials Unit was established at RAF Odiham. The Wessex HC2 became the service's first twin-engined, single-rotor helicopter when it entered operational service with No 18 Squadron at Odiham in February 1964. As well as UK operations, it was also active in Aden, Cyprus, Germany, Hong Kong and Singapore.

As recently as May 1992, No 60 Squadron was reformed at RAF Benson, flying HC2s with the UK Support Helicopter Force for five years. A total of 382 Wessex had been built when production ended in 1981. The last RAF Wessex, the final quartet of HC2s operated by No 84 Squadron at RAF Akrotiri, Cyprus, were retired in January 2003 after nearly 40 years RAF service.

Westland Wessex *One of No 28 Squadron's Westland Wessex HC2s, based at Kai Tak, delivers supplies to an army unit near Hong Kong.*

Lockheed Tristar

Military use of the Lockheed Tristar civil airliner (which first flew on 16 November 1970) is confined to the UK, with the RAF having obtained nine former civil L-1011-500s (either British Airways or PanAm) examples for service with No 216 Squadron at RAF Brize Norton. These were extensively modified into four different configurations by Marshall Aerospace during the late 1980s and early 1990s. The RAF examples comprise the K1 tanker/transport (two), KC1 tanker/cargo aircraft (four), C2 transport (two) and C2A transport (one). First flight of the initial conversion was on 9 July 1985 and the type entered operational service in March 1986. These perform in-flight refuelling, troop transport and cargo airlift missions.

It is a low-wing design with two engines in pods suspended from the wing and a third engine buried in the aft fuselage, and fed by an air intake duct forward and faired into the vertical tail surface. RAF tanker versions are fitted with additional cells in the former baggage holds, as well as an in-flight refuelling probe above the cockpit. They also have two hose drum units beneath the aft fuselage section.

A No 216 Squadron Tristar pilot reported on his time in the Gulf in 1990/91:

"The UK build-up at Dhahran in Saudi Arabia began on 9 August with the arrival of our two Tristar K1s carrying administrative and support personnel, and the Tornado F3s flew in two days later. We

Lockheed Tristar *Providing an essential service during the Gulf War, a Lockheed Tristar K1 tanker from No 216 Squadron refuels a Jaguar whilst a Buccaneer waits its turn.*

subsequently flew from King Khalid airfield and Muharraq, Bahrain to refuel the F3s, our main customers, on Combat Air Patrols (CAPs). In addition we not only passed our fuel to our Jaguars and Buccaneers, but also to Canadian CF-18 Hornets, French Mirage 2000s and a variety of US Navy and Marine Corps warplanes. The K1s were involved in deploying combat aircraft to the Gulf theatre before, during and after Desert Storm, being able to carry heavy equipment as well as to refuel aircraft in flight."

BAe (Hawker Siddeley) 125/BAe 146

As one of the world's first executive jets, the then de Havilland 125 was quickly identified by the RAF for the Dominie T1 navigation trainer. In addition the RAF has operated the 125 in the communications/transport role. At the time of the Golden Jubilee Flypast in 2002, No 32 (The Royal) Squadron at RAF Northolt was operating six CC3s (Series 700), powered by Garrett TFE731 turbofans. The type has found particular use by military air arms as a VIP transport, thanks to its roomy cabin of constant cross-section which allows a wide range of VIP interior layouts. Though initially entering service in the 1970s upgrading has resulted in a long production life and excellent performance in relation to today's contemporary types.

The BAe 146/RJ Series originates from a 1973 proposal by Hawker Siddeley for a new short-range, low-noise civil transport as the HS146. Design resumed in July 1978 and the first prototype flew on 3 September 1981 having four Textron Lycoming turbofans with a very low-noise signature. The high lift, high-mounted wing has large Fowler-type trailing edge flaps giving the aircraft the ability to operate from short or semi-prepared strips with minimum ground facilities. The RAF currently operates two (originally three) CC2s, which were acquired in 1986, with No 32 (The Royal) Squadron at RAF Northolt as a VIP transport and are fitted with Loral Matador infrared jamming systems, offering an ECM capability.

BAe (Hawker Siddeley) 125 and BAe 146 *A BAe 146 and two BAe 125CC2s of No 34 (The Royal) Squadron from RAF Northolt, in echelon formation low over Buckingham Palace, as part of the RAF fly-past for The Queen's Jubilee Celebrations in June 2002.*

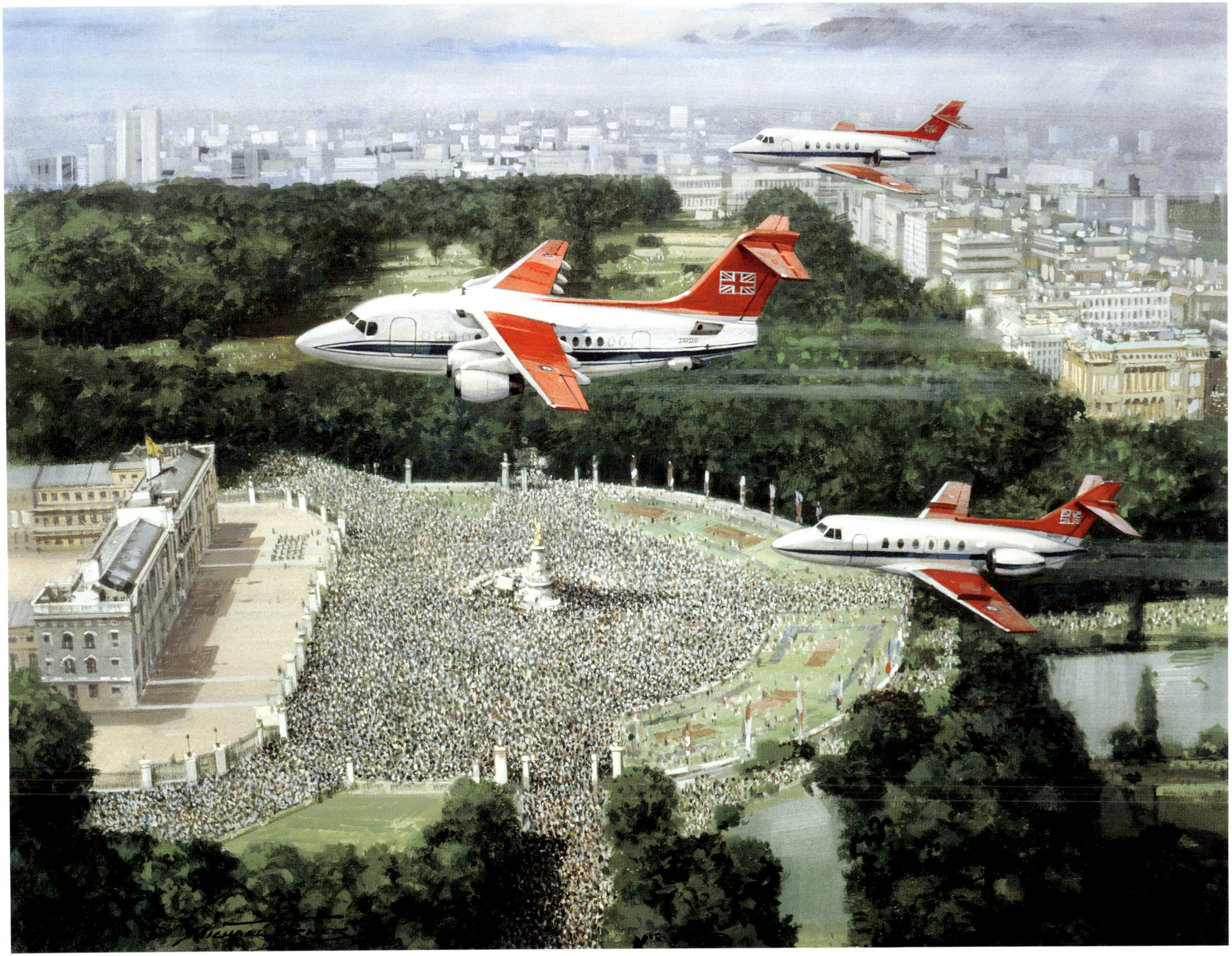

204

BAe Harrier GR7

British Aerospace initiated development of an advanced Harrier during the late 1979s to succeed the GR3. By that time the US became involved and a partnership between BAe and McDonnell Douglas ensued, to proceed with the development of the 'big wing' V/STOL Harrier. The British version, initially the GR5, but subsequently converted to the GR7, is basically the equivalent of the night-attack US AV-8B, using the same equipment and avionics. The GR5 first flew on 30 April 1985 and the GR7 on 18 May 1990. The first GR7s replaced Harrier GR3 squadrons in Germany.

The RAF's Nos 1, 3 and 4 Squadrons are based at RAF Cottesmore as part of Joint Force Harrier. No 20(R) Squadron is based at RAF Wittering. Fitted with an NVG compatible cockpit, the GR7 is fitted with a TIALD pod to enable it to automatically launch laser-guided PGMs. Provision of a dedicated Sidewinder pylon allows adequate defence capability, even when carrying a full offensive load.

In the 1990s RAF Harriers were deployed in Operation *Bolton,* monitoring the No Fly Zone over Southern Iraq and as part of Operation *Warden,* protecting Kurdish settlements in Northern Iraq. They have also been involved in Operation *Telic* in Iraq in April 2003.

Its warload is two 25mm cannon on an under-fuselage station and nine weapons pylons with 4,900kg (10,800lb) payload. A range of freefall and retarded bombs, including 1,000lb laser-guided and cluster bombs can be carried. Alternatively, or as a mix, rocket launchers, ASMs, Sidewinder/Magic AAMs can be carried. Storm Shadow and Brimstone missiles will be carried on the upgraded GR9 version, which is now in the pipe-line.

BAe Harrier GR7 *RAF Harrier GR7s of No 3 Squadron at RAF Cottesmore deployed aboard HMS Invincible in January 1998, as part of the UK's response to problems in the Balkans, took part in live-armed operational missions over Kosovo. Here two fully-armed Harriers have just taken-off from the 'ski-jump' on the carrier, climbing out and heading for their targets.*

EH 101 Merlin

EH Industries was formed as a collaborative venture between Westland Helicopters and Agusta in June 1980, to develop a new generation anti-submarine warfare three-engined helicopter for the Royal Navy and Italian Navy to replace the Sea King. A support transport version was developed for the RAF and 22 HC3s were delivered, with the first examples entering operational service in autumn 2000 and are fully integrated into the Joint Helicopter Command. They are based with No 28 (AC) Squadron at RAF Benson. Extra power and safety is provided by the use of three engines. British versions have the Rolls-Royce/Turboméca RTM 322s, whereas civil and Italian EH 101s are fitted with General Electric C77 engines.

The Merlin has long-range deployment capabilities, using either air-to-air refuelling or internal ferry tanks. It can lift 24 troops in full crash-worthy seats, each with its own individual headset, at 150kts in all weather conditions. As well as troops the HC3 can use its rear-loading ramp to carry an assortment of motorbikes or quad bikes, as well as internal cargo and carry under-slung loads of up to 12,000lb (5,445kg). Its wide capability make the helicopter ideally suited to other more specialised missions such as combat recovery and long-range insertions. In addition the HC3 has provision for pintle-mounted machine guns in the main doors and has provision for FLIR and AAR probe. Its operational début was in Afghanistan in 2002.

EH 101 Merlin *Exercise Pegasus Trial, which took place during September 2001, saw the first field deployment of the new RAF EHI Merlin HC3, and the first tactical troop lift by No 29 (Army Co-operation) Squadron from RAF Benson in an exercise scenario. It was the first time that the Merlin had been cleared to operate with 24 troops.*

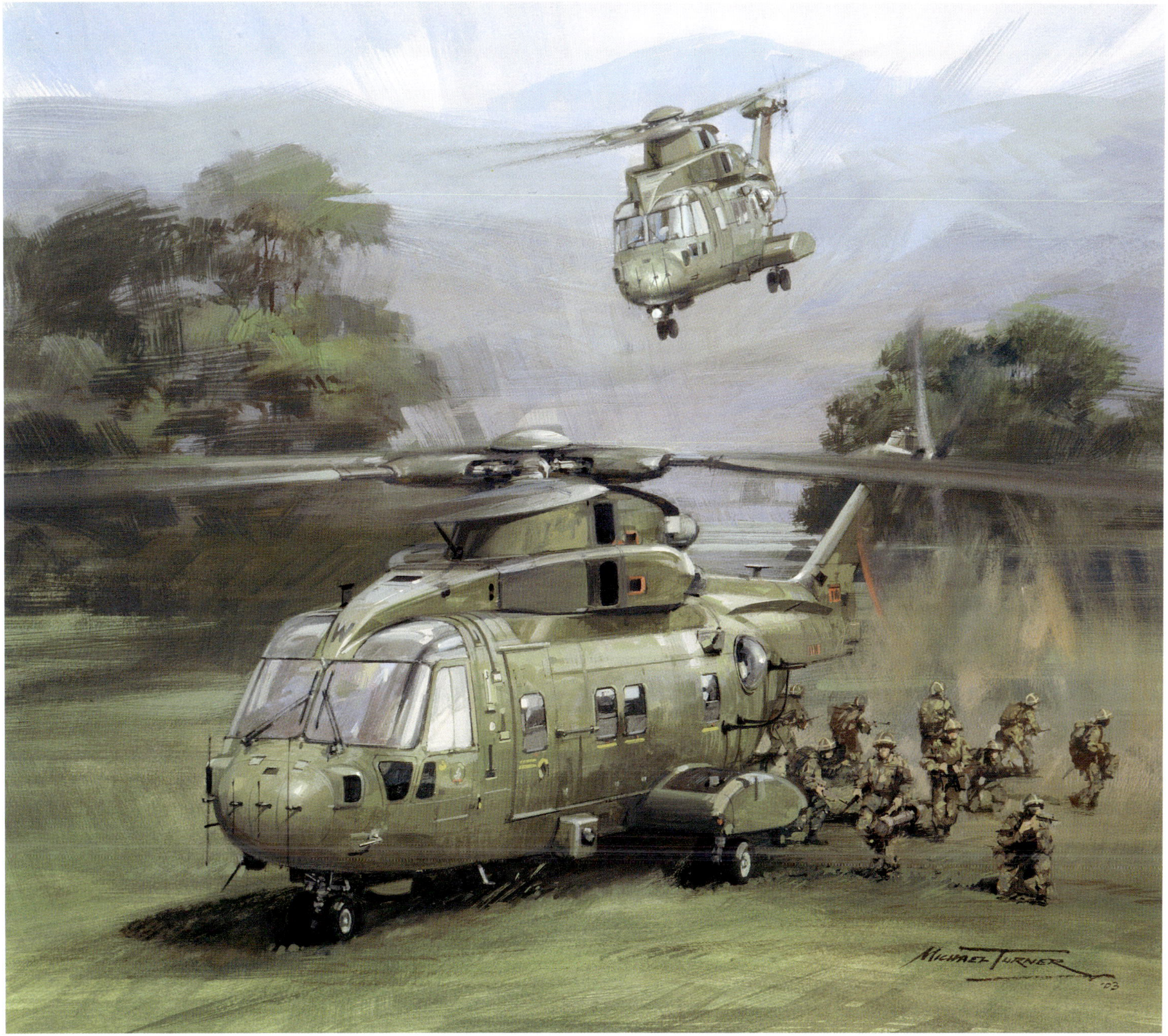
MICHAEL TURNER
'03

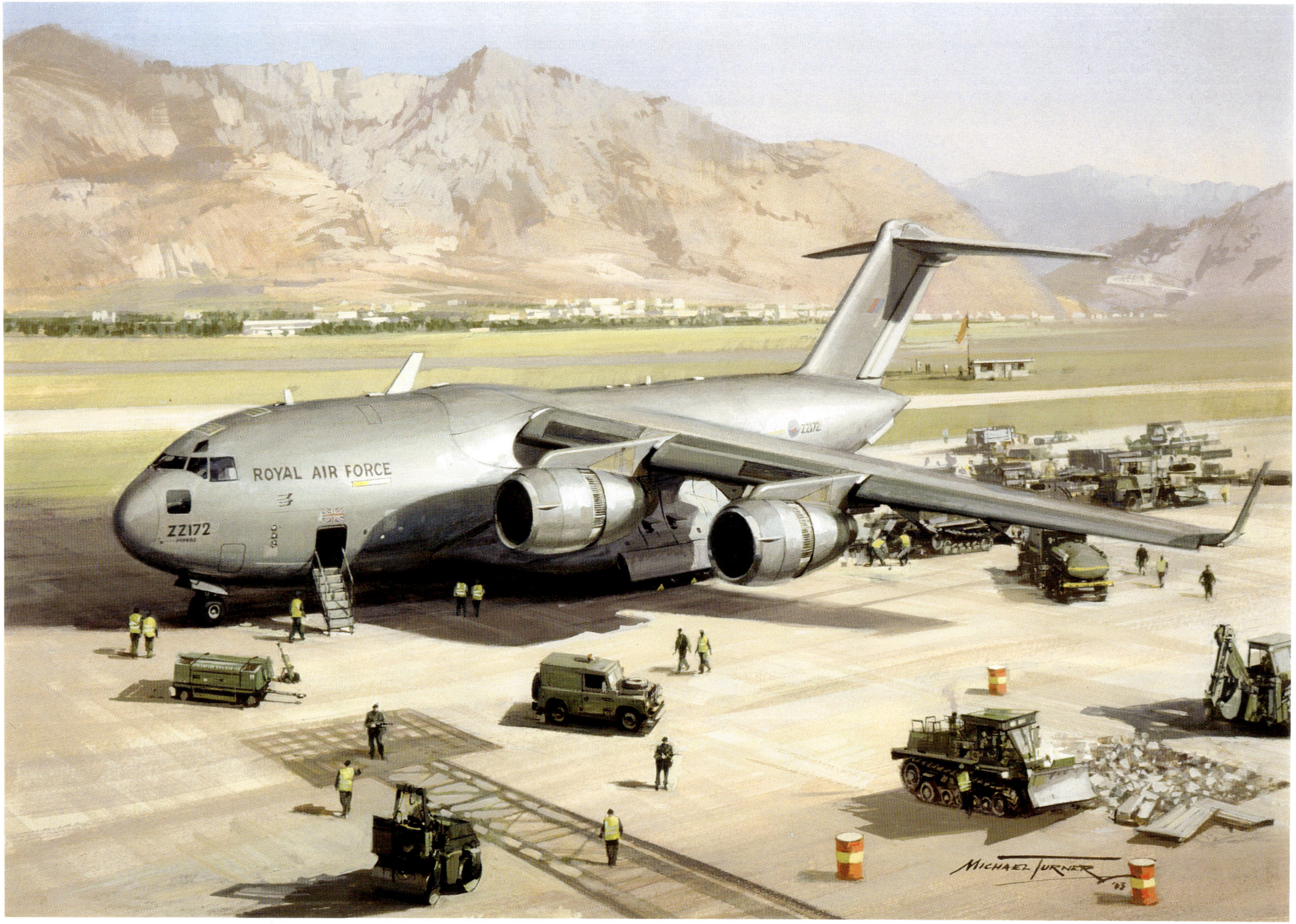
ROYAL AIR FORCE
ZZ172
ZZ172
MICHAEL TURNER

Boeing C-17 Globemaster III

Programme go-ahead occurred in the early 1980s when McDonnell Douglas (since merged with Boeing) was selected by the US Air Force to develop the C-17 Globemaster III four-turbofan, in response to the C-X aircraft requirement to replace the C-141 StarLifter. It made its maiden flight in September 1991 and entered USAF operational service in June 1993.

The C-17 incorporates a number of classic cargo aircraft features. Foremost amongst these is the choice of a high-wing configuration, with podded underslung engines, that allows unobstructed access to the cargo hold, as well as a rear ramp that combines with a sharply upswept aft fuselage to offer a good clearance for bulky and outsize loads. It also has a T-tail and winglets, as well as flap-blowing to enhance short-field performance.

Four C-17s joined the Royal Air Force on a lease basis in Summer 2001 (with the possibility of more joining the RAF in the years to come), as a temporary measure pending the availability of the forthcoming Airbus A400M, as a strategic airlifter, transporting heavy equipment and bulky loads over long distances. These are based with No 99 Squadron at RAF Brize Norton and have been fully utilised in the Afghanistan operations of 2002 and the Iraqi War of 2003. Its crew comprises pilot, co-pilot and loadmaster plus up to 102 paratroops. As a cargo transport its payload is 169,000lb (76,655kg). Impressively sprightly for its size, the C-17 can haul a full load off a very meagre stretch of runway and climb at an exceptional rate. Aircraft, too, can be carried in a disassembled state. Another time-critical load is helicopters. The capacious hold can accommodate one complete Chinook package, two Pumas or four Lynxes.

Boeing C-17 Globemaster III The first major operational challenge for the RAF's C-17 Globemaster IIIs of No 99 Squadron from RAF Brize Norton came in Afghanistan in 2002. Each mission was staged through Bahrain to Kabul and Bagram to ferry in essential supplies. Here ZZ172 is on the ramp at Kabul airport, 5,800ft above sea-level with 20,000ft plus mountains in the vicinity.

Eurofighter Typhoon

The Eurofighter consortium of British, German, Italian and Spanish manufacturers was established to develop and produce a new-generation air superiority fighter. From the outset the Typhoon was designed to have an unstable aerodynamic configuration for increased agility in both the beyond visual range (BVR) and close-in spheres of air combat. The design incorporated prominent canard foreplanes and an active digital fly-by-wire system. Its Eurojet EJ200 turbofans develop power for employment in the 'supercruise' mode at high-level without recourse to afterburning. It is one of the world's most advanced fighters and offers a steep jump in capability compared to the aircraft types it replaces.

The first Eurofighter made its maiden flight in 1994 and entered RAF operational evaluation units in 2002, with the first operational squadrons to form in 2004. The RAF version has a multi-role capability for operation in the air-to-surface mode and the initial order was for 232 examples. In RAF service the Typhoon has no provision for fixed cannon. Its warload of 14,300lb (6,500kg) includes BVRAAMs, ASRAAM, AIM-9L Sidewinders, bombs/cluster bombs/laser-guided bombs (GBU-24 and Paveway III) and ALARMS in the air-to-surface role. Future stores will include Storm Shadow, Brimstone, JDAMs and Harpoon.

The Typhoon will replace Tornado F3s in air defence squadrons and subsequently Jaguars in the multi-role units. Even with a full air-to-air weapon load the aircraft has a thrust-to-weight ratio greater than parity, and acceleration in all flight regimes is phenomenal.

An RAF test pilot on the Typhoon reported: *"The Typhoon is one of the world's most advanced fighters, and offers a step jump in capability compared to the aircraft types it replaces. Pooling the technological skills of four nations has produced an aircraft which breathes 'smartness' from every pore, while the involvement of front-line pilots at all stages of development has ensured that the Typhoon has the most 'user-friendly cockpit' to be found anywhere. Furthermore, the Typhoon has been designed to new levels of ease of production and maintenance, and unprecedented levels of reliability.*

The Typhoon has considerable growth potential, and the enhancements being planned and studied for '2010 Eurofighters' of the third production batch - such as 'e-scan' radar, Meteor and Storm Shadow, terrain-referenced navigation, conformal fuel tanks and increased-thrust engines - should keep the aircraft at the forefront of fighter design for many decades."

Eurofighter Typhoon *Two RAF Typhoon F1s demonstrate, in 2003, the ability to take-off and accelerate rapidly to provide a high launch speed for its weapons, in turn producing longer missile ranges and shorter fly-out times. No 17 Squadron will be the first front-line RAF squadron and a NATO declaration with FOC (Full Operating Capability) is expected by the middle of the decade.*

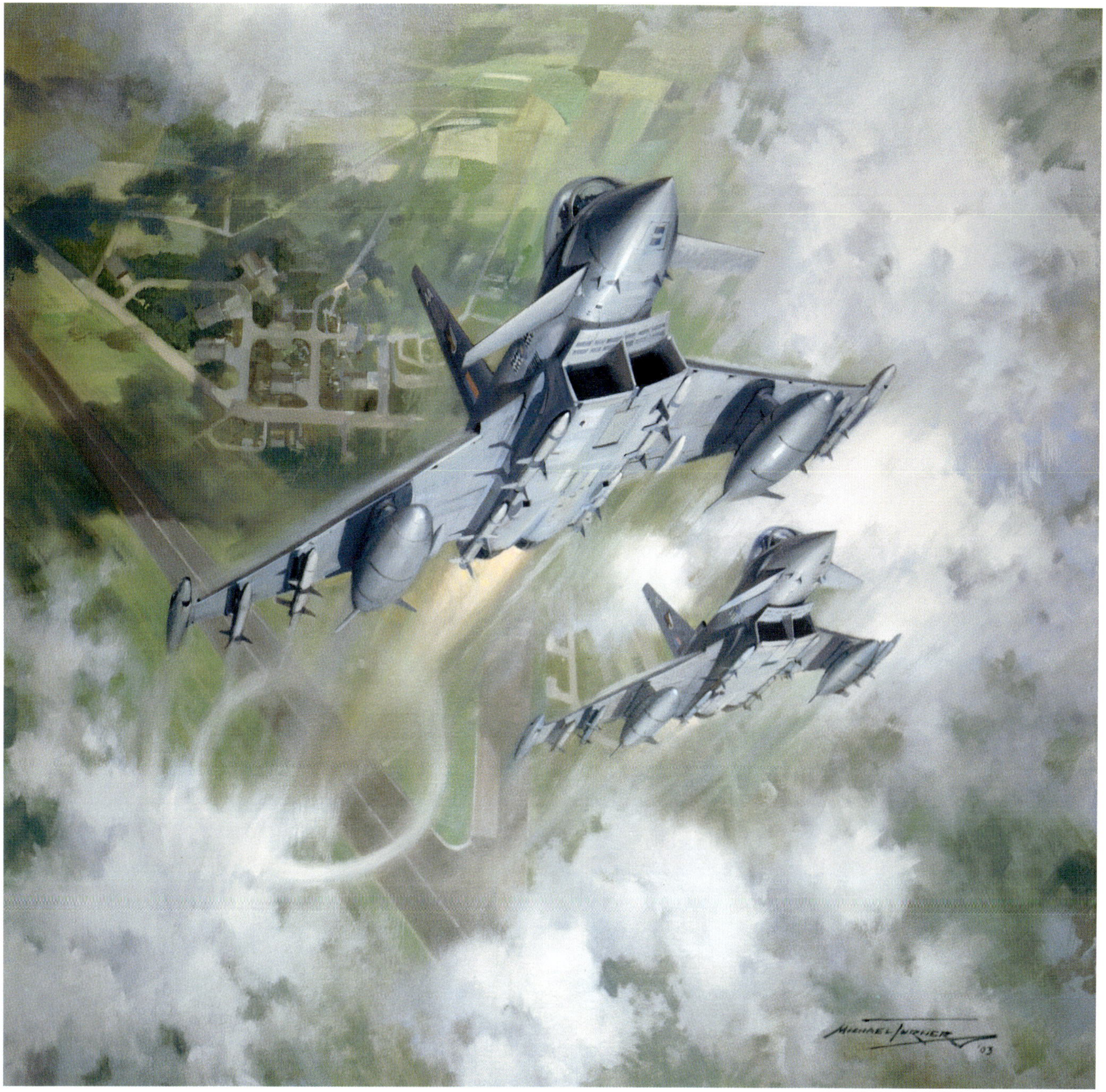

Michael Turner is one of the most highly regarded and long established aviation and motorsport artists in the country and abroad. He was born in Harrow in 1934, and began drawing 'planes whilst still at school during WWII, being particularly inspired by the exploits of the RAF. After a year in art school and two years National Service, he gained experience in advertising studios for three years before becoming a freelance artist at the age of 23.

Elected a member of the now defunct Society of Aviation artists in the 1950's, he became a founder member of the Guild of Aviation Artists in 1971, of which he has been President since 1988. In his search for first-hand experience and subjects for his paintings, he has flown in a wide variety of RAF aircraft over the years, from Tiger Moth, Lancaster, Hercules and Canberra, to aerobatic sorties with the Red Arrows and fast jets including Lightning, Hunter, Jaguar, Harrier and Tornado. He is also a qualified private pilot and flies his own ex-RAF Chipmunk.

His high regard for the Royal Air Force has led to this collection of paintings, which form a unique record of the multitude of aircraft types seen in service throughout the world during its long history.

Each painting is accompanied by an account of the history and development of the aircraft illustrated, which has been written mainly by Chaz Bowyer - with the more modern aircraft accounts provided by Peter R March. Chaz joined the RAF as a Halton Aircraft Apprentice (a 'Trenchard Brat'), at the age of 16. He completed 26 years' regular service before voluntarily retiring from the RAF to take up aviation history research and authorship as a full-time profession. Peter is a leading aviation author and photo-journalist. He has contributed a monthly column to Aircraft Illustrated for over 30 years and also writes a column for Pilot Magazine.

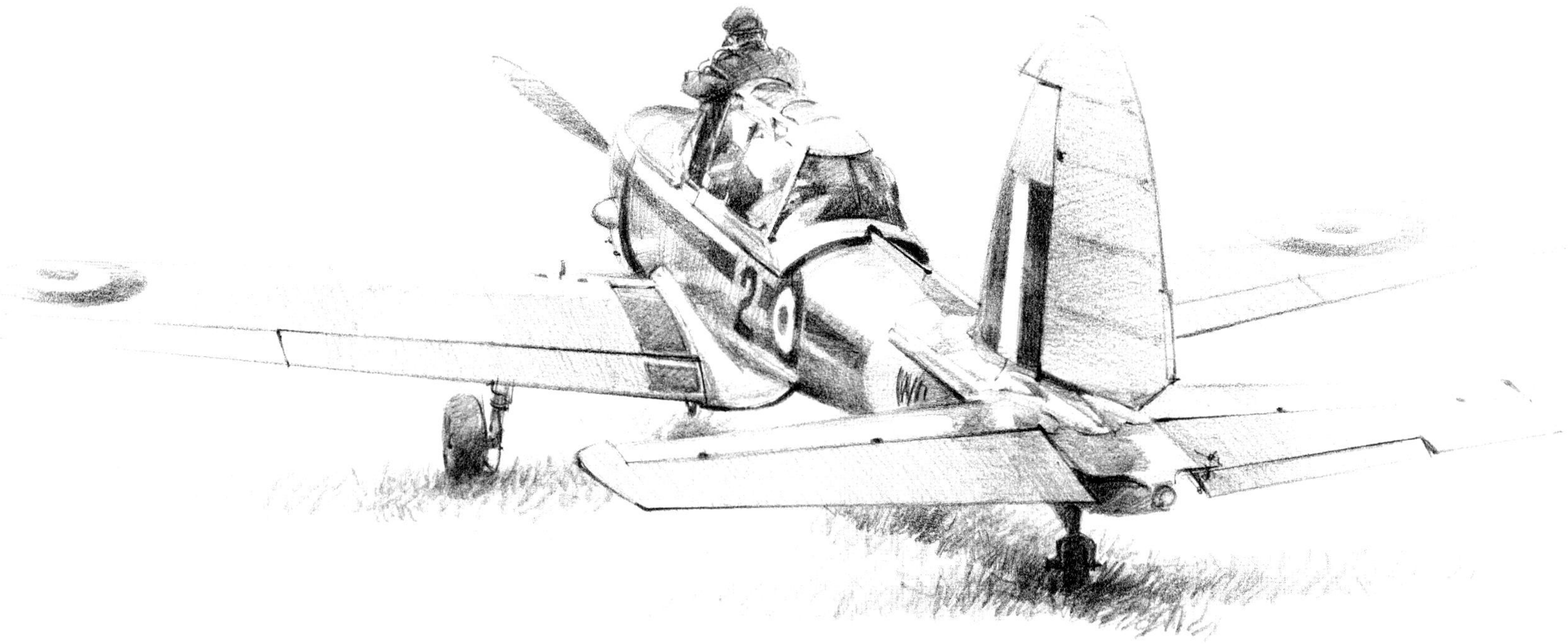